Excellent English 3
Language Skills for Success

Mary Ann Maynard
Ingrid Wisniewska

Jan Forstrom
Marta Pitt
Shirley Velasco

 **McGraw-Hill**

Excellent English Student Book 3

ISBN 13: 978-0-07-329182-6 (Student Book)
ISBN 10: 0-07-329182-X
7 8 9 10 11 12 RMN 11

ISBN 13: 978-0-07-719286-0 (Student Book with Audio Highlights)
ISBN 10: 0-07-719286-9
7 8 9 10 11 12 RMN 11

Series editor: Nancy Jordan
Developmental editor: Eve Einselen
Cover designer: Witz End Design
Interior designer: NETS

McGraw-Hill

The McGraw·Hill Companies

Acknowledgements

The authors and publisher would like to thank the following individuals who reviewed the *Excellent English* program at various stages of development and whose comments, reviews, and field-testing were instrumental in helping us shape the series.

Tony Albert • Jewish Vocational Service; San Francisco, CA

Alex Baez • The Texas Professional Development Group; Austin, TX

Katie Blackburn • Truman College; Chicago, IL

Robert Breitbard • Collier County Adult Education; Naples, FL

Jeff Bright • McHenry County College; Crystal Lake, IL

Sherrie Carroll • Montgomery College; Conroe, TX

Georges Colin • Lindsey Hopkins Technical Education Center; Miami, FL

Irene Dennis • Palo Alto College; Palo Alto, CA

Terry Doyle • City College of San Francisco, Alemany Campus; San Francisco, CA

Rolly Fanton • San Diego City College; San Diego, CA

Ingrid Farnbach • City College of San Francisco; San Francisco, CA

Colleen Fitzmaurice • San Diego Community College District, Mid-City; San Diego, CA

Phil Garfinkel • Adult & Family Education of Lutheran Medical Centers; Brooklyn, New York

Ana Maria Guaolayol • Miami-Dade College, Kendall Campus; Miami, FL

Shama Hasib • City College of San Francisco; San Francisco, CA

Margaret Hass • San Diego Community College District, Mid-City; San Diego, CA

Kathleen Hiscock • Portland Adult Education; Portland, ME

Giang Hoang • Evans Community Adult School, Los Angeles Unified School District; Los Angeles, CA

Armenuhi Hovhannes • City College of San Francisco, Mission Campus; San Francisco, CA

Vivian Ikeda • City College of San Francisco, Teacher Resource Center; San Francisco, CA

Sally Ruth Jacobson • San Diego Community College District, Centre City; San Diego, CA

Kathleen Jimenez • Miami-Dade College, Kendall Campus; Miami, FL

Nancy Johansen • San Diego Community College District, Mid-City; San Diego, CA

Mary Kapp • City College of San Francisco, Chinatown Campus; San Francisco, CA

Caryn Kovacs • Brookline Adult Education; Brookline, MA

Linda Kozin • San Diego Community College District, North City Center; San Diego, CA

Gretchen Lammers-Ghereben • Martinez Adult Education School; Martinez, CA

Paul Mayer • Glendale Community College; Glendale, CA

Cathleen McCargo • Arlington Education and Employment Program (REEP); Arlington, VA

Lee Mosteller • San Diego Community College District, North City; San Diego, CA

Virginia Parra • Miami Dade College; Miami, FL

Iliana Pena • Lindsey Hopkins Technical Education Center; Miami, FL

Howard Riddles • Tomlinson Adult Learning Center; St. Petersburg, FL

Lisa Roberson • Mission Language and Vocational School; San Francisco, CA

Renata Russo Watson • Harris County Department of Education; Harris County, TX

Francisco Sanchez • Miami-Dade College, Kendall Campus; Miami, FL

Curt Sanford • City College of San Francisco, Alemany Campus; San Francisco, CA

Laurie Shapero • Miami-Dade College, Kendall Campus; Miami, FL

Eileen Spada • Max Hayes Adult School; Detroit, IL

Margaret Teske • Mt. San Antonio College; Walnut, CA

Theresa Warren • East Side Independence Adult Center; San Jose, CA

D. Banu Yaylali • Miami-Dade College, Kendall Campus; Miami, FL

Scope and Sequence

Unit	Grammar Point	Vocabulary	Listening/ Speaking/ Pronunciation	Reading	Writing
Pre-unit *page 2*	• Review parts of speech: noun, verb, preposition, adjective, article, and adverb • Review verb forms	• Introductions • School	• Listen to introductions • Practice introducing yourself to others • Use expressions to check and confirm understanding • Use the dictionary for pronunciation	• Read definitions from a dictionary • Read a conversation script • Read a sample paragraph by students	• Write a sentence in the negative form • Write a paragraph about yourself • Edit your writing
1 **Study Skills and Learning Styles** *page 6*	• Simple present and present continuous • Simple past • Future with *be going to*	• School verbs • Study habits • School employees	• Talk about academic life • Understand advice for succeeding in school • Listen to a teacher giving advice • Discuss goals with an academic counselor • **Pronunciation:** Identify word stress	• Read a paragraph using the simple past • Read a picture • Read quotes from students • Read an article about learning styles • **FOCUS:** Preview and skim an article	• Write about your plans • Create sentences to describe school staff • Write about your ideas • Write and revise a paragraph • **FOCUS:** Paragraph outline
2 **Get Value for Your Money** *page 22*	• The comparative form of adjectives • (*not*) *as* + adjective + *as* • The superlative adjectives • Superlatives with *most* and *least*	• Household appliances • Clothing • Household cleaning supplies • Department store names • Text messaging	• Compare home goods • Discuss advertisements • Talk to a salesclerk • Talk about a faulty appliance • Describe product characteristics • Explain why you like a product • **Pronunciation:** Blending *Is/Was* + *as*	• Read a formal letter of complaint • Read job ads • Read article about a cell phone survey • Read an energy label • **FOCUS:** Use prior knowledge	• Write a formal letter of complaint • Write notes about products • Complete a product comparison chart • Write an advertisement • **FOCUS:** Notice the format of a formal letter
3 **Traffic and Work Safety** *page 38*	• Past continuous • Past continuous with *when* clauses • *Wh-* questions with the past continuous • Past continuous with *while* clauses	• Safe and unsafe driving • Accidents • Job benefits	• Understand people's descriptions of a traffic accident • Talk to manager about a workplace accident • Create dialogues between a police officer and a driver • Give reasons for being late • **Pronunciation:** *Is/was/does/yes* with *she* and *he*	• Scan for specific information • Read a story about two drivers • **FOCUS:** Scan for specific information	• Write an accident description • Take notes about an accident • Write times related to travel • **FOCUS:** *Wh-* questions
4 **Laws, Rules, and Regulations** *page 54*	• *May* and *can* to indicate that something is allowed, and *may not* and *cannot* to indicate prohibition • *Must* and *have to* for necessity, *must not* for prohibition, and *don't have to* for lack of necessity	• Workplace rules • Park rules • Resident rules • School rules	• Understand conversations about workplace rules • Talk to a manager about not following the rules • Tell your classmates about dress code in your country • **Pronunciation:** Reduction and word stress: *can* and *can't*	• Read an employee dress code • Read a list of school rules • Read park signs • Read an article on citizenship requirements • **FOCUS:** Use context to guess the meanings of new words	• Write employee dress-code rules • Write a paragraph about school rules • **FOCUS:** Avoid run-on sentences

Civics/Lifeskills	Math	Critical Thinking	CASAS	SCANS	EFF Content Standards
• Introduce yourself and others	• Use language for asking about differences between number words	• Locate parts of speech • Correct errors in writing	• 0.1.1 • 0.1.2 • 0.1.3 • 0.1.4 • 0.1.6	• Participates as a member of a team • Interprets and communicates information • Negotiates	• Listen actively • Speak so others can understand • Cooperate with others
• Attend a school • Follow a schedule • Manage school and work stress	• Calculate elapsed time using class schedules • Work with time and schedules	• Devise a plan for your future • Decide about training sessions you'd like to take • Assess problems and give advice	• **1:** 0.1.5, 7.1.1, 7.1.3, 7.3.2, 7.4.2, 0.2.4, 7.5.1 • **2:** 7.2.1, 0.1.6, 0.1.2 • **3:** 6.0.4, 6.1.1, 6.1.5, 0.1.4, 0.2.4 • **4:** 7.1.1, 7.1.3, 7.5.2 • **5:** 0.1.2, 7.2.1, 7.4.2, 7.2.5 • **6:** 7.4.1, 7.4.5, 7.4.3, 7.4.9, 7.2.6, 7.2.1 7.4.8 • **7:** 7.2.1, 7.4.2 • **8:** 7.1.1, 7.1.3	• Allocates material and facility resources • Participates as a member of a team • Teaches others • Interprets and communicates information • Organizes and maintains information • Allocates time • Teaches others	• Read with understanding • Observe critically • Speak so others can understand • Listen actively • Reflect and evaluate • Plan • Convey ideas in writing • Take responsibility for learning • Learn through research
• Shop for appliances • Read a home energy guide • Interpret job ads	• Calculate kilowatt usage of an appliance • Determine hourly wages	• Examine alternatives and choose using information • Role-play to explain reasons	• **1:** 1.2.5, 1.2.2, 7.2.1, 7.2.4, 7.4.2 • **2:** 7.4.2, 1.2.1, 1.2.5, 1.3.7 • **3:** 0.1.6, 1.2.1, 1.2.2, 6.1.5, 6.2.5, 6.4.5, 6.9.2 • **4:** 0.1.6, 1.3.9, 1.2.2, 1.3.1, 7.4.2 • **5:** 1.2.2, 1.1.4, 1.3.1, 7.4.2, 7.2.3 • **6:** 7.2.1, 7.2.3, 7.4.2 • **7:** 7.4.2, 0.2.3 • **8:** 0.1.4, 0.2.4, 4.1.7, 4.1.3	• Participates as a member of a team • Acquires and evaluates information • Interprets and communicates information • Negotiates • Allocates money • Organizes and maintains information	• Read with understanding • Listen actively • Observe critically • Solve problems and make decisions • Convey ideas in writing • Speak so others can understand • Reflect and evaluate • Guide others • Cooperate with others
• Fill out an employee accident report • Read about worker's compensation	• Discuss hospital expenses • Calculate miles per hour under and over the speed limit	• Decide on issues related to employee accidents • Identify the type of accident you witness	• **1:** 1.9.1, 2.2.2, 2.2.3, 7.2.1, 7.4.2 • **2:** 1.9.1, 2.2.2, 7.2.1, 7.4.2 • **3:** 0.2.1, 0.1.6, 1.9.4, 2.2.5, 7.2.1, 7.4.2 • **4:** 0.1.3, 0.1.6, 1.9.1, 7.2.1, 7.4.2 • **5:** 0.1.6, 7.2.1, 7.2.2, 7.2.5, 7.4.2 • **6:** 0.1.6, 7.2.1, 7.2.2, 7.2.5, 7.4.2 • **7:** 0.1.6, 7.2.1, 7.4.2 • **8:** 7.2.1, 7.2.5, 7.4.2	• Participates as a member of a team • Acquires and evaluates information • Interprets and communicates information • Organizes and maintains information • Teaches others	• Read with understanding • Convey ideas in writing • Observe critically • Speak so others can understand • Listen actively • Reflect and evaluate • Learn through research • Cooperate with others
• Follow rules in public places • Read signs in a park	• Calculate costs after expenses of a fishing trip	• Say your opinions about school rules • Think about workplace safety rules and why they are important	• **1:** 0.1.6, 7.2.1, 4.2.4 • **2:** 4.6.3, 4.2.4 7.2.1, 7.3.1, 4.6.1 • **3:** 4.2.4, 4.6.5, 4.6.3, 4.6.1 • **4:** 5.6.1, 2.5.4, 1.4.5, 1.4.7 • **5:** 0.1.6, 2.5.4, 5.7.1, 7.2.1, 7.4.2 • **6:** 7.4.2, 5.3.7, 5.3.1, 5.3.6, 2.5.2 • **7:** 7.4.2, 2.5.5, 0.1.6 • **8:** 0.1.6, 0.2.1, 4.2.4	• Acquires and evaluates information • Interprets and communicates information • Participates as a member of a team • Teaches others • Negotiates • Organizes and maintains information • Exercises leadership	• Read with understanding • Speak so others can understand • Observe critically • Listen actively • Guide others • Solve problems and make decisions • Reflect and evaluate • Convey ideas in writing • Plan

Civics/ Lifeskills	Math	Critical Thinking	CASAS	SCANS	EFF Content Standards
• Learn about healthy eating • Understand the use of over-the-counter drugs • Realize exercise is part of a healthy lifestyle	• Determine percentage of daily nutrition values in a serving • Interpret nutrition labels	• Make suggestions on healthier living habits • Recognize common symptoms for health problems • Compare lifestyles from the past to today	**1:** 3.1.1, 3.1.3 **2:** 3.1.1, 3.1.3, 7.4.2 **3:** 3.1.1, 3.1.2, 3.1.3 **4:** 3.5.9, 3.5.1, 3.5.2, 3.5.3 **5:** 3.4.1, 3.5.4, 3.5.8, 3.5.9 **6:** 3.5.9, 3.5.1, 3.5.2 **7:** 3.1.1, 3.4.2, 7.4.2 **8:** 3.5.4, 3.5.8, 3.5.9, 7.4.2	• Organizes and maintains information • Interprets and communicates information • Participates as a member of a team • Teaches others • Negotiates • Acquires and evaluates information • Exercises leadership	• Read with understanding • Speak so others can understand • Cooperate with others • Listen actively • Observe critically • Convey ideas in writing • Guide others • Solve problems and make decisions • Plan
• Learn about volunteering • Decide how to spend your free time in the community	• Calculate monthly expenses	• Decide what type of entertainment meets your budget • Distinguish between fact and opinion	**1:** 7.1.1, 7.1.2, 7.4.2 **2:** 7.1.1, 7.4.2, 7.5.1 **3:** 0.1.6, 0.2.1, 0.2.4, 7.4.2 **4:** 0.1.2, 0.1.4, 7.4.2 **5:** 0.1.2, 0.1.4, 7.4.2 **6:** 7.2.1, 7.2.2 **7:** 7.4.2 **8:** 4.4.1, 4.8.2, 4.9.3	• Participates as a member of a team • Acquires and evaluates information • Organizes and maintains information • Interprets and communicates information • Teaches others • Negotiates	• Read with understanding • Listen actively • Observe critically • Convey ideas in writing • Speak so others can understand • Guide others • Advocate and influence
• Make a complaint about poor service • Use proper etiquette when conversing at work	• Review a utility bill • Calculate energy cost of household appliances • Multiply kilowatts • Examine a hotel bill	• Generate a list of ways to save energy at home • Offer solutions to workplace problems	**1:** 2.5.1, 5.1.6, 5.6.1, 5.7.1 **2:** 2.2.1, 2.2.3, 2.5.4, 2.6.3 **3:** 1.4.4, 1.5.3, 6.03, 6.04, 7.3.2 **4:** 5.7.1, 5.7.2, 5.7.3, 5.8.3 **5:** 1.4.7, 3.4.2, 6.1.3, 6.1.5, 7.5.5 **6:** 1.2.5, 5.6.1, 5.6.3 **7:** 5.7.1, 7.4.2, 7.4.3, 7.5.7 **8:** 4.5.5, 4.6.2, 4.6.4, 4.6.5, 4.7.2, 4.8.5, 4.8.7	• Monitors and corrects performance • Allocates time • Allocates material and facility resources • Negotiates • Allocates money • Understands systems • Organizes and maintains information • Applies technology to task • Serves clients/customers • Uses computers to process information	• Take responsibility for learning • Listen actively • Reflect and evaluate • Observe critically • Convey ideas in writing • Advocate and influence • Use math to solve problems and make decisions • Speak so others can understand • Use information and communications technology • Resolve conflict and negotiate • Guide others
• Help a newcomer to your city • Interpret a charge about paying for medical services • Talk about jobs that are available including skills required	• Calculate health care costs • Understand sliding payment scales	• Offer suggestions and opinions to a variety of issues • Recall your past experiences • Share advice with others	**1:** 0.1.5, 2.6.3, 2.5.6 **2:** 0.1.2, 2.5.5, 2.6.1 **3:** 4.2.1, 4.7.1, 6.1.5, 6.4.3 **4:** 3.1.1, 3.2.3, 7.4.4 **5:** 0.1.3, 0.2.1, 7.4.2 **6:** 2.6.1, 7.3.4, 7.4.8 **7:** 6.6.5, 6.6.6, 7.2.6 **8:** 4.1.3, 4.1.8, 7.4.7	• Teaches others • Monitors and corrects performance • Participates as a member of a team • Exercises leadership • Acquires and evaluates information • Organizes and maintains information • Improves and designs systems • Negotiates • Understands systems	• Cooperate with others • Read with understanding • Listen actively • Observe critically • Convey ideas in writing • Take responsibility for learning • Guide others • Speak so others can understand • Advocate and influence • Plan

Correlations

Civics/ Lifeskills	Math	Critical Thinking	CASAS	SCANS	EFF Content Standards
• Respond to criticism at work • Converse about ways to encourage others	• Calculate people's ages • Calculate work time	• Describe a time when you made a mistake at work • Make inferences about positive attitudes at work	**1:** 0.1.4, 0.2.1 **2:** 0.2.4, 1.4.1 **3:** 4.4.1, 4.4.2 **4:** 7.1.3, 8.3.2 **5:** 4.7.4, 4.8.5 **6:** 4.1.9, 4.4.2, 4.4.5 **7:** 4.6.1, 4.6.4 **8:** 4.4.2, 4.4.7, 4.5.2, 4.5.5	• Interprets and communicates information • Allocates material and facility resources • Exercises leadership • Monitors and corrects performance • Acquires and evaluates information • Improves and designs systems • Applies technology to task	• Observe critically • Read with understanding • Convey ideas in writing • Guide others • Speak so others can understand • Cooperate with others • Use math to solve problems and communicate • Take responsibility for learning • Reflect and evaluate
• Solve problems at the office • Comprehend the usage of items in a first-aid kit • Calling 911 • Solve school problems • Use a blood pressure machine • Operate a copy machine	• Calculate elapsed time • Budget time	• Choose the correct action to respond to an emergency • Decide which health items are useful for the workplace7	**1:** 4.5.1, 4.5.4, 4.5.6, 4.5.7 **2:** 1.4.8, 2.5.1 **3:** 1.3.1, 1.3.3, 1.8.1 **4:** 4.4.1, 4.6.4, 4.8.1, 4.8.3, 4.8.6 **5:** 7.2.4, 7.2.7, 7.3.4 **6:** 2.5.1, 3.1.1, 7.5.5 **7:** 3.1.3, 3.5.9 **8:** 7.2.6, 7.3.2, 7.3.4	• Maintains and troubleshoots technology • Understands systems • Exercises leadership • Uses computers to process information • Interprets and communicates information • Participates as a member of a team • Acquires and evaluates information • Applies technology to a task • Selects technology	• Read with understanding • Cooperate with others • Convey ideas in writing • Speak so others can understand • Guide others • Use math to solve problems and communicate • Observe critically • Take responsibility for learning • Use information and communications technology • Learn through research
• Determine what expenses are needed to move • Understand landlord/tenant agreement	• Determine moving costs	• Prioritize a list of needs when looking for housing • Respond to a letter of complaint while role-playing with a partner	**1:** 7.4.5 **2:** 7.1.1 **3:** 1.4.1, 1.4.7 **4:** 1.4.5, 1.4.7, 7.2.3 **5:** 1.4.3, 1.4.7 **6:** 1.4.3, 1.4.7 **7:** 0.1.3, 4.8.1, 4.8.5 **8:** 1.4.5, 1.4.7, 5.1.6, 5.3.1	• Allocates material and facility resources • Negotiates • Works with cultural diversity • Allocates time • Monitors and corrects performance • Allocates money • Monitors and corrects performance • Understands systems	• Observe critically • Read with understanding • Speak so others can understand • Convey ideas in writing • Cooperate with others • Guide others • Solve problems and make decisions • Use math to solve problems and communicate
• Use the Internet to find information • Make goals for the future • Communicate with an academic adviser	• Compare tuition fees to determine unit cost • Follow an enrollment schedule using time, date, and credits	• Interpret data from a bar graph • Create a career plan and discuss • Recognize the relationship between education and salary	**1:** 4.8.2, 7.2.7, 7.3.1, 7.3.2 **2:** 7.2.1, 7.5.1 **3:** 2.1, 4.1.6, 4.1.8 **4:** 1.5.1, 1.8.1, 3.5.7 **5:** 4.1.9, 4.4.5 **6:** 4.1.8, 4.2.1, 4.4.3 **7:** 4.6.5, 7.4.2 **8:** 7.1.1, 7.1.2, 7.1.3	• Applies technology to a task • Participates as a member of a team • Takes responsibility for learning • Exercises leadership • Organizes and maintains information • Acquires and evaluates information	• Cooperate with others • Listen actively • Observe critically • Reflect and evaluate • Use math to solve problems and communicate • Solve problems and make decisions • Learn through research • Take responsibility for learning

To The Teacher

PROGRAM OVERVIEW

> **Excellent English: Language Skills for Success** equips students with the grammar and skills they need to access community resources, while developing the foundation for long-term career and academic success.

Excellent English is a four-level, grammar-oriented series for English learners featuring a *Grammar Picture Dictionary* approach to vocabulary building and grammar acquisition. An accessible and predictable sequence of lessons in each unit systematically builds language and math skills around life-skill topics. *Excellent English* is tightly correlated to all of the major standards for adult instruction.

What has led the *Excellent English* team to develop this new series? The program responds to the large and growing need for a new generation of adult materials that provide a more academic alternative to existing publications. *Excellent English* is a natural response to the higher level aspirations of today's adult learners. Stronger reading and writing skills, greater technological proficiency, and a deeper appreciation for today's global economy—increasingly, prospective employees across virtually all industries must exhibit these skill sets to be successful. Interviews with a wide range of administrators, instructors, and students underscore the need for new materials that more quickly prepare students for the vocational and academic challenges they must meet to be successful.

The Complete Excellent English Program

- The **Student Book** features twelve 16-page units that integrate listening, speaking, reading, writing, grammar, math, and pronunciation skills with life-skill topics, critical thinking activities, and civics concepts.

- The **Student Book with Audio Highlights** provides students with audio recordings of all of the Grammar Picture Dictionary, pronunciation, and conversation models in the Student Book.

- The **Workbook with Audio CD** is an essential companion to the Student Book. It provides:
  - Supplementary practice activities correlated to the Student Book.

- Application lessons that carry vital, standards-based learning objectives through its *Family Connection, Community Connection, Career Connection*, and *Technology Connection* lessons.
  - Practice tests that encourage students to assess their skills in a low-stakes environment, complete with listening tasks from the Workbook CD.

- The **Teacher's Edition with Tests** provides:
  - Step-by-step procedural notes for each Student Book activity.
  - Expansion activities for the Student Book, many of which offer creative tasks tied to the "big picture" scenes in each unit, including photocopiable worksheets.
  - Culture, Grammar, Academic, Vocabulary, and Pronunciation Notes.
  - A two-page written test for each unit.
  - Audio scripts for audio program materials.
  - Answer keys for Student Book, Workbook, and Tests.

- The **Interactive Multimedia Program** in *Excellent English* Levels 1 and 2 incorporates and extends the learning goals of the Student Book by integrating language, literacy, and numeracy skill-building with multimedia practice on the computer. A flexible set of activities correlated to each unit builds vocabulary, listening, reading, writing, and test-taking skills.

- The **Color Overhead Transparencies** encourage instructors to present new vocabulary and grammar in fun and meaningful ways. This component provides a full color overhead transparency for each "big picture" scene, as well as transparencies of the grammar charts in each unit.

- The **Big Picture PowerPoint® CD-ROM** includes the "big picture" scenes for all four Student Books. Instructors can use this CD-ROM to project the scenes from a laptop through an LCD or data projector in class.

- The **Audio CDs** and **Audiocassettes** contain recordings for all listening activities in the Student Book. Listening passages for the unit tests are provided on a separate Assessment CD or cassette.

- The **EZ Test® CD-ROM Test Generator** provides a databank of assessment items from which instructors can create customized tests within minutes. The EZ Test assessment materials are also available online at www.eztestonline.com.

Student Book Overview

Consult the *Welcome to Excellent English* guide on pages xiv-xviii. This guide offers instructors and administrators a visual tour of one Student Book unit.

Excellent English is designed to maximize accessibility and flexibility. Each unit in Levels 3 and 4 contain the following sequence of eight, two-page lessons that develop vocabulary and build language, grammar, and math skills around life-skill topics:

- Lesson 1: Grammar and Vocabulary (1)
- Lesson 2: Grammar Practice Plus
- Lesson 3: Listening and Conversation
- Lesson 4: Grammar and Vocabulary (2)
- Lesson 5: Grammar Practice Plus
- Lesson 6: Reading
- Lesson 7: Writing
- Lesson 8: Career Connection and Check Your Progress

Each lesson in *Excellent English* is designed as a two-page spread. Lessons 1 and 4 introduce new grammar points and vocabulary sets that allow students to practice the grammar in controlled and meaningful ways. Lessons 2 and 5—the Grammar Practice Plus lessons—provide more opened-ended opportunities for students to use their new language productively. Lesson 3 allows students to hear a variety of listening inputs and to use their new language skills in conversation. In Lessons 6 and 7, students develop the more academic skills of reading and writing through explicit teaching of academic strategies and through exposure to multiple text types and writing tasks. Each unit ends with Lesson 8, an exciting capstone that offers both Career Connection—a career-oriented lesson that presents a variety of workplace situations and provides language-oriented problem-solving tasks—and Check Your Progress—a self-evaluation task. Each lesson addresses a key adult standard, and these standards are indicated in the scope and sequence and in the footer at the bottom of the left-hand page in each lesson.

SPECIAL FEATURES IN EACH STUDENT BOOK UNIT

- **Grammar Picture Dictionary**. Lessons 1 and 4 introduce students to vocabulary and grammar through a picture dictionary approach. This context-rich approach allows students to acquire grammatical structures as they build vocabulary.

- **Grammar Charts**. Also in Lessons 1 and 4, new grammar points are presented in clear paradigms, providing easy reference for students and instructors.

- **"Grammar Professor" Notes**. Additional information related to key grammar points is provided at point of use through the "Grammar Professor" feature. A cheerful, red-haired character appears next to each of these additional grammar points, calling students' attention to learning points in an inviting and memorable way.

- **Math**. Learning basic math skills is critically important for success in school, on the job, and at home. As such, national and state standards for adult education mandate instruction in basic math skills. In each unit, a Math box is dedicated to helping students develop the functional numeracy and language skills they need for success with basic math.

- **Pronunciation**. This special feature has two major goals: (1) to help students hear and produce specific sounds, words, and phrases so they become better listeners and speakers; and (2) to address issues of stress, rhythm, and intonation so that students' spoken English becomes more comprehensible.

- ***What about you?*** Throughout each unit of the Student Book, students are encouraged to apply new language to their own lives through personalization activities.

- **"Big Picture" scenes**. Lesson 2 in each unit introduces a "big picture" scene. This scene serves as a springboard to a variety of activities provided in the Student Book, Teacher's Edition, Color Overhead Transparencies package and the Big Picture PowerPoint CD-ROM. In the Student Book, the "big picture" scene features key vocabulary and serves as a prompt for language activities that practice the grammar points of the unit. The scene features characters with distinct personalities for students to enjoy, respond to, and talk about.

CIVICS CONCEPTS

Many institutions focus direct attention on the importance of civics instruction for English language learners. Civics instruction encourages students to become active and informed community members. The Teacher's Edition includes multiple *Community Connection* activities in each unit. These activities encourage learners to become more active and informed members of their communities.

ACADEMIC SKILL DEVELOPMENT

Many adult programs recognize the need to help students develop important academic skills that will facilitate lifelong learning. The *Excellent English* Student Book addresses this need through explicit teaching of reading and writing strategies, explicit presentation and practice of grammar, and academic notes in the Teacher's Edition. The Teacher's Edition also includes multiple *Academic Connection* activities in each unit. These activities encourage learners to become more successful in an academic environment.

CASAS, SCANS, EFF, AND OTHER STANDARDS

Instructors and administrators benchmark student progress against national and/or state standards for adult instruction. With this in mind, *Excellent English* carefully integrates instructional elements from a wide range of standards including CASAS, SCANS, EFF, TABE CLAS-E, the Florida Adult ESOL Syllabi, and the Los Angeles Unified School District Course Outlines. Unit-by-unit correlations of some of these standards appear in the Student Book scope and sequence on pages iv-ix. Other correlations appear in the Teacher's Edition. Here is a brief overview of our approach to meeting the key national and state standards:

- **CASAS.** Many U.S. states, including California, tie funding for adult education programs to student performance on the Comprehensive Adult Student Assessment System (CASAS). The CASAS (www.casas.org) competencies identify more than 30 essential skills that adults need in order to succeed in the classroom, workplace, and community. *Excellent English* comprehensively integrates all of the CASAS Life Skill Competencies throughout the four levels of the series.

- **SCANS.** Developed by the United States Department of Labor, SCANS is an acronym for the Secretary's Commission on Achieving Necessary Skills (wdr.doleta.gov/SCANS/). SCANS competencies are workplace skills that help people compete more effectively in today's global economy. A variety of SCANS competencies is threaded throughout the activities in each unit of *Excellent English*.

The incorporation of these competencies recognizes both the intrinsic importance of teaching workplace skills and the fact that many adult students are already working members of their communities.

- **EFF.** Equipped for the Future (EFF) is a set of standards for adult literacy and lifelong learning, developed by The National Institute for Literacy (www.nifl.gov). The organizing principle of EFF is that adults assume responsibilities in three major areas of life – as workers, as parents, and as citizens. These three areas of focus are called "role maps" in the EFF documentation. Each *Excellent English* unit addresses all three of the EFF role maps in the Student Book or Workbook.

- **Florida Adult ESOL Syllabi** provide the curriculum frameworks for all six levels of instruction; Foundations, Low Beginning, High Beginning, Low Intermediate, High Intermediate, and Advanced. The syllabi were developed by the State of Florida as a guide to include the following areas of adult literacy standards: workplace, communication (listen, speak, read, and write), technology, interpersonal communication, health and nutrition, government and community resources, consumer education, family and parenting, concepts of time and money, safety and security, and language development (grammar and pronunciation). *Excellent English* Level 3 incorporates into its instruction the vast majority of standards at the Low Intermediate level.

- **TABE Complete Language Assessment System— English (CLAS-E)** has been developed by CTB/ McGraw-Hill and provides administrators and teachers with accurate, reliable evaluations of adult students' English language skills. TABE CLAS-E measures students' reading, listening, writing, and speaking skills at all English proficiency levels and also assesses critically important grammar standards. TABE CLAS-E scores are linked to TABE 9 and 10, providing a battery of assessment tools that offer seamless transition from English language to adult basic education assessment.

- **Los Angeles Unified School District (LAUSD) Course Outlines.** LAUSD Competency-Based Education (CBE) Course Outlines were developed to guide teachers in lesson planning and to inform students about what they will be able to do after successful completion of their course. The CBE Course outlines focus on acquiring skills in listening, speaking, reading and writing in the context of everyday life. *Excellent English* addresses all four language skills in the contexts of home, community and work, appropriately targeting Intermediate Low adult ESL students.

TECHNOLOGY

Technology plays an increasingly important role in our lives as students, workers, family members, and citizens. Every unit in the Workbook includes a one-page lesson titled *Technology Connection* that focuses on some aspect of technology in our everyday lives.

The EZ Test® CD-ROM Test Generator—and its online version, available at www.eztestonline.com—allow instructors to easily create customized tests from a digital databank of assessment items.

NUMBER OF HOURS OF INSTRUCTION

The *Excellent English* program has been designed to accommodate the needs of adult classes with 100–180 hours of classroom instruction. Here are three recommended ways in which various components in the *Excellent English* program can be combined to meet student and instructor needs.

- **80–100 hours.** Instructors are encouraged to work through all of the Student Book materials. The Color Overhead Transparencies can be used to introduce and/or review materials in each unit. Instructors should also look to the Teacher's Edition for teaching suggestions and testing materials as necessary. *Time per unit: 8–10 hours.*

- **100–140 hours.** In addition to working through all of the Student Book materials, instructors are encouraged to incorporate the Workbook activities for supplementary practice. *Time per unit: 10–14 hours.*

- **140–180 hours.** Instructors and students working in an intensive instructional setting can take advantage of the wealth of expansion activities threaded through the Teacher's Edition to supplement the Student Book, and Workbook. *Time per unit: 14–18 hours.*

ASSESSMENT

The *Excellent English* program offers instructors, students, and administrators the following wealth of resources for monitoring and assessing student progress and achievement:

- **Standardized testing formats.** *Excellent English* is comprehensively correlated to the CASAS competencies and all of the other major national and state standards for adult learning. Students have the opportunity to practice answering CASAS-style listening questions in Lessons 3 of each Student Book unit, and both listening and reading questions in the Unit tests in the Teacher's Edition and practice tests in the Workbook. Students practice with the same items types and bubble-in answer sheets they encounter on CASAS and other standardized tests.

- **Achievement tests.** The *Excellent English* Teacher's Edition includes paper-and-pencil end-of-unit tests. In addition, the *EZ Test® CD-ROM Test Generator* provides a databank of assessment items from which instructors can create customized tests within minutes. The EZ Test assessment materials are also available online at www.eztestonline.com. These tests help students demonstrate how well they have learned the instructional content of the unit. Adult learners often show incremental increases in learning that are not always measured on the standardized tests. The achievement tests may demonstrate learning even in a short amount of instructional time. Twenty percent of each test includes questions that encourage students to apply more academic skills such as determining meaning from context, making inferences, and understanding main ideas. Practice with these question types will help prepare students who may want to enroll in academic classes.

- **Performance-based assessment.** *Excellent English* provides several ways to measure students' performance on productive tasks, including the Writing tasks in Lesson 7 of each Student Book unit. In addition, the Teacher's Edition suggests writing and speaking prompts that instructors can use for performance-based assessment.

- **Portfolio assessment.** A portfolio is a collection of student work that can be used to show progress. Examples of work that the instructor or the student may submit in the portfolio include writing samples, speaking rubrics, audiotapes, videotapes, or projects.

- **Self-assessment.** Self-assessment is an important part of the overall assessment picture, as it promotes student involvement and commitment to the learning process. When encouraged to assess themselves, students take more control of their learning and are better able to connect the instructional content with their own goals. The Student Book includes Check Your Progress activities at the end of each unit, which allow students to assess their knowledge of vocabulary and grammar. Students can chart their mastery of the key language lessons in the unit, and use this information to set new learning goals.

Welcome to Excellent English!

Grammar Picture Dictionary uses engaging illustrations to showcase target grammar and vocabulary.

Clear and thorough **grammar charts** make target grammar points accessible and easily comprehensible.

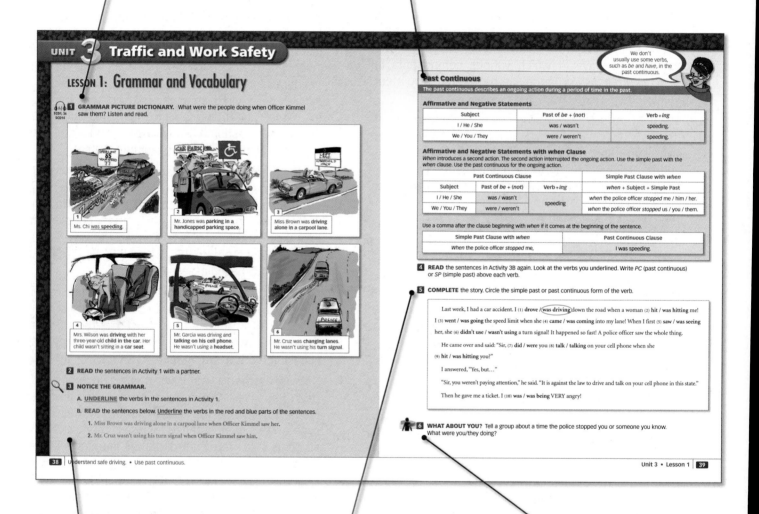

Notice the Grammar activities make students aware of the form and function of new grammar points.

Scaffolded grammar activities systematically expose, stress, and review each key grammar structure.

Personalization activities encourage students to use new grammar to talk about their own experiences.

A **Grammar Professor** calls students' attention to additional grammar points in an inviting and memorable way.

Grammar Practice Plus lessons introduce additional vocabulary while recycling and practicing the target grammar.

Notebook **Writing Activities** encourage students to write more freely.

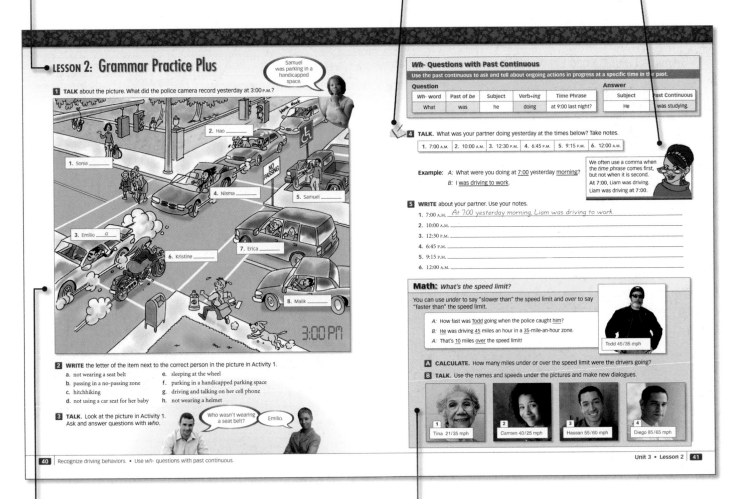

Big Picture activities provide rich opportunities for classroom discussion and practice with new language.

Math activities allow students to activate newly acquired vocabulary and grammar as they learn and apply everyday math skills.

Listening comprehension activities provide students with opportunities to build practical listening skills.

Life skills-based listening activities integrate grammar and vocabulary to provide students with models of everyday conversation.

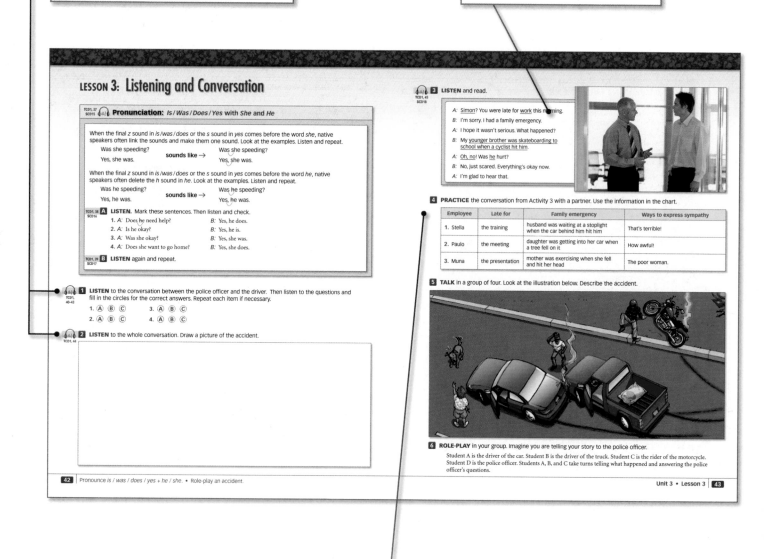

LESSON 3: Listening and Conversation

TCD1, 37
SCD15 **Pronunciation:** *Is / Was / Does / Yes* with *She* and *He*

When the final *z* sound in *is / was / does* or the *s* sound in *yes* comes before the word *she*, native speakers often link the sounds and make them one sound. Look at the examples. Listen and repeat.

Was she speeding?
Yes, she was.
sounds like →
Was she speeding?
Yes, she was.

When the final *z* sound in *is / was / does* or the *s* sound in *yes* comes before the word *he*, native speakers often delete the *h* sound in *he*. Look at the examples. Listen and repeat.

Was he speeding?
Yes, he was.
sounds like →
Was he speeding?
Yes, he was.

TCD1, 38
SCD16 **A LISTEN.** Mark these sentences. Then listen and check.
1. A: Does he need help? B: Yes, he does.
2. A: Is he okay? B: Yes, he is.
3. A: Was she okay? B: Yes, she was.
4. A: Does she want to go home? B: Yes, she does.

TCD1, 39
SCD17 **B LISTEN** again and repeat.

TCD1, 40-43 **1 LISTEN** to the conversation between the police officer and the driver. Then listen to the questions and fill in the circles for the correct answers. Repeat each item if necessary.
1. Ⓐ Ⓑ Ⓒ   3. Ⓐ Ⓑ Ⓒ
2. Ⓐ Ⓑ Ⓒ   4. Ⓐ Ⓑ Ⓒ

TCD1, 44 **2 LISTEN** to the whole conversation. Draw a picture of the accident.

TCD1, 45
SCD18 **3 LISTEN** and read.

A: Simon? You were late for work this morning.
B: I'm sorry. I had a family emergency.
A: I hope it wasn't serious. What happened?
B: My younger brother was skateboarding to school when a cyclist hit him.
A: Oh, no! Was he hurt?
B: No, just scared. Everything's okay now.
A: I'm glad to hear that.

4 PRACTICE the conversation from Activity 3 with a partner. Use the information in the chart.

Employee	Late for	Family emergency	Ways to express sympathy
1. Stella	the training	husband was waiting at a stoplight when the car behind him hit him	That's terrible!
2. Paulo	the meeting	daughter was getting into her car when a tree fell on it	How awful!
3. Muna	the presentation	mother was exercising when she fell and hit her head	The poor woman.

5 TALK in a group of four. Look at the illustration below. Describe the accident.

6 ROLE-PLAY in your group. Imagine you are telling your story to the police officer.
Student A is the driver of the car. Student B is the driver of the truck. Student C is the rider of the motorcycle. Student D is the police officer. Students A, B, and C take turns telling what happened and answering the police officer's questions.

42 | Pronounce is / was / does / yes + he / she. • Role-play an accident.

Unit 3 • Lesson 3 43

Guided speaking activities provide controlled practice of new grammar and vocabulary while building students' confidence with the target language.

Pre-reading tasks activate prior knowledge and introduce the reading passage.

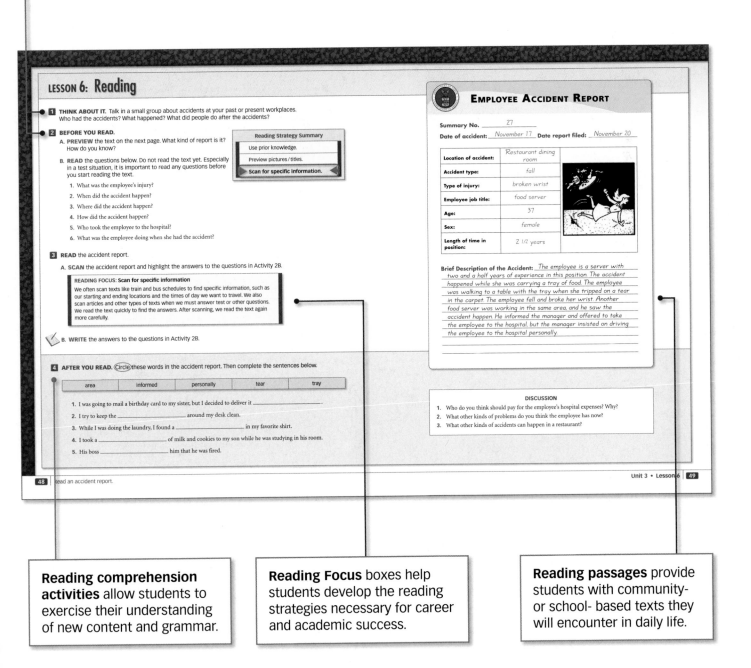

LESSON 6: Reading

1 THINK ABOUT IT. Talk in a small group about accidents at your past or present workplaces. Who had the accidents? What happened? What did people do after the accidents?

2 BEFORE YOU READ.

A. **PREVIEW** the text on the next page. What kind of report is it? How do you know?

B. **READ** the questions below. Do not read the text yet. Especially in a test situation, it is important to read any questions before you start reading the text.

1. What was the employee's injury?
2. When did the accident happen?
3. Where did the accident happen?
4. How did the accident happen?
5. Who took the employee to the hospital?
6. What was the employee doing when she had the accident?

Reading Strategy Summary

Use prior knowledge.

Preview pictures / titles.

Scan for specific information.

3 READ the accident report.

A. **SCAN** the accident report and highlight the answers to the questions in Activity 2B.

READING FOCUS: Scan for specific information
We often scan texts like train and bus schedules to find specific information, such as our starting and ending locations and the times of day we want to travel. We also scan articles and other types of texts when we must answer test or other questions. We read the text quickly to find the answers. After scanning, we read the text again more carefully.

B. **WRITE** the answers to the questions in Activity 2B.

4 AFTER YOU READ. Circle these words in the accident report. Then complete the sentences below.

| area | informed | personally | tear | tray |

1. I was going to mail a birthday card to my sister, but I decided to deliver it _____.
2. I try to keep the _____ around my desk clean.
3. While I was doing the laundry, I found a _____ in my favorite shirt.
4. I took a _____ of milk and cookies to my son while he was studying in his room.
5. His boss _____ him that he was fired.

48 | Read an accident report.

EMPLOYEE ACCIDENT REPORT

Summary No. _____ 27

Date of accident: _November 17_ Date report filed: _November 20_

Location of accident:	Restaurant dining room
Accident type:	fall
Type of injury:	broken wrist
Employee job title:	food server
Age:	37
Sex:	female
Length of time in position:	2 1/2 years

Brief Description of the Accident: _The employee is a server with two and a half years of experience in this position. The accident happened while she was carrying a tray of food. The employee was walking to a table with the tray when she tripped on a tear in the carpet. The employee fell and broke her wrist. Another food server was working in the same area, and he saw the accident happen. He informed the manager and offered to take the employee to the hospital, but the manager insisted on driving the employee to the hospital personally._

DISCUSSION
1. Who do you think should pay for the employee's hospital expenses? Why?
2. What other kinds of problems do you think the employee has now?
3. What other kinds of accidents can happen in a restaurant?

Reading comprehension activities allow students to exercise their understanding of new content and grammar.

Reading Focus boxes help students develop the reading strategies necessary for career and academic success.

Reading passages provide students with community- or school- based texts they will encounter in daily life.

Writing Focus boxes help students develop critical academic skills.

Students write a **variety of text types** such as accident reports, applications, letters, and essays.

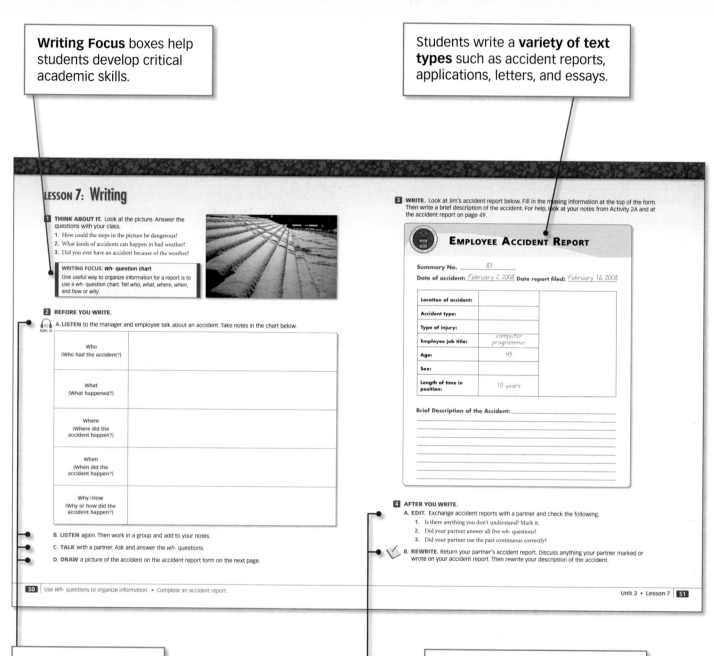

LESSON 7: Writing

1 THINK ABOUT IT. Look at the picture. Answer the questions with your class.
1. How could the steps in the picture be dangerous?
2. What kinds of accidents can happen in bad weather?
3. Did you ever have an accident because of the weather?

WRITING FOCUS: *Wh*- question chart
One useful way to organize information for a report is to use a *wh*- question chart. Tell *who, what, where, when,* and *how* or *why.*

2 BEFORE YOU WRITE.

A. **LISTEN** to the manager and employee talk about an accident. Take notes in the chart below. (TCD1, 47)

Who (Who had the accident?)	
What (What happened?)	
Where (Where did the accident happen?)	
When (When did the accident happen?)	
Why / How (Why or how did the accident happen?)	

B. **LISTEN** again. Then work in a group and add to your notes.

C. **TALK** with a partner. Ask and answer the *wh*- questions.

D. **DRAW** a picture of the accident on the accident report form on the next page.

3 WRITE. Look at Jim's accident report below. Fill in the missing information at the top of the form. Then write a brief description of the accident. For help, look at your notes from Activity 2A and at the accident report on page 49.

EMPLOYEE ACCIDENT REPORT

Summary No. _____83_____

Date of accident: *February 2, 2008* Date report filed: *February 16, 2008*

Location of accident:		
Accident type:		
Type of injury:		
Employee job title:	*computer programmer*	
Age:	*43*	
Sex:		
Length of time in position:	*10 years*	

Brief Description of the Accident: _____
_____
_____
_____
_____
_____
_____

4 AFTER YOU WRITE.

A. **EDIT.** Exchange accident reports with a partner and check the following.
1. Is there anything you don't understand? Mark it.
2. Did your partner answer all five *wh*- questions?
3. Did your partner use the past continuous correctly?

B. **REWRITE.** Return your partner's accident report. Discuss anything your partner marked or wrote on your accident report. Then rewrite your description of the accident.

50 | Use *Wh*- questions to organize information. • Complete an accident report.

Unit 3 • Lesson 7 **51**

A series of **highly-scaffolded tasks** culminates in an academic or practical writing task.

Editing and **revising activities** encourage students to be more effective and accurate writers.

The **Career Connection** develops students' problem-solving skills in a variety of workplace situations.

Check Your Progress ensures student comprehension and retention of each unit's target grammar and vocabulary.

Career Connection

1 **LISTEN** to the conversation. Then practice the conversation with a partner.

TCD1, 48

Jason: What happened?

Tomás: I was climbing the ladder when I slipped and fell. I think I hurt my wrist.

Jason: You should go to the emergency room.

Tomás: I don't have insurance. And a visit to the emergency room is really expensive.

Jason: But you were working when you had the accident. I think workers' compensation will cover the cost.

Tomás: Workers' compensation? What's that?

2 **TALK** with a partner. Answer the questions.
1. What are Jason's and Tomás's jobs?
2. What are they talking about?
3. What is Jason's suggestion?

3 **WRITE.** Why do you think workers sometimes don't get medical treatment for accidents at work? Use ideas from Activity 1 and your own ideas.

Example: _They don't know about workers' compensation._

4 **READ** about workers' compensation.

WORKERS' COMPENSATION

State laws say that employers must pay for workers' compensation insurance for their employees. That means that if employees are injured or become sick while they are doing their work, all their medical costs will be covered. Workers' compensation also includes disability payments if the worker cannot work, and physical therapy to help the worker return to work. Employees do not have to pay for this insurance.

5 **READ** the text above again. Check ☑ the benefits workers' compensation provides.

☐ visit to the emergency room   ☐ medications and treatment
☐ physical therapy   ☐ payments if you can't work

6 **WHAT ABOUT YOU?** Talk in small groups. Tell about a time you or someone you know had an accident at work or school. What happened? What did the person do after the accident?

Check Your Progress!

Skill	Circle the answers	Is it correct?
A. Use the past continuous with *when* clauses.	1. Angela **talk** / **was talking** / **talks** on her cell phone when she hit the tree.	☐
	2. **Were** / **Was** / **Are** they speeding when she saw them?	☐
	3. David was changing lanes when he **hit** / **was hitting** / **hits** the truck.	☐
	4. Were you speeding when you **had** / **was having** / **has** the accident?	☐

Number Correct   0   1   2   3   4

Skill	Circle the answers	Is it correct?
B. Use the past continuous with *while* clauses.	5. May sprained her ankle while she **play** / **plays** / **was playing** soccer.	☐
	6. While Dan **running** / **run** / **was running**, he dislocated his knee.	☐
	7. Sharon **broke** / **was breaking** / **breaking** her arm while she was playing basketball.	☐
	8. She **hurting** / **was hurting** / **hurt** her back while she was lifting the box.	☐

Number Correct   0   1   2   3   4

Skill	Circle the answers	Is it correct?
C. Talk about traffic safety.	9. Babies should sit in a **seat belt** / **car seat**.	☐
	10. Use your **turn signal** / **carpool lane** when you change lanes.	☐
	11. She got a ticket. She was **speeding** / **parking** in a handicapped parking space.	☐
	12. You should use a **headset** / **carpool lane** while you're driving and talking on your cell phone.	☐

Number Correct   0   1   2   3   4

Skill	Circle the answers	Is it correct?
D. Understand work safety and injuries.	13. Alex **dislocated** / **tripped** his shoulder at work.	☐
	14. Clean up the wet floor before someone **slips** / **hurts** on it.	☐
	15. I hurt my back while I was **lifting** / **unloading** the truck.	☐
	16. Did you fall while you were getting **down** / **out of** the elevator?	☐

Number Correct   0   1   2   3   4

COUNT the number of correct answers above. Fill in the bubbles.

Chart Your Success					
Skill	Need Practice	Okay	Good	Very Good	Excellent!
A. Use the past continuous with *when* clauses.	⓪	①	②	③	④
B. Use the past continuous with *while* clauses.	⓪	①	②	③	④
C. Talk about traffic safety.	⓪	①	②	③	④
D. Understand work safety and injuries.	⓪	①	②	③	④

Language in the Classroom

 1 **LISTEN** to the introductions. Then practice them with a partner.

Shirley:	Hi. I'm Shirley. Are you a new student?
Carl:	Yes, I am. My name is Carl.
Shirley:	Nice to meet you, Carl. I was a student in this class last term.
Carl:	Nice to meet you, Shirley.

Shirley:	Carl, let me introduce you to another student in this class. This is Luisa. Luisa, this is Carl.
Luisa:	Nice to meet you, Carl. Welcome to our class.
Carl:	Thank you, Luisa. Nice to meet you, too.

 2 **LISTEN** and repeat the phrases. You can use these phrases with your classmates.

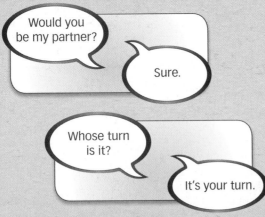

Would you be my partner?

Sure.

Whose turn is it?

It's your turn.

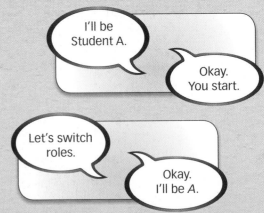

I'll be Student A.

Okay. You start.

Let's switch roles.

Okay. I'll be A.

3 **TALK.** Work in a group of three. Practice introducing yourselves. Use the conversations in Activity 1 and the phrases in Activity 2.

4 **COMPLETE** the sentences below with a word from the box. Then write answers to the questions.

from	live	did	language	new	What

1. _____ is your first name? _____

2. Where are you _____? _____

3. Are you a _____ student? _____

4. Where do you _____? _____

5. What _____ do you speak? _____

6. When _____ you move here? _____

5 **LISTEN** and repeat the following questions.

TCD1, 4

Ask to hear something again
Excuse me. Could you repeat that, please?
Could you please say that again?
Can you please repeat that?
Did you say *fourteen* or *forty*?
Could you spell that, please?
Check for understanding
Do you understand what I said?
Do you know what I mean?

6 **WHAT ABOUT YOU?** Work with a partner. Take turns asking and answering the questions in Activity 4. Use the expressions in the box in Activity 5 to check for or confirm understanding.

Hi. What's your name?

Shirley.

I'm sorry. Could you spell that, please?

Sure. S-H-I-R-L-E-Y. *Shirley.*

Grammar Review

1 **MATCH.** For each **bold** word below, write the letter of the correct grammar word. Then ask and answer the questions with a partner.

1. _g_ How many students are **in** your class?
2. _____ What kinds of movies do you **like**?
3. _____ Where do you **usually** study?
4. _____ Do **you** have a computer?
5. _____ Are you **single**?
6. _____ What is your favorite **subject**?
7. _____ Where **do** you shop?
8. _____ Is there **a** library at this school?

a. adjective
b. adverb
c. article
d. helping/auxiliary verb
e. main verb
f. noun
g. preposition
h. pronoun

2 **MATCH** the verbs in **bold** with the correct verb form.

1. _d_ She **goes** to the library every day.
2. _____ I **passed** my exam last week.
3. _____ You**'re studying** English right now.
4. _____ We**'ll apply** for college next year.
5. _____ He**'s going to get** a job as an office manager.

a. simple past
b. present continuous
c. future with *be going to*
d. simple present
e. future with *will*

3 **WRITE** each sentence in Activity 2 in the *negative* form. Write in your notebook.

1. *She doesn't go to the library every day.*

4 **MATCH** the mistakes in the paragraph with the type of mistake in the box. Then correct the mistake.

_b._ punctuation	_____ spelling	_____ verb form	_____ capitalization

My name is Francine Perera. I <u>come</u> to this school three months ago. <u>Im</u> taking ESL and
a. *b.*
computer classes this semester. I want to get a job as an accountant. <u>everyone</u> in my new class
c.
is kind and <u>freindly</u>. I want to study hard and learn a lot!
d.

5 **WRITE** a paragraph about yourself in your notebook. Use the paragraph in Activity 4 as a model.

Review parts of speech, verb forms, and punctuation. • Practice using a dictionary.

Use Your Dictionary

1 **READ** the definitions of *student, studious,* and *study* from the dictionary. Then (circle) the correct answer to each question below.

An **accent mark** shows stress and comes <u>before</u> the stressed syllable.

stu•dent /ˈstudnt/ *n.* 1. a person who learns from teachers or professors at any school, college, or university: *She is a high-school student and will start college next fall.*
2. a person who studies seriously, in or out of school: *a student of football*

These dots divide the **syllables** in a word

stu•di•ous /ˈstudiəs/ *adj.* liking or tending to study: *I see a studious young woman in the library every day.*

These are the **parts of speech**: noun (n.), verb (v.), adjective (adj.), adverb (adv.).

stud•y /ˈstʌdi/ *n.* –ies 1. a room in a living space for reading, writing, and other quiet activities: *Her study is filled with books.* 2. the act of learning: *the study of a foreign languages* 3. a report on a specific topic: *a governmental study on poverty*

v. **–ied, -ying, -ies** 1. to work, to learn, by practicing, reading, and listening: *She studied for her math test.* 2. to look carefully at: *I study the chessboard carefully before I make a move.*

The **definition** is the meaning of the word. There are three definitions for the word *study.*

---

1. What part of speech is *student*?   **a.** noun   **b.** verb   **c.** adjective   **d.** adverb

2. How many syllables does *student* have?   **a.** one   **b.** two   **c.** three   **d.** four

3. What part of speech is *studious*?   **a.** noun   **b.** verb   **c.** adjective   **d.** adverb

4. How many syllables does *studious* have?   **a.** one   **b.** two   **c.** three   **d.** four

5. How many syllables does *study* have?   **a.** one   **b.** two   **c.** three   **d.** four

6. Which syllable is stressed in *study*?   **a.** first   **b.** second   **c.** third   **d.** fourth

2 **COMPLETE.** Use your dictionary to complete the chart.

	What part of speech is it?	How many syllables are there?	What is the definition?
weekend			
understand			
fascinating			

3 **WHAT ABOUT YOU?** Read the questions below. Then ask and answer the questions with a partner.

1. What do you do on the **weekends**?
2. Do you **understand** television shows in English?
3. Who is the most **fascinating** person you know?

LESSON 1: Grammar and Vocabulary

TCD1, 5
SCD2

1 GRAMMAR PICTURE DICTIONARY. What are the students doing at school? Listen and read.

1
Ratna is talking with her **academic counselor** about her goals. Ratna's counselor always gives her good **advice**.

2
Leslie is meeting with her **tutor** right now. Her tutor is helping her with an **assignment**. Leslie meets with her tutor twice a week.

3
Binh is using a **CD-ROM** in the computer lab now. He goes to the lab every day. An **assistant** in the lab helps students.

4
These students are taking a **tour** of the library. There are tours every month. The library has many **resources** for students.

5
Greg is asking his **instructor** questions about his class. Greg often goes to his instructor's office during **office hours**.

6
This is a **study group**. The students are helping each other with homework. They meet once a week in the **cafeteria**.

2 READ the sentences in Activity 1 with a partner.

3 NOTICE THE GRAMMAR. Underline the verbs in the simple present in the sentences in Activity 1. Circle the verbs in the present continuous.

Simple Present and Present Continuous Review

- Use the simple present to talk about facts or repeated actions.
- Use the present continuous to talk about actions that are happening right now.

Simple Present
We often use the simple present with the adverbs *always, usually, sometimes, never,* and *every day / week / month / year.*

Affirmative Statements

Subject	*be*	
I	am	
You	are	a student.
He / She	is	
We / You / They	are	students.

Subject	Verb	
I / You	study	
He / She	studies	every day.
We / You / They	study	

Negative Statements

Subject	*be + not*	
I	am not	
You	are not	a student.
He / She	is not	
We / You / They	are not	students.

Subject	*do + not + Verb*	
I / You	don't study	
He / She	doesn't study	every day.
We / You / They	don't study	

Present Continuous
We often use the present continuous with *now* or *right now.*

Affirmative and Negative Statements

Subject	*be + (not) + verb + ing*	
I	am (not) using	
You	are (not) using	a computer.
He / She	is (not) using	
We / You / They	are (not) using	

Contractions with *be*

Affirmative	Negative
I'm	I'm not
You're	You're not / You aren't
They're	They're not / They aren't
He's	He's not / He isn't
She's	She's not / She isn't
We're	We're not / We aren't

*See spelling rules for present and present continuous verbs on page 198.

4 COMPLETE the sentences with the simple present or present continuous.

1. Claudia _____ (talk) with her academic counselor right now. Her counselor always _____ (help) her set goals.

2. Bruce _____ (use) a CD-ROM in the lab right now. A lab assistant _____ (be) there every weekday until 9:00 P.M.

3. The librarian _____ (give) her daily tour right now. She usually _____ (not / finish) until 3:00.

4. Gerald's study group _____ (meet) in the library now. They usually _____ (not / meet) there. They usually_____ (study) in the cafeteria.

 5 WHAT ABOUT YOU? Complete the sentence. Then tell your class.

I want to…

| find a tutor. | take a library tour. | join a study group. | use the computer lab. |

LESSON 2: Grammar Practice Plus

1 **LISTEN** and write the number of the activity next to the correct student in the picture.

TCD1, 6

1. meeting with his study group
2. talking about an assignment
3. using a CD-ROM
4. highlighting important information

5. drawing illustrations of new words
6. typing his notes
7. listening to a CD
8. writing notes on index cards

2 **TALK** with a partner. Ask and answer questions about people in the picture.

Example: *A:* Is Pam writing notes on index cards?

B: No, she isn't. She's listening to a CD.

3 **WHAT ABOUT YOU?** Talk with a partner. Ask and answer questions about your study habits.

Example: *A:* Do you type your notes?

B: No. But I read them after class and rewrite them in my notebook.

8 | Learn about services in a school library. • Talk about school jobs.

4 **MATCH** the people who work at school with the things they do.

_____ 1. counselor   a. gives students extra help with their assignments

_____ 2. instructor   b. helps students check out books and use other resources

_____ 3. tutor   c. helps students use the computers in the lab

_____ 4. librarian   d. teaches classes and meets students during office hours

_____ 5. lab assistant   e. answers the telephone and greets visitors

_____ 6. secretary   f. helps students solve problems and gives them advice

5 **TALK.** Ask and answer questions about the words in Activity 4 with a partner.

Example: *A:* What does a counselor do?

          B: A counselor helps students solve problems and gives them advice.

> **Remember:**
> Some verbs, such as *be*, *like*, *need*, and *want*, are rarely used in the present continuous form.

6 **COMPLETE.** Write the correct form of the verb. Use the simple present or the present continuous.

It's 4:30, but many people at Washington Adult School (1) _____*are working*_____ (work).

Mrs. Lifson, the counselor, (2) _____ (talk) with a new student right now.

She (3) _____ (tell) him about classes at the school. Mr. Mitchell

(4) _____ (be) the custodian. He usually (5) _____ (start) work

around 4:00 and (6) _____ (work) until 10:00 at night. Right now he

(7) _____ (clean) the cafeteria. A few instructors (8) _____ (be)

also still in the building. Mr. Jacobson, the writing instructor, (9) _____ (have)

office hours every day from 4:00 to 5:00. He (10) _____ (help) a student with a

homework assignment now. Ms. Perez, the Spanish teacher, (11) _____ (not / teach)

a class now. Her students (12) _____ (take) a tour of the library, so she

(13) _____ (grade) papers. Everyone is busy at the Washington Adult School!

7 **WRITE** four sentences about someone you know. Write what they *never* do, *often* do, *usually* do, and/or *always* do. Then tell, or guess, what that person is doing *now*.

Example: *The secretary at our school never takes a break.*

          She is friendly and often speaks to students.

          She usually answers the telephone in the mornings.

          Now, I think she is giving visitors a tour of the school.

LESSON 3: Listening and Conversation

TCD1, 7-10

1 **LISTEN** to the question. Then listen to Mr. Smith talk to his students. Listen to the question again. Fill in the circle for the correct answer. Repeat each item if necessary.

1. Ⓐ Ⓑ Ⓒ   3. Ⓐ Ⓑ Ⓒ
2. Ⓐ Ⓑ Ⓒ   4. Ⓐ Ⓑ Ⓒ

TCD1, 11

2 **LISTEN** again. Check the suggestions you hear.

☐ Come to every class.
☐ Spend 30 minutes on homework every day.
☐ Get to know your classmates.
☐ Go to the library every day.
☐ Schedule time to study.
☐ Make vocabulary flashcards.

Math: Calculating Hours

A **READ** Melissa's schedule for the week. What types of activities do the colors indicate?

Monday	– work 8:00–4:00 – English class 6:00–8:00	Friday	– work 10:00–4:00 – English class in computer lab 6:00–8:00
Tuesday	– work 8:00–12:00 – English tutor 1:00–3:00	Saturday	– work 8:00–4:00
Wednesday	– work 8:00–4:00 – English class 6:00–8:00 – English study group 8:00–9:00	Sunday	– homework, library 10:00–12:00 – English study group, cafeteria 12:00–1:00 (bring lunch)
Thursday	– work 12:00–4:00	Notes:	

B **CALCULATE.** Read the schedule again and answer the questions with a partner.

1. How many hours is Melissa in her English class? _____

2. How many hours does she study in the library? _____

3. How many hours does she work in the computer lab? _____

4. What is the total number of hours Melissa spends learning English? _____

5. On Monday, Wednesday, Friday, and Saturday, Melissa has a one-hour lunch break.

   How many hours does she work this week? _____

3 **LISTEN** and read.

A: Hi! How are you?

B: Good. How are you?

A: Great. How's your family?

B: Oh, everyone's fine.

I'd love to stop and talk, but

I'm on my way to the computer lab.

A: Well, it was good to see you.

B: Good to see you, too. Let's get together soon.

A: Sounds good. I'll call you this weekend.

B: Okay. Great! See you!

A: Bye!

4 **PRACTICE** the conversation in Activity 3 with a partner. Use the information in the chart below.

Expression when you are too busy to talk	Excuse	Expression of agreement
1. I wish I could talk longer	I have to meet with my study group.	Good idea.
2. I wish I could stop and chat	I have to run; I'm on my way to class.	Yes, I'd love to.
3. I'd like to stop and chat	I'm going to the library for a 3:00 tour.	Yes, let's do that.

5 **WHAT ABOUT YOU?** Read the suggestions in Activity 2. Write the three ideas that you think are best for you. Then tell your class why you chose them.

1. _____

2. _____

3. _____

I'll come to every class. I don't want to miss anything!

I'll go to the library every day. I need to learn how to use the computers.

LESSON 4: Grammar and Vocabulary

1 **GRAMMAR PICTURE DICTIONARY.** What do the students say after their last class? Listen and read.

1. I **made** learning a priority. I decided my class was more important than other things. I studied every day. I'm going to study hard in my next class, too.

2. I **stuck to a schedule**. It helped me to plan my time and complete my assignments. I usually followed my plan. Next year I'm going to go to community college.

3. I **set goals**. I always knew what I wanted to do during the year, the term, the month, the week, and the class. Now, I'm going to get a job. That's my new goal.

4. I **was motivated**. I needed English for my job. I wanted to understand my children's homework assignments, too. I need to study more. I'm going to come back next term!

5. I **had support**. My instructor, my study group, the librarian, and the lab assistant all helped me. I cooperated with them. My husband cooked dinner every night. Now, *he's* going to take a class!

6. I **took responsibility** for learning. I paid attention, asked questions, and was courteous in class. I looked for ways to use English outside of class. Next, I'm going to join a study group.

7. I **attended every class**. I was never absent. I'm not going to miss a class next term, either!

2 **READ** the sentences in Activity 1 with a partner.

3 **NOTICE THE GRAMMAR.** Underline verbs in the simple past in sentences in Activity 1. Circle *be going to* + verb in sentences about the future.

Simple Past Review

Remember to use the simple past to talk about actions in the past.

Affirmative Statements

Subject	Verb	
I / You / He / She	attended	class.
We / You / They		

Negative Statements

Subject	Verb	
I / You / He / She	didn't attend	class.
We / You / They		

Questions

	Subject	Verb	
Did	I / you / he / she	attend	class?
	we / you / they		

Short Answers

	Subject	Verb
Yes,	I / you / he / she	did.
No,	we / you / they	didn't.

Future with *be going to*

Use *be going to* + verb for future planned actions.

Affirmative Statements

Subject	*be*	*going to* + Verb
I	am	going to study.
You	are	
He / She	is	
We / You / They	are	

Negative Statements

Subject	*be*	*going to* + Verb
I	am not	going to study.
You	aren't	
He / She	isn't	
We / You / They	aren't	

Questions

be	Subject	*going to* + Verb
Are	you	going to study?
Is	he / she	

Short Answers

	Subject	Verb
Yes,	I	am.
No,	he / she	isn't.

4 **WRITE.** Read the sentences with the bold words in Activity 1. Rewrite them as questions in the simple past.

Example: I made learning a priority. → *Did you make learning a priority?*

5 **WRITE.** Read the sentences with the bold words in Activity 1 again. Rewrite them as sentences about future plans.

Example: I made learning a priority. → *I am going to make learning a priority.*

6 **WHAT ABOUT YOU?** Choose a sentence from Activity 5 about a future activity that you plan to do. Tell the group how you are going to do it.

Example: I'm going to make learning a priority. I'm going to study for ten minutes every morning. At night, I'm going to finish my homework before I watch TV.

LESSON 5: Grammar Practice Plus

1 **MATCH** the words or phrases with their meanings or explanations.

1. _____ courteous   a. to finish
2. _____ to complete   b. to listen carefully
3. _____ to cooperate   c. something important
4. _____ to pay attention   d. help or assistance
5. _____ support   e. excited about doing something
6. _____ priority   f. to work well with others
7. _____ motivated   g. polite

2 **READ** the paragraph about Brenda. <u>Underline</u> the verbs in the simple past.

> Brenda <u>was</u> a good student last term. She set goals and she was very motivated. She cooperated with her classmates, and she paid attention when they spoke. She was very courteous and helpful. Brenda completed all of her assignments on time. She asked her family and friends for support, and they helped her find time to study. Brenda made learning a priority. She was very happy with her grades.

3 **WRITE** about Jim. He didn't do any of the things that Brenda did. Make changes to the paragraph in Activity 2 to describe Jim and his behavior last term.

Jim wasn't a good student last term. He didn't...

_____

_____

_____

_____

_____

_____

_____

_____

_____

_____

_____

_____

_____

_____

Pronunciation: Identify Word Stress

You can use your dictionary to find out which syllable in a word is the stressed (strong) syllable. Many dictionaries show the phonetic spelling of a word. An accent mark comes *before* the stressed syllable. In both examples below, the second syllable has the stress. Listen and repeat.

Examples: ad•<u>vice</u> = əd•văĭs   at•<u>ten</u>•tion = ə•ten•ʃən
                                         accent mark   accent mark

TCD1,15 SCD5 **A** **LISTEN** to the words. <u>Underline</u> the stressed syllable in each word. Use a dictionary to check your answers.

1. <u>stu</u>•dent
2. ve•ry
3. cour•te•ous
4. as•sign•ments
5. fam•i•ly
6. pri•or•i•ty
7. com•plete
8. mo•ti•vate
9. co•op•er•ate

TCD1,16 **B** **LISTEN** again and repeat.

TCD1, 17 **4** **LISTEN** to Jim talk with his academic counselor, and answer the questions.

1. What was Jim's biggest problem last term?
2. Why did he have this problem?

5 **LISTEN** again. What is Jim going to do next term? Check ☑ the things you hear.

Jim is going to…

☐ ask his instructor for help when he needs it.
☐ study in the computer lab.
☐ pay attention.
☐ ask his wife for help.
☐ complete all his assignments.

☐ stick to a schedule.
☐ attend every class.
☐ remember to do his homework.
☐ be friendly.
☐ get phone numbers from his classmates.

6 **TALK** in a group. List three problems that students have. What is good advice for someone with each problem?

1. _____

2. _____

3. _____

Students don't always complete their assignments.

They should make studying a priority.

LESSON 6: Reading

1 **THINK ABOUT IT.** Talk in a small group about how you study.

1. Do you have a favorite way of studying?
2. Do you have a favorite place to study?
3. Do you learn better by seeing something, hearing something, or doing something?

2 **BEFORE YOU READ.** Preview and skim the article on the next page. What are the three types of learners you will read about? Guess the meaning of *visual, auditory,* and *kinesthetic*.

> **READING FOCUS: Preview and skim an article**
> To preview, look at the pictures and read the title and subtitles. Skim by reading the first sentence in each paragraph and the headings in charts.

3 **READ** about the three learning styles in the article on the next page.

A. READ the article. Did you guess the meaning of *visual, auditory,* and *kinesthetic*?

B. READ the tips for studying English below. Write the learning styles that match the tips. (More than one answer may be correct.)

1. Draw pictures of new vocabulary words.
   _____

2. Work with a study group, tutor, or partner. Listen carefully to others, and repeat key information.
   _____

3. Tape notes around your house. Remove them as you learn the information.
   _____

4 **AFTER YOU READ.**

A. VOCABULARY. The chart at the end of the article gives study tips for each type of learner. Look at these bold words in the chart at the end of the article. Guess the meaning of each. Be sure to notice the parts of speech—noun (n), verb (v), or adjective (adj).

| colored (adj) | key (adj) | make up (v) | pace (n) | record (v) | underline (v) |

Now check in a dictionary. Were your guesses correct?

B. TALK about these questions in a group.

1. Which of the strategies in the article do you use?
2. What is your learning style?
3. What are other learning strategies that you should try?
4. Can you think of other strategies for each type of learner?

Discuss study habits. • Read about learning styles.

Learning Styles

People learn new information in different ways.

1 **Visual learners** like to see what they are learning. They like to have a "picture" of information. Visual learners understand more when they read information before listening to a lecture. Listening to an instructor for a long time can be difficult for visual learners. It is easier for them when the
5 instructor writes information on the board. Charts, graphs, and pictures are helpful for visual learners.

Auditory learners like to hear information. If they listen to an instructor explain something, they might "hear" the instructor's words again later when they study. They learn well in study groups or when they work with
10 tutors or partners — any time they can talk and listen to other people. Some auditory learners record a teacher speaking, then listen to the recording again later. This helps them study the information. Auditory learners also remember written information better when they read it out loud.

Kinesthetic learners like to do things and to take action. They like to
15 move their bodies. Sometimes it is difficult for them to sit and listen to a lecture or to read for a long time. They like to act out situations, or role-play. They learn well when they can move or touch things as they study. For example, it's good for them to use flashcards, or to write on a large board with chalk or a marker.

What's your learning style? What learning strategies are best for you? The chart below gives suggestions.

Visual Learners	Auditory Learners	Kinesthetic Learners
Write sentences to practice grammar. Use **colored** pens or pencils for different parts of speech (nouns, verbs, adjectives,...)	Listen to music while you study grammar or vocabulary.	Write new definitions of words on index cards. Then move the cards around and organize them into categories.
Use a different colored pen or pencil to **underline** new words when you read.	Read sentences with new vocabulary out loud and **record** them. Then listen to the recording.	Walk at a steady **pace**, snap your fingers as you practice reading sentences or new words.
Highlight important information with different **colored** highlighters.	**Make up** a new song including the vocabulary and grammar you want to learn. Then sing it whenever you have a chance.	Draw or cut out pictures of **key** vocabulary words. Label each picture and make a mini-dictionary.

LESSON 7: Writing

1 **THINK ABOUT IT.** Talk about these questions with your class.

1. What is a goal?

2. How is a goal different from a dream?

3. What goals do you have?

2 **BEFORE YOU WRITE.**

A. READ about the parts of a paragraph. A paragraph is a group of sentences about one idea.

- **Topic sentence:** There is always a topic sentence in a paragraph. The topic sentence gives the main idea. The topic sentence is usually the first sentence.

- **Supporting sentences:** There are usually two or more supporting sentences. The supporting sentences tell more about the topic sentence.

- **Examples and details:** Often, after each supporting sentence, there are one or more sentences that give examples or details about the information in the supporting sentence.

- **Concluding sentence:** There is usually a concluding sentence. The concluding sentence restates the main idea of the topic sentence in different words.

B. READ the paragraph.

> *I have two main goals for this term. My first goal is to pass this class. I'm going to complete all my class work and homework assignments. I'm also going to see my instructor during office hours once a month. My second goal is to use English more outside of class. I'm going to speak more. I'm not going to worry about mistakes. I'm going to try to use new grammar and vocabulary outside of class three times a week. I'm going to work hard to reach these important goals this term.*

C. COMPLETE. Write the correct part of the paragraph to complete each sentence below.

1. The blue line is under the ____*topic sentence*_____.

2. The green lines are under the _____.

3. The red lines are under the _____.

4. The purple line is under the _____.

D. **TALK** with a partner. Discuss two main goals you have for this class. Talk about what you are going to do to reach them.

E. **WRITE** your goals.

Goal 1: _____

_____

Goal 2: _____

_____

> **WRITING FOCUS: Paragraph outline**
> Organize the parts of your paragraph with an outline. Write your ideas in the outline, and then write your paragraph.

F. **COMPLETE** this paragraph outline using the goals you listed in Activity E.

Topic sentence: _____ *I have two important goals for this class.* _____

Supporting sentence (Goal 1): _____

_____

  Detail or example (one thing you are going to do to reach the goal):

  _____

  Detail or example (another thing you are going to do to reach the goal):

  _____

Supporting sentence (Goal 2): _____

_____

  Detail or example (one thing you are going to do to reach the goal):

  _____

  Detail or example (another thing you are going to do to reach the goal):

  _____

Concluding sentence (the main idea from the topic sentence in different words):

  _____

3 **WRITE.** Use your outline to write your paragraph. Remember to indent (leave space) at the beginning of the first line.

4 **AFTER YOU WRITE.**

  A. **EDIT** your paragraph.

   1. Did you discuss two important goals?

   2. Did you include the parts of a paragraph from your outline?

   3. Did you use *going to* correctly?

  B. **REWRITE** your paragraph with corrections.

Career Connection

1 **LISTEN** to the conversation. Then practice with a partner.

TCD1, 18

Mario: I'm going to sign up for a training session.

Curtis: Which one?

Mario: Well, I have a lot of stress right now, so I'm going to take Stress Management.

Curtis: That's a good idea. I need advice about finishing my work on time. I have so much work to do every day! Maybe I should take Time Management.

Mario: Yes, I want to go to that training session, too. Actually, I want to attend all of them!

Curtis: That's a great goal.

2 **MATCH** the work issue with the training session.

WORK ISSUE	TRAINING SESSION
1. _____ stress	a. Conflict Resolution
2. _____ difficulty finishing work on time	b. Communication in the Workplace
3. _____ not knowing the best way to write e-mails	c. Stress Management
4. _____ difficulty expressing your feelings and ideas at work	d. E-mail Etiquette
5. _____ trouble getting along with coworkers	e. Time Management

3 **WRITE** about two training sessions you would like to take and why. Use ideas from Activity 2 and your own ideas.

Example: *I want to take Stress Management. I have a lot of stress at home and work.*

4 **WHAT ABOUT YOU?** Talk about the questions in a group.

1. What kind of training would help you at work or school?

2. Do you know about training sessions at work, school, the library, a workforce development center, or other places in your community? What kinds of training can you get at these places?

3. What other ways can you take responsibility for learning at school or work?

Check Your Progress!

Skill	Circle the answers.	Is it correct?
A. Use the simple present and present continuous.	1. Allen **am** / **is** / **are** in the language lab every morning. 2. I am **do** / **does** / **doing** my homework right now. 3. Do you **work** / **works** / **working** at the library? 4. Is she **talking** / **talks** / **talk** to her teacher right now?	☐ ☐ ☐ ☐

Number Correct | 0 | 1 | 2 | 3 | 4

Skill	Circle the answers.	Is it correct?
B. Use simple past and the future with *be going to*.	5. **Did** / **Is** / **Was** the English class start last week? 6. No, it **starts** / **started** / **starting** two weeks ago. 7. **Is** / **Are** / **Am** you going to complete the course? 8. Yes, I am going to **complete** / **completes** / **completing** it.	☐ ☐ ☐ ☐

Number Correct | 0 | 1 | 2 | 3 | 4

Skill	Circle the answers.	Is it correct?
C. Talk about learning.	9. Sharon's counselor gives good **tutor** / **advice**. 10. The **study group** / **resource** meets every Thursday. 11. The **lab assistant** / **academic counselor** helps students use computers. 12. I want to talk to Professor Kim. When are her **tours** / **office hours**?	☐ ☐ ☐ ☐

Number Correct | 0 | 1 | 2 | 3 | 4

Skill	Circle the answers.	Is it correct?
D. Demonstrate understanding of ways to support learning.	13. I took **responsibility** / **priority** for my learning this year. 14. They **had support** / **set goals** from their instructor. 15. Ellen planned every minute of her day. She **made learning a priority** / **stuck to a schedule**. 16. Ellen set a **goal** / **responsibility** to get a new job.	☐ ☐ ☐ ☐

Number Correct | 0 | 1 | 2 | 3 | 4

COUNT the number of correct answers above. Fill in the bubbles.

Chart Your Success

Skill	Need Practice	Okay	Good	Very Good	Excellent!
A. Use the simple present and present continuous.	⓪	①	②	③	④
B. Use simple past and the future with *be going to*.	⓪	①	②	③	④
C. Talk about learning.	⓪	①	②	③	④
D. Demonstrate understanding of ways to support learning.	⓪	①	②	③	④

LESSON 1: Grammar and Vocabulary

1 GRAMMAR PICTURE DICTIONARY. What are people saying about the appliances?
Listen and read.

TCD1, 19
SCD6

1
A: This **air conditioner** is larger and cheaper.
B: Yes, but it uses a lot of electricity. The smaller air conditioner is more energy efficient.

2
A: Which **microwave** do you think is better?
B: Well, the Colby microwave is smaller, but it isn't as **powerful** as the Deluxe. So, I'd say the Deluxe.

3
A: Do you like the Buzz **mixer**? It's not expensive.
B: It's cheaper, but it isn't as **reliable** as this Wizz mixer. Last year I bought a mixer like this and it broke after a month. Before that, I had a Wizz for many years.

4
A: Let's get this **coffeemaker**. We can make real espresso coffee!
B: But the Quick Cup coffeemaker is less **complicated**, and regular coffee is just as good.

2 READ the conversations with a partner.

3 NOTICE THE GRAMMAR. Circle the adjectives in each conversation in Activity 1. Which adjectives are comparatives? How many different ways of making comparisons with adjectives can you find?

Comparisons with Adjectives

Use comparative adjectives to compare two things. Short adjectives have just one syllable (*large, small*). Long adjectives have two or more syllables (*re-li-a-ble*).

Subject + *be*	Comparative (Short Adjectives)	
The Buzz mixer is	cheaper than	the Wizz food mixer.
cheap → cheaper, heavy → heavier, big → bigger (*See spelling rules page 200.*)		

Subject + *be*	Comparative (Long Adjectives)	
The Espressomix coffeemaker is	more complicated than	the Quick Cup coffeemaker.
The Quick Cup coffeemaker is	less complicated than	the Espressomix coffeemaker.
complicated → more complicated/less complicated (*less* is the opposite of *more*)		

Use *as…as* to say things are the same or equal.
The Espressomix coffee is *as good as* the Quick Cup coffee. (Both items are equal, or the same.)

Use *not as…as* to say things are not the same or equal.
The Colby microwave *isn't as powerful as* the Deluxe microwave. (The first item is less powerful than the second.)

4 **UNDERLINE** the correct word.

1. The large air conditioner is less energy efficient *as/than* the small one.

2. The small mixer isn't as reliable *as/than* the large one.

3. The Colby microwave is *as/less* powerful than the Deluxe.

4. The Quick Cup coffeemaker isn't *as/more* expensive as the Espressomix.

5. The Espressomix coffeemaker is *as/more* complicated than the Quick Cup.

5 **COMPLETE** the sentences. Look at Activity 1. Then use adjectives to make comparisons.

1. The large air conditioner isn't _____as energy efficient as_____ (energy efficient) the small one.

2. The Colby microwave isn't _____ (large) the Deluxe.

3. The Wizz mixer is _____ (reliable) the Buzz mixer.

4. The Deluxe microwave is _____ (powerful) the Colby.

5. The Quick Cup coffee is _____ (good) the Espressomix coffee.

6 **WHAT ABOUT YOU?** Which of these appliances do you have at home? Describe them to a partner. Then compare your appliances with those in Activity 1. Use *as…as, not as…as,* and *less…than.*

I have a small microwave. It's less powerful than the Deluxe microwave.

LESSON 2: Grammar Practice Plus

TCD1, 20

1 **TALK** about the picture. Then listen and write the letter of each word in the green box next to the correct product in the picture. How many other products can you name?

| a. sofa | b. hair dryer | c. vacuum cleaner | d. TV |

3. _____

1. _____Furniture_____

4. _____

2. _____

Cosmetics   1st floor
Electronics   2nd floor
Fashion   1st floor
Furniture   2nd floor
Household appliances 2nd floor
Lawn and garden   basement
Personal Care   1st fl

5. _____

2 **MATCH.** Write the department name from the directory in the correct red box in the picture. What items do you think are in the other departments? Discuss with your class.

3 **TALK** with a partner. Compare products in the picture using the adjectives in the box.

Example: The blue vacuum cleaner *isn't as heavy as* the brown vacuum cleaner.

convenient	heavy	modern	comfortable	attractive
inconvenient	light	old-fashioned	uncomfortable	ugly

Pronunciation: Blending *is + as* and *was + as*   TCD1, 21

In spoken English, an *s* at the end of one word is often linked to the vowel at the beginning of the next word. Listen to and repeat the following examples:

Is as   **sounds like →**   Is as

Was as   **sounds like →**   Was as

 A **LISTEN.** Draw marks to predict the linking in the sentences below. Then listen and check.   TCD1, 22 SCD7

1. My microwave is as expensive as yours.
2. My sofa is as old as your sofa.
3. This test was as hard as last week's test.
4. This hair dryer is as powerful as mine.
5. This mixer is as cheap as that one.
6. The Quick Cup was as complicated as Espressomix.

 B **LISTEN** again and repeat.   TCD1, 23

4 **WRITE** two sentences about each pair of products in the pictures. Use the adjectives in the box.

Example: *A regular toothbrush is less expensive than an electric toothbrush.*
It isn't as powerful.

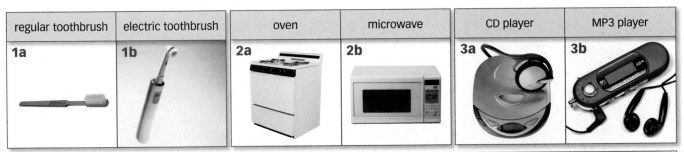

regular toothbrush	electric toothbrush	oven	microwave	CD player	MP3 player
1a	1b	2a	2b	3a	3b

complicated	expensive	old-fashioned	reliable
convenient	heavy	powerful	safe

Questions with Comparatives

Question	1st Choice	2nd Choice
Which are better,	regular toothbrushes	or electric toothbrushes?
Which is more expensive,	a CD player	or an MP3 player?

5 **TALK** with a partner. Ask and answer questions about the products in Activity 4.

Example A: Which do you think are better, regular toothbrushes or electric toothbrushes?
B: I'd say regular toothbrushes. They're easier to use, and they aren't as expensive.
A: True, but don't you think they're less powerful?
B: I guess so.

 6 **WHAT ABOUT YOU?** Do you have any of the products in Activity 4? Why do you use them?
Tell a partner.

LESSON 3: Listening and Conversation

1 **LISTEN** to the question and to each advertisement. Listen to the question again. Fill in the circle for the correct answer. Repeat each item if necessary.

TCD1, 24–26

1. (A) (B) (C)
2. (A) (B) (C)
3. (A) (B) (C)

2 **LISTEN** to the questions and to the conversation. Then listen to the questions again. Fill in the circle for the correct answer. Repeat each item if necessary.

TCD1, 27–29

1. (A) (B) (C)
2. (A) (B) (C)
3. (A) (B) (C)

Tip
When you want to buy something, say: *I'll take this one, please.*
If you are not sure you want it, say: *Thank you, I'm going to think about it.*

3 **LISTEN** again to the conversation in Activity 2. Make notes about each product in the chart below.

TCD1, 30

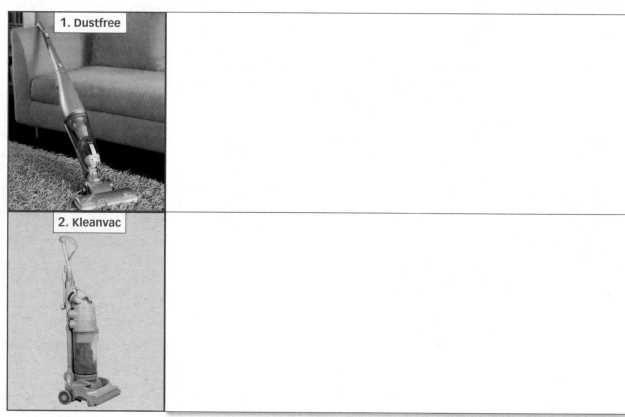

1. Dustfree

2. Kleanvac

4 **TALK** with a partner about the vacuum cleaners in Activity 3. Discuss the questions.

1. Which one does the customer buy?
2. Which one do you think is better? Why?

Compare vacuum cleaners. • Calculate energy costs.

5 **LISTEN** and read.

Goodtoast

A: Excuse me. How much are these <u>toaster ovens</u>?

B: The <u>Goodtoast</u> is $29.50 and the <u>Mr. Toastee</u> is $59.99.

A: I see, the Goodtoast is less expensive, but which one is better?

B: They're both good, but the <u>Goodtoast</u> <u>has a single setting</u> and the Mr. Toastee <u>has multi-settings</u>.

A: So the <u>Mr. Toastee</u> is <u>more complicated</u>?

B: Yes, that's right.

A: Hmmm. I think I'll take <u>the Goodtoast</u>.

Goodtoast	
$29.50	single setting

Mr. Toastee	
$59.99	multi-settings

6 **PRACTICE** the conversation in Activity 5 with a partner. Use the information in the chart below.

Products to compare	Brand names and prices	Information about the products	Adjective
1. microwaves	Spencer is $99 / Heatum Up is $149	Spencer has 800 watts and the Heatum Up has 1200 watts	powerful
2. washing machines	Everbrite is $450 / King is $789	Everbrite's energy cost is $123 per year, and the King's is $78 per year	energy efficient

Math: Calculating the cost of using an appliance

A **READ** the energy efficiency label for the refrigerator. How many kilowatt hours per year (kWh/year) does this refrigerator use?

_____

B **CALCULATE** the cost of using this refrigerator in each situation below.

1. Your electricity is 10 cents per kWh. Calculate the cost of using this appliance for a year.

2. Your electricity is 15 cents per kWh. Calculate the cost of using this appliance for a year.

Based on standard U.S. Government tests

ENERGY GUIDE

Compare the Energy Use of this Refrigerator with Others before You Buy.

This model Uses
776 kWh/year

Energy Use (kWh//year) range of all similar models

Uses Least Energy 742

Uses Most Energy 836

Refrigerators using more energy cost more to operate. This model's estimated yearly operating cost is:

$68

LESSON 4: Grammar and Vocabulary

 1 GRAMMAR PICTURE DICTIONARY. What items are Sam and Tina comparing while they shop? Listen and read.

TCD1, 32
SCD9

1

A: I want to get a sweatshirt for my sister. Which one should I get?

B: This sweatshirt is the <u>cheapest</u>, but it's also the <u>least colorful</u> one.

A: This <u>gray</u> and <u>silver</u> one is the <u>most</u> **stylish**.

2

B: I love that green bag. It's so **pretty**.

A: Yes, but it's probably the least **durable** one here. This blue **suitcase** is the strongest.

B: But it's the heaviest, too!

3

B: The black **boots** look the most **practical**. They're good for rainy days and for working in the garden.

A: Do you think they're comfortable, too?

4

A: I need some **socks**. Which are the least expensive?

B: Well, the white ones are the **best value**. There are three in a package.

2 PRACTICE the conversations with a partner.

3 NOTICE THE GRAMMAR. <u>Underline</u> the adjectives in each conversation in Activity 1. Which ones are superlatives? How many different ways of making superlatives with adjectives can you find? What kind of adjectives use *most or least* before them in the superlative form?

Practice words for comparison shopping. • Use superlative adjectives.

Remember:
Some adjectives are irregular in the comparative and superlative.
good → better → best
bad → worse → worst

Superlative Adjectives

Use superlative adjectives to compare one thing to two or more things in the same set or group

Subject + *be*	Superlative with Short Adjectives (Use *the* + adjective + *est*)
The white sweatshirt is	the cheapest.
large → largest, heavy → heaviest, big → biggest *(See spelling rules page 201.)*	

Subject + *be*	Superlative with Long Adjectives (Use *the* + *most / least* + adjective)
The black boots are	the most / least practical.
least expensive = cheapest (*least* is the opposite of *most*)	

Questions and Answers

Often you can use *one* or *ones* instead of the noun in the answer. *One* or *ones* points to the noun in the question. This is more natural in conversation than repeating the noun.

Which **sweatshirt** is the cheapest? ↑ The white **one**.	Which **boots** are the most practical? ↑ The black **ones**.

4 **COMPLETE** the sentences about the items in Activity 1. Use *most, least,* or *-est.*

1. The brown boots are _____ (nice).
2. The white sweatshirt is _____ (colorful).
3. The blue suitcase is _____ (strong).
4. The green bag is _____ (attractive).
5. The white socks are _____ (expensive).

5 **COMPLETE** the questions about the items in Activity 1. Use *most, least,* or *-est.* Then ask and answer questions with a partner.

1. (comfortable) Which boots are _the   most   comfortable_? The black ones.
2. (heavy) Which suitcase is _____? The blue one.
3. (colorful) Which sweatshirt is _____? The red and yellow one.
4. (expensive) Which socks are _____? The black ones.
5. (durable) Which suitcase is _____? The green one.
6. (stylish) Which sweatshirt is _____? The white one.

6 **WHAT ABOUT YOU?** Choose an item from each section in Activity 1. Tell a partner why you like it.

I like the black boots. They look the most comfortable.

LESSON 5: Grammar Practice Plus

1 **MATCH.** Write the name of the product under the correct picture.

bath oil	glass cleaner	laundry detergent	stain remover

1. _____
2. _____
3. _____
4. _____

2 **LISTEN** to four people talking about why they buy different products. Then complete the chart.

TCD1, 33

Name of person	Type of product	Reason for buying
1. Tina	*laundry detergent*	*nicest smell*
2. Bruno		
3. Leon		
4. Isabella		

3 **COMPLETE** the sentences about the people in Activity 2. Use the superlative.

1. Tina buys Everclean ___*laundry detergent*___ because ___*it has the nicest smell*___.

2. Bruno buys Brite Lite _____ because _____.

3. Leon buys Stainaway _____ because _____.

4. Isabella buys Spa _____ because _____.

4 **WHAT ABOUT YOU?** Tell your partner about products you like. Explain why you like them.

I usually buy Soft and Smooth hand lotion. It's more expensive than other lotions, but it really works!

5 **READ** the information about cell phones.

	Talktime	Pexagon	Interstar
Cell phone			
Product description	Size: 4 inches × 2 inches Weight: 5.8 ounces Price: $79	Size: 4.5 inches × 2 inches Weight: 4.6 ounces Price: $49	Size: 3.7 inches × 1.9 inches Weight: 3.1 ounces Price: $129

6 **COMPLETE** the comparison chart. Write numbers 1, 2, or 3 (1 = the best, 3 = the worst).

Cell Phone Comparison Chart			
	Talktime	**Pexagon**	**Interstar**
Size			
Weight			
Price			

7 **WRITE** five questions about the cell phones in Activity 5. Use the superlative form of the words in the box. Then ask and answer questions about the cell phones with a partner.

Example: *A:* Which phone is the cheapest?
B: The Pexagon.

cheap	heavy	small	durable	practical
expensive	light	large	good value	stylish

8 **TALK** in a group. Choose one popular type of household appliance or product. Think of a name for it. Write an advertisement for your product. Use as many adjectives, comparatives, and superlatives as you can.

Happylife Toaster Oven

The Happylife toaster oven makes the best toast and the most delicious pizza! It's faster, safer, and quieter than any other toaster oven. The design is simple and stylish. It's the least complicated and the most convenient toaster oven you can find.

LESSON 6: Reading

1 **THINK ABOUT IT.** Use prior knowledge. Talk with your class.

   1. Do you like to use cell phones? Why or why not?

   2. Do you have a cell phone?

2 **BEFORE YOU READ.** Preview and skim the article on the next page. What is the article about?

READING FOCUS: Use prior knowledge

Before you start reading, think about what you already know about the topic. What opinions do you have about the topic? This will help you to understand the text and to remember new information more easily.

3 **READ** the article on the next page and highlight the advantages of texting. Then write a list and compare with your partner.

Reading Strategy Summary

Use prior knowledge.

Preview and skim an article.

   1. _It's easier to text if you don't want to disturb someone._

   2. _____

   3. _____

   4. _____

   5. _____

4 **AFTER YOU READ.**

  A. VOCABULARY. Find and circle these words in the article. Then match each word with the definition you think is the best. Use your dictionary to check.

      _____ **1.** unlimited   **a.** polite conversation

      _____ **2.** disturb   **b.** dangerous

      _____ **3.** small talk   **c.** describe

      _____ **4.** risky   **d.** as many or as much as you like

      _____ **5.** express   **e.** annoy or interrupt

  B. WRITE. With a partner, make a list of advantages of talking on the phone, compared with texting.

  C. TALK. Group A likes texting. Group B likes talking. In your groups, think of as many reasons as you can. Then take turns telling the other group your reasons.

    Example *Group A:* We like texting because it's more private. You can text in class or on the bus and no one can hear you.

               Group B: We like to talk on the phone because it is faster. It takes a long time to type text messages.

Are You a Texter or a Talker?

1   Do you use your cell phone for talking — or for texting? A recent survey in the United States shows that cell phone users over 45 prefer to talk, but younger cell phone users, especially teens, prefer to text and sometimes send
5 more than 200 text messages every day. So why is texting so popular?

> ❯ *I have unlimited text messages on my phone plan. It's easier to send a text message to my boyfriend; he can answer whenever. I don't want to disturb him at work.*
> 10 *Phone calls take longer.* **Cindy**

> ❯ *On the phone, you have to be polite and have small talk. But with a text message, you can get to the point¹.* **Luis**

> ❯ *Texting is great at work or in a loud place, like at a concert. It's more polite than talking on the phone if*
> 15 *you are on a train or in a movie theater. You don't disturb other people.* **Fabian**

> ❯ *I can talk to my friends and family in class and the teacher doesn't know! I text over 3,000 messages every month.* **Joel**

> ❯ *It's more private than a phone conversation. No one can hear you text!* **Shirlee**

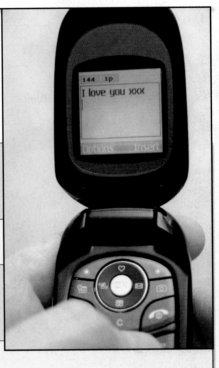

20   So, why else do people prefer to text? Shy or lonely teens like to text because it is less risky. It's easier to answer a text message than a surprise phone call. It's personal — but you don't have to talk directly, so it's easier to express your feelings.

    Texting has created its own language, too, using abbreviated words that are shorter and take less time to send. For example,
25 PCM means "Please call me." NP means "No problem." Texters sometimes create their own language — and often parents or teachers are not included. It seems, however, that older people still prefer the old-fashioned voice-to-voice method of communicating by phone.

ASAP = as soon as possible
BLNT = better luck next time
TTYL = talk to you later
BTW = by the way

---

¹*get to the point* = talk about the main topic right away

LESSON 7: Writing

1 **THINK ABOUT IT.** Tell your classmates about an appliance that broke or that didn't work after you bought it.

2 **BEFORE YOU WRITE.**

TCD1, 34

A. LISTEN to the conversation. Answer the questions.

1. What did Rachel buy? _____

2. Why did she like it? _____

3. What is the problem? _____

B. READ Rachel's letter of complaint.

> **WRITING FOCUS: Notice the format of a formal letter**
>
> Most formal letters follow a similar format. First, the sender's address appears at the top left side of the page. Below that are: the receiver's address, the date, the greeting, the body of the letter, the closing, the signature, and the typed name.

> **Tip**
>
> Appliances, cars, and electronics often come with a warranty. The **warranty** promises that the company will repair or replace the item if it breaks within a certain time limit.

25 Palm Tree Lane
Miami, FL 33128 —— Rachel's address

Keepcool Air Conditioner Co.
2390 South Main Drive
Los Angeles, CA 90003 —— Recipient's address

November 28, 2008 —— Date

Dear Sir or Madam: —— Greeting

I purchased a Keepcool air conditioner from Ben's Electrical Appliance Store on September 8, 2008. It cost $450. At first I was very pleased because it was smaller and quieter than my old air conditioner, but now there is a problem. It's not working. I have a three-year warranty. Could you please repair my air conditioner or replace it as soon as possible? I am enclosing a copy of my receipt and my warranty information. —— Body of letter

Yours truly, —— Closing

Rachel Gomez —— Signature

Rachel Gomez —— Typed name
(786) 555-1968
RGmz@yahaaa.com

C. MATCH. Read the list of problems. Match them with the appliances.

1. __e__ caught on fire
2. _____ stained my clothes
3. _____ destroyed my CDs
4. _____ leaked water
5. _____ damaged my rug

a. washing machine
b. dishwasher
c. vacuum cleaner
d. CD player
e. tumble dryer

D. WRITE. Imagine that you bought one of the appliances in Activity C. Answer the questions.

1. What did you buy? _____

2. Where did you buy it? _____

3. What is wrong with it? _____

4. What do you want the company to do? _____

3 **COMPLETE** the chart with information you need to write your letter. Then use the information to write a letter in the correct format in your notebook. Use Rachel's letter and your answers from Activity 2D to help you.

	Information
Your address	
Receiver's address	
Date	
Greeting	
Closing	

4 **AFTER YOU WRITE.**

A. EDIT. Look at your letter.
1. Did you include all of the information from Activity 2D?
2. Did you use the correct format?
3. Did you use the correct punctuation?

B. EXCHANGE letters with a partner. Can you find two mistakes in the format or punctuation of your partner's letter? Mark them.

 C. REWRITE. Discuss anything your partner marked or wrote on your paper. Then rewrite it.

Career Connection

1 **LISTEN** to the conversation. Then practice the conversation with a partner.

Lila: Hi, Jean! What's up?

Jean: I'm looking at the job ads.

Lila: Oh, are you looking for another job?

Jean: Yes, a job with better pay and shorter hours!

Lila: Do you find anything interesting?

Jean: Yes, there's a good job at the Beacon Restaurant. It pays more than my job now, and the hours are shorter.

Lila: That sounds great!

Jean: Yes, but it isn't as close to my home. I really like my coworkers at my current job, too.

Lila: Hmm… maybe you should ask for a raise before you apply for another job.

Jean: That's a good idea.

2 **COMPLETE** the chart with ideas from Activity 1.

Advantages of Jean's current job	Advantages of the Beacon Restaurant job
1.	1.
2.	2.

3 **DISCUSS** in a group. What do you think are the most important things to have in a job? Number in order of importance (1 = most important, 5 = least important).

_____ Pay   _____ Hours   _____ Benefits   _____ Friendly co-workers   _____ Location

4 **READ** the job ads. Find and circle the abbreviations for: *full-time, part-time, hour, experienced, plus, benefits, opportunity, professional,* and *resume*.

Job #1

Paradise Restaurant is looking for: exp. prof. FT and PT waiters and waitresses. Apply today and receive introductory starting rate of $6.50 per hr. Hours: 10:30 A.M.– 2 P.M., 6:30 P.M.–11 P.M. Health ben. for full-time workers. Company uniforms. Join our friendly team! Fax resume to 801-555-6653.

Job #2

Rossi's Café and Restaurant WAITERS, WAITRESSES needed for busy department store restaurant. Exp. Full-time, Part-time, $9/hour + tips. Hours: 9 A.M.– 6:30 P.M. Convenient downtown location. Hurry while oppty lasts. Please fax res. to 516-555-2771.

5 **WHAT ABOUT YOU?** Compare two of your past jobs or the two jobs above. Explain which one is better and why.

Check Your Progress!

Skill	Circle the answers.	Is it correct?
A. Make comparisons with adjectives.	1. My coffeemaker is **more big** / **bigger** / **as big** than yours. 2. The small microwave is **not as expensive** / **more expensive** / **less expensive** as the big one. 3. The Buzz mixer is **more cheap** / **cheaper** / **cheap** than my mixer. 4. That sofa is **as nice** / **nicer** / **nice** as my sofa.	☐ ☐ ☐ ☐

| | | Number Correct | 0 | 1 | 2 | 3 | 4 |

Skill	Circle the answers.	Is it correct?
B. Use superlative adjectives.	5. All the cars are new, but this car is **the most new** / **the newest** / **most new**. 6. The brown coat is **the most** / **the more** / **the best** attractive. 7. Which sweater is the most **colorful** / **smaller** / **nice**? 8. Which shoes are **the more new** / **the newest** / **the most new**.	☐ ☐ ☐ ☐

| | | Number Correct | 0 | 1 | 2 | 3 | 4 |

Skill	Circle the answers.	Is it correct?
C. Talk about appliances.	9. It's too hot! We need a new **air conditioner** / **mixer**. 10. I can't make cookies because **the coffeemaker** / **mixer** is broken. 11. My TV is **reliable** / **energy efficient**. I never have problems with it. 12. I don't understand the instructions. They're too **complicated** / **reliable**.	☐ ☐ ☐ ☐

| | | Number Correct | 0 | 1 | 2 | 3 | 4 |

Skill	Circle the answers.	Is it correct?
D. Understand product qualities.	13. I can wear these boots with many outfits. They are very **colorful** / **practical**. 14. This suitcase is strong! It's very **durable** / **stylish**. 15. This shirt is plain and boring. It's not very **stylish** / **practical**. 16. The black boots are **the best value** / **prettiest**. They are as stylish as the brown ones, but they cost $50 less.	☐ ☐ ☐ ☐

| | | Number Correct | 0 | 1 | 2 | 3 | 4 |

COUNT the number of correct answers above. Fill in the bubbles.

Chart Your Success					
Skill	Need Practice	Okay	Good	Very Good	Excellent!
A. Make comparisons with adjectives.	⓪	①	②	③	④
B. Use superlative adjectives.	⓪	①	②	③	④
C. Talk about appliances.	⓪	①	②	③	④
D. Understand product qualities.	⓪	①	②	③	④

LESSON 1: Grammar and Vocabulary

1 **GRAMMAR PICTURE DICTIONARY.** What were the people doing when Officer Kimmel saw them? Listen and read.

TCD1, 36
SCD10

1 Ms. Chi was **speeding**.

2 Mr. Jones was **parking in a handicapped parking space**.

3 Miss Brown was **driving alone in a carpool lane**.

4 Mrs. Wilson was **driving** with her three-year-old **child in the car**. Her child wasn't sitting in a **car seat**.

5 Mr. Garcia was driving and **talking on his cell phone**. He wasn't using a **headset**.

6 Mr. Cruz was **changing lanes**. He wasn't using his **turn signal**.

2 **READ** the sentences in Activity 1 with a partner.

3 **NOTICE THE GRAMMAR.**

A. <u>UNDERLINE</u> the verbs in the sentences in Activity 1.

B. **READ** the sentences below. <u>Underline</u> the verbs in the red and blue parts of the sentences.

    1. Miss Brown was driving alone in a carpool lane when Officer Kimmel saw her.

    2. Mr. Cruz wasn't using his turn signal when Officer Kimmel saw him.

Past Continuous

The past continuous describes an ongoing action during a period of time in the past.

Affirmative and Negative Statements

Subject	Past of *be* + (*not*)	Verb + *ing*
I / He / She	was / wasn't	speeding.
We / You / They	were / weren't	speeding.

Affirmative and Negative Statements with *when* Clause

When introduces a second action. The second action interrupted the ongoing action. Use the simple past with the *when* clause. Use the past continuous for the ongoing action.

Past Continuous Clause			Simple Past Clause with *when*
Subject	**Past of *be* + (*not*)**	**Verb + *ing***	***when* + Subject + Simple Past**
I / He / She	was / wasn't	speeding	*when* the police officer *stopped* me / him / her.
We / You / They	were / weren't		*when* the police officer *stopped* us / you / them.

Use a comma after the clause beginning with *when* if it comes at the beginning of the sentence.

Simple Past Clause with *when*	Past Continuous Clause
When the police officer *stopped* me,	I was speeding.

4   **READ** the sentences in Activity 3B again. Look at the verbs you underlined. Write *PC* (past continuous) or *SP* (simple past) above each verb.

5   **COMPLETE** the story. Circle the simple past or past continuous form of the verb.

> Last week, I had a car accident. I (1) **drove /** **was driving** down the road when a woman (2) **hit / was hitting** me!
>
> I (3) **went / was going** the speed limit when she (4) **came / was coming** into my lane! When I first (5) **saw / was seeing** her, she (6) **didn't use / wasn't using** a turn signal! It happened so fast! A police officer saw the whole thing.
>
> He came over and said: "Sir, (7) **did / were** you (8) **talk / talking** on your cell phone when she
>
> (9) **hit / was hitting** you?"
>
> I answered, "Yes, but…"
>
> "Sir, you weren't paying attention," he said. "It is against the law to drive and talk on your cell phone in this state."
>
> Then he gave me a ticket. I (10) **was / was being** VERY angry!

6   **WHAT ABOUT YOU?** Tell a group about a time the police stopped you or someone you know. What were you/they doing?

LESSON 2: Grammar Practice Plus

1 **TALK** about the picture. What did the police camera record yesterday at 3:00 P.M.?

> Samuel was parking in a handicapped space.

1. Sonia _____

2. Hao _____

3. Emilio ___a___

4. Nisma _____

5. Samuel _____

6. Kristine _____

7. Erica _____

8. Malik _____

NO PASSING

Honk Honk

3:00 PM

2 **WRITE** the letter of the item next to the correct person in the picture in Activity 1.

a. not wearing a seat belt

b. passing in a no-passing zone

c. hitchhiking

d. not using a car seat for her baby

e. sleeping at the wheel

f. parking in a handicapped parking space

g. driving and talking on her cell phone

h. not wearing a helmet

3 **TALK.** Look at the picture in Activity 1. Ask and answer questions with *who*.

> Who wasn't wearing a seat belt?

> Emilio.

40 | Recognize driving behaviors. • Use *wh-* questions with past continuous.

Wh- Questions with Past Continuous

Use the past continuous to ask and tell about ongoing actions in progress at a specific time in the past.

Question						**Answer**	
Wh- word	Past of *be*	Subject	Verb+*ing*	Time Phrase		Subject	Past Continuous
What	was	he	doing	at 9:00 last night?		He	was studying.

4 **TALK.** What was your partner doing yesterday at the times below? Take notes.

| **1.** 7:00 A.M. | **2.** 10:00 A.M. | **3.** 12:30 P.M. | **4.** 6:45 P.M. | **5.** 9:15 P.M. | **6.** 12:00 A.M. |

Example: *A:* What were you doing at <u>7:00</u> yesterday <u>morning</u>?

           B: I <u>was driving to work</u>.

We often use a comma when the *time phrase* comes first, but not when it is second.
At 7:00, Liam was driving.
Liam was driving **at 7:00.**

5 **WRITE** about your partner. Use your notes.

1. 7:00 A.M. *At 7:00 yesterday morning, Liam was driving to work.*

2. 10:00 A.M. _____

3. 12:30 P.M. _____

4. 6:45 P.M. _____

5. 9:15 P.M. _____

6. 12:00 A.M. _____

Math: *What's the speed limit?*

You can use *under* to say "slower than" the speed limit and *over* to say "faster than" the speed limit.

> *A:* How fast was <u>Todd</u> going when the police caught <u>him</u>?
>
> *B:* <u>He</u> was driving <u>45</u> miles an hour in a <u>35</u>-mile-an-hour zone.
>
> *A:* That's <u>10</u> miles <u>over</u> the speed limit!

Todd 45/35 mph

A **CALCULATE.** How many miles under or over the speed limit were the drivers going?

B **TALK.** Use the names and speeds under the pictures and make new dialogues.

Tina 21/35 mph

Carmen 40/25 mph

Hassan 55/60 mph

Diego 85/65 mph

LESSON 3: Listening and Conversation

TCD1, 37 🎧 **Pronunciation:** *Is / Was / Does / Yes* with *She* and *He*

When the final *z* sound in *is / was / does* or the *s* sound in *yes* comes before the word *she*, native speakers often link the sounds and make them one sound. Look at the examples. Listen and repeat.

Was she speeding?

Yes, she was.

sounds like →

Was she speeding?

Yes, she was.

When the final *z* sound in *is / was / does* or the *s* sound in *yes* comes before the word *he*, native speakers often delete the *h* sound in *he*. Look at the examples. Listen and repeat.

Was he speeding?

Yes, he was.

sounds like →

Was he speeding?

Yes, he was.

TCD1, 38
SCD11 **A** **LISTEN.** Mark these sentences. Then listen and check.

1. *A:* Does he need help? *B:* Yes, he does.
2. *A:* Is he okay? *B:* Yes, he is.
3. *A:* Was she okay? *B:* Yes, she was.
4. *A:* Does she want to go home? *B:* Yes, she does.

TCD1, 39 **B** **LISTEN** again and repeat.

TCD1,
40–43 **1** **LISTEN** to the conversation between the police officer and the driver. Then listen to the questions and fill in the circles for the correct answers. Repeat each item if necessary.

1. (A) (B) (C)   3. (A) (B) (C)
2. (A) (B) (C)   4. (A) (B) (C)

TCD1, 44 **2** **LISTEN** to the whole conversation. Draw a picture of the accident.

Pronounce *is / was / does / yes + he / she.* • Role-play an accident.

3 **LISTEN** and read.

TCD1, 45
SCD12

> A: <u>Simon</u>? You were late for <u>work</u> this morning.
>
> B: I'm sorry. I had a family emergency.
>
> A: I hope it wasn't serious. What happened?
>
> B: My <u>younger brother was skateboarding to school when a cyclist hit him.</u>
>
> A: <u>Oh, no</u>! Was <u>he</u> hurt?
>
> B: No, just scared. Everything's okay now.
>
> A: I'm glad to hear that.

4 **PRACTICE** the conversation from Activity 3 with a partner. Use the information in the chart.

Employee	Late for	Family emergency	Ways to express sympathy
1. Stella	the training	husband was waiting at a stoplight when the car behind him hit him	That's terrible!
2. Paulo	the meeting	daughter was getting into her car when a tree fell on it	How awful!
3. Muna	the presentation	mother was exercising when she fell and hit her head	The poor woman.

5 **TALK** in a group of four. Look at the illustration below. Describe the accident.

6 **ROLE-PLAY** in your group. Imagine you are telling your story to the police officer.

Student A is the driver of the car. Student B is the driver of the truck. Student C is the rider of the motorcycle. Student D is the police officer. Students A, B, and C take turns telling what happened and answering the police officer's questions.

LESSON 4: Grammar and Vocabulary

1 **GRAMMAR PICTURE DICTIONARY.** What happened while they were working? Listen and read.

1

A: Did you hear about Lia's accident?
B: No, what happened?
A: She **slipped** and sprained her ankle while she was walking **down the hall**.
B: I'm sorry to hear that. Thanks for letting me know.

2

A: Did you hear about Tanya's accident?
B: No, what happened?
A: She **tripped** and sprained her wrist while she was getting **out of an elevator**.
B: I'm sorry to hear that. Thanks for letting me know.

3

A: Did you hear about Larry's accident?
B: No, what happened?
A: He **dislocated** his shoulder while he was **unloading** a truck.
B: That's too bad. Thanks for telling me.

4

A: Did you hear about Rupert's accident?
B: No, what happened?
A: He **hurt** his back while he was **lifting** a heavy box.
B: That's too bad. Thanks for telling me.

2 **PRACTICE** the conversations with a partner.

3 **NOTICE THE GRAMMAR.** Circle the simple past verbs in the conversations above. Draw a rectangle around the word *while*. Underline the past continuous verbs.

Talk about workplace accidents. • Use *while* with past continuous.

Past Continuous with *while* Clause

While means "during the time." *While* introduces the continuous action. Use the past continuous after *while*.

Simple Past Clause		Past Continuous Clause with *while*		
Subject	**Simple past**	***while***	**Subject**	**Past continuous**
She	cut her hand	while	she	was unpacking boxes.
He	burned his arm	while	he	was cooking dinner.

Use a comma after the clause beginning with *while* if it comes at the beginning of the sentence.

Past Continuous clause with *while*			Simple Past Clause	
While	**Subject**	**Past Continuous**	**Subject**	**Simple Past**
While	she	was unpacking boxes,	she	cut her hand.
While	he	was cooking dinner,	he	burned his arm.

4 **WRITE.** Read the conversations. Then write past continuous sentences with *while*.

1. *A:* Claudia broke her arm.
   B: How did she do that?
   A: Playing soccer.

   Claudia broke her arm while she was playing soccer.

2. *A:* Dang burned her hand.
   B: How did she do that?
   A: Taking a cake out of the oven.

   _____

3. *A:* George slipped and broke his arm.
   B: How did he do that?
   A: Running in the rain.

   _____

4. *A:* Ai dislocated her shoulder.
   B: How did she do that?
   A: Moving furniture.

   _____

5. *A:* Liam tripped and hurt his knee.
   B: How did he do that?
   A: Running down the hall at school.

   _____

6. *A:* Anna hurt her back.
   B: How did she do that?
   A: Lifting her son out of the pool.

   _____

5 **ACT OUT** an accident from Activity 1 or 4 for a partner. Your partner will guess the accident.

LESSON 5: Grammar Practice Plus

1 **TALK** about the picture. What was everyone doing at the park last Saturday? Were there any accidents?

2 **COMPLETE.** Write the names of the people in the picture in the first space of each sentence. Then write the simple past or past continuous to complete the sentences about each person.

1. _____Linda_____ _____cut_____ (cut) her hand while she _____was unpacking_____ (unpack) the picnic basket.

2. _____ _____ (burn) his hand while he _____ (grill) hamburgers.

3. _____ _____ (trip) and _____ (sprain) his ankle while he _____ (run).

4. _____ _____ (hurt) her back while she _____ (play) soccer.

5. _____ _____ (bump) his head while he _____ (take) his bicycle out of the car.

6. _____ _____ (slip) on a banana peel and _____ (sprain) her wrist while she _____ (walk) to the picnic area.

7. _____ _____ (fall) and hurt his knee while he _____ (play) on the swings.

3 **TALK.** Look at the picture. Ask and answer questions with *how*.

> How did Linda cut herself?

> Unpacking the picnic basket.

Describe park events. • Talk about accidents.

4 **WHAT ABOUT YOU?** Talk with a group about an accident you had. Complete the chart with your classmates' accidents.

What happened?	What was the person doing?
Example: *Simon cut his hand.*	*washing dishes*
1.	
2.	
3.	
4.	
5.	

5 **WRITE** about your classmates' accidents. Use the information in your chart and *while*.

Example: _Simon cut his hand while he was washing dishes._

1. _____

2. _____

3. _____

4. _____

5. _____

6 **TALK.** Ask and answer questions about the accidents in your chart.

Simon, did you go to the emergency room?

No. It wasn't serious.

Do you remember how to form simple past questions with *be*, *do*, and *wh-* words?

Were you okay?

Did you go to the doctor?

When did the accident happen?

Where did it happen?

What did you do?

LESSON 6: Reading

1 **THINK ABOUT IT.** Talk in a small group about accidents at your past or present workplaces. Who had the accidents? What happened? What did people do after the accidents?

2 **BEFORE YOU READ.**

A. **PREVIEW** the text on the next page. What kind of report is it? How do you know?

B. **READ** the questions below. Do not read the text yet. Especially in a test situation, it is important to read any questions before you start reading the text.

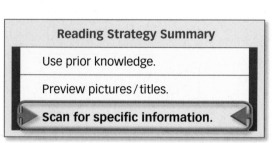

Reading Strategy Summary
Use prior knowledge.
Preview pictures / titles.
Scan for specific information.

1. What was the employee's injury?

2. When did the accident happen?

3. Where did the accident happen?

4. How did the accident happen?

5. Who took the employee to the hospital?

6. What was the employee doing when she had the accident?

3 **READ** the accident report.

A. **SCAN** the accident report and highlight the answers to the questions in Activity 2B.

> **READING FOCUS: Scan for specific information**
>
> We often scan texts like train and bus schedules to find specific information, such as our starting and ending locations and the times of day we want to travel. We also scan articles and other types of texts when we must answer test or other questions. We read the text quickly to find the answers. After scanning, we read the text again more carefully.

 B. **WRITE** the answers to the questions in Activity 2B.

4 **AFTER YOU READ.** Circle these words in the accident report. Then complete the sentences below.

area	informed	personally	tear	tray

1. I was going to mail a birthday card to my sister, but I decided to deliver it _____.

2. I try to keep the _____ around my desk clean.

3. While I was doing the laundry, I found a _____ in my favorite shirt.

4. I took a _____ of milk and cookies to my son while he was studying in his room.

5. His boss _____ him that he was fired.

EMPLOYEE ACCIDENT REPORT

Summary No. _____27_____

Date of accident: _November 17_ Date report filed: _November 20_

Location of accident:	Restaurant dining room	
Accident type:	fall	
Type of injury:	broken wrist	
Employee job title:	food server	
Age:	37	
Sex:	female	
Length of time in position:	2 1/2 years	

Brief Description of the Accident: _The employee is a server with two and a half years of experience in this position. The accident happened while she was carrying a tray of food. The employee was walking to a table with the tray when she tripped on a tear in the carpet. The employee fell and broke her wrist. Another food server was working in the same area, and he saw the accident happen. He informed the manager and offered to take the employee to the hospital, but the manager insisted on driving the employee to the hospital personally._

DISCUSSION

1. Who do you think should pay for the employee's hospital expenses? Why?
2. What other kinds of problems do you think the employee has now?
3. What other kinds of accidents can happen in a restaurant?

LESSON 7: Writing

1 **THINK ABOUT IT.** Look at the picture. Answer the questions with your class.

1. How could the steps in the picture be dangerous?
2. What kinds of accidents can happen in bad weather?
3. Did you ever have an accident because of the weather?

> **WRITING FOCUS:** *Wh*- question chart
>
> One useful way to organize information for a report is to use a *wh*- question chart. Tell *who, what, where, when,* and *how* or *why.*

2 **BEFORE YOU WRITE.**

TCD1, 47

A. LISTEN to the manager and employee talk about an accident. Take notes in the chart below.

Who (Who had the accident?)	
What (What happened?)	
Where (Where did the accident happen?)	
When (When did the accident happen?)	
Why / How (Why or how did the accident happen?)	

B. LISTEN again. Then work in a group and add to your notes.

C. TALK with a partner. Ask and answer the *wh*- questions.

D. DRAW a picture of the accident on the accident report form on the next page.

Use *Wh*- questions to organize information. • Complete an accident report.

3 **WRITE.** Look at Jim's accident report below. Fill in the missing information at the top of the form. Then write a brief description of the accident. For help, look at your notes from Activity 2A and at the accident report on page 49.

EMPLOYEE ACCIDENT REPORT

Summary No. _____83_____

Date of accident: _February 2, 2008_ Date report filed: _February 16, 2008_

Location of accident:	
Accident type:	
Type of injury:	
Employee job title:	computer programmer
Age:	43
Sex:	
Length of time in position:	10 years

Brief Description of the Accident: _____

_____

_____

_____

_____

_____

_____

_____

_____

4 **AFTER YOU WRITE.**

A. EDIT. Exchange accident reports with a partner and check the following.

1. Is there anything you don't understand? Mark it.
2. Did your partner answer all five *wh-* questions?
3. Did your partner use the past continuous correctly?

B. REWRITE. Return your partner's accident report. Discuss anything your partner marked or wrote on your accident report. Then rewrite your description of the accident.

TCD1, 48

1 **LISTEN** to the conversation. Then practice the conversation with a partner.

> *Jason:* What happened?
>
> *Tomás:* I was climbing the ladder when I slipped and fell. I think I hurt my wrist.
>
> *Jason:* You should go to the emergency room.
>
> *Tomás:* I don't have insurance. And a visit to the emergency room is really expensive.
>
> *Jason:* But you were working when you had the accident. I think workers' compensation will cover the cost.
>
> *Tomás:* Workers' compensation? What's that?

2 **TALK** with a partner. Answer the questions.

1. What are Jason's and Tomas's jobs?
2. What are they talking about?
3. What is Jason's suggestion?

3 **WRITE.** Why do you think workers sometimes don't get medical treatment for accidents at work? Use ideas from Activity 1 and your own ideas.

Example: *They don't know about workers' compensation.*

4 **READ** about workers' compensation.

> **WORKERS' COMPENSATION**
>
> State laws say that employers must pay for workers' compensation insurance for their employees. That means that if employees are injured or become sick while they are doing their work, all their medical costs will be covered. Workers' compensation also includes disability payments if the worker cannot work, and physical therapy to help the worker return to work. Employees do not have to pay for this insurance.

5 **READ** the text above again. Check ☑ the benefits workers' compensation provides.

- ◯ visit to the emergency room
- ◯ physical therapy
- ◯ medications and treatment
- ◯ payments if you can't work

6 **WHAT ABOUT YOU?** Talk in small groups. Tell about a time you or someone you know had an accident at work or school. What happened? What did the person do after the accident?

Check Your Progress!

Skill	Circle the answers	Is it correct?
A. Use the past continuous with _when clauses_.	1. Angela **talk** / **was talking** / **talks** on her cell phone when she hit the tree. 2. **Were** / **Was** / **Are** they speeding when she saw them? 3. David was changing lanes when he **hit** / **was hitting** / **hits** the truck. 4. Were you speeding when you **had** / **was having** / **has** the accident?	☐ ☐ ☐ ☐

		Number Correct	0	1	2	3	4

Skill	Circle the answers	Is it correct?
B. Use the past continuous with _while clauses_.	5. May sprained her ankle while she **play** / **plays** / **was playing** soccer. 6. While Dan **running** / **run** / **was running**, he dislocated his knee. 7. Sharon **broke** / **was breaking** / **breaking** her arm while she was playing basketball. 8. She **hurting** / **was hurting** / **hurt** her back while she was lifting the box.	☐ ☐ ☐ ☐

		Number Correct	0	1	2	3	4

Skill	Circle the answers	Is it correct?
C. Talk about traffic safety.	9. Babies should sit in a **seat belt** / **car seat**. 10. Use your **turn signal** / **carpool lane** when you change lanes. 11. She got a ticket. She was **speeding** / **parking** in a handicapped parking space. 12. You should use a **headset** / **carpool lane** while you're driving and talking on your cell phone.	☐ ☐ ☐ ☐

		Number Correct	0	1	2	3	4

Skill	Circle the answers	Is it correct?
D. Understand work safety and injuries.	13. Alex **dislocated** / **tripped** his shoulder at work. 14. Clean up the wet floor before someone **slips** / **hurts** on it. 15. I hurt my back while I was **lifting** / **unloading** the truck. 16. Did you fall while you were getting **down** / **out of** the elevator?	☐ ☐ ☐ ☐

		Number Correct	0	1	2	3	4

COUNT the number of correct answers above. Fill in the bubbles.

Chart Your Success					
Skill	Need Practice	Okay	Good	Very Good	Excellent!
A. Use the past continuous with _when_ clauses.	⓪	①	②	③	④
B. Use the past continuous with _while_ clauses.	⓪	①	②	③	④
C. Talk about traffic safety.	⓪	①	②	③	④
D. Understand work safety and injuries.	⓪	①	②	③	④

LESSON 1: Grammar and Vocabulary

1 **GRAMMAR PICTURE DICTIONARY.** What are the rules and regulations at this restaurant? Listen and read.

TCD2, 2
SCD14

WEEKLY SCHEDULE

MON	BOB
TUES	JOHN ED
WED	ED
THURS	BOB
FRI	ED JOHN
SAT	JOHN

1

Employees <u>may not</u> exchange **shifts** with each other.

HI, MOM!

PLEASE WAIT TO BE SEATED

2

Employees may not make **personal calls** during work hours.

EMPLOYEES ONLY

3

Employees may **chat with each other** behind the restaurant.

4

We can't use iPods® or MP3 players in the **dining area**.

5

We can't wear **flip-flops**.

BILL
EMPLOYEE MEAL--
NO CHARGE
TOTAL $0.00

6

We can have one **free meal** per six-hour shift.

2 **TALK** with a partner about what the restaurant employees can and can't do.

Example: *A:* Can the restaurant employees make personal calls?
B: No, they can't.

3 **NOTICE THE GRAMMAR.** <u>Underline</u> *may, may not, can,* and *can't* in the sentences in Activity 1. What is the difference between *may* and *can*?

> We write *can* + *not* together: *cannot* or *can't* (contracted). There is no contraction for *may not*.

May and *Can* for What is Allowed

Use *may* to say an action is okay or allowed. Use *may not* to say that an action is not allowed. It is common to use *may* and *may not* in formal writing or in listing rules. *May* and *may not* are less common in informal conversation. Use the base form of the verb after *may* and *can*.

Subject	*may* (*not*)	Base Verb
Employees / You / They	may may not	exchange shifts.

Use *can* to say that an action is allowed. Use *cannot* to say that an action is not allowed. *Can* is more common in informal conversation than in formal writing or listing rules.

Subject	*can* (*not*)	Base Verb
I / You / He / She	can can't	exchange shifts.
We / You / They		

4 **COMPLETE** the restaurant rules. Use *may* or *may not*.

1. Employees _____*may not*_____ make personal calls or send text messages during work hours. However, employees _____*may*_____ make personal calls during breaks.

2. Employees _____ use iPods in the dining area. However, employees _____ change the radio station in the restaurant.

3. Employees _____ have one free meal per six-hour shift. However, tables are for customers only. Employees _____ eat at the tables. They should eat at the counter.

4. Employees _____ only chat with each other behind the restaurant. Employees _____ chat with each other in the dining area or in the kitchen.

5. Employees _____ wear flip-flops or sandals for health and safety reasons. Employees _____ wear black or white sneakers, but they must be clean.

6. Employees _____ exchange shifts with each other. Employees _____ ask for time off, but not more than two weeks.

5 **ROLE-PLAY** with a partner. Imagine you are employees at the restaurant in Activity 1. The new employee asks questions about the rules. The old employee answers using information from Activities 1 and 4.

Can we listen to music at work?

We can only listen to the radio. We can't listen to iPods or MP3 players.

LESSON 2: Grammar Practice Plus

1 **READ** the office rules. Write the letter of the rule next to the person who is breaking it in the picture.

> **Employees may not:**
>
> **a.** surf the Internet during work hours.
> **b.** make personal calls during work hours.
> **c.** use the copier to make personal copies.
> **d.** chat in the work area.
>
> **e.** wear flip-flops.
> **f.** play music without headphones or earbuds.
> **g.** use cooking appliances at their desks.
> **h.** use obscene language.

2 **ROLE-PLAY** with a partner. Imagine you are office employees. Partner B acts out breaking a rule. Partner A tells Partner B the rule. Follow the example below.

Example: *A:* Excuse me.
   B: Hi, what's up?
   A: We can't play music without headphones or earbuds. It's an office rule.
   B: Oh, I didn't know that. Thanks for telling me.

3 **READ** the summer dress code for the employees in the office in Activity 1.

Employee Summer Dress Code	
Men	**Women**
Allowed: • pants, colored jeans (black, white, green) • shirts, sweaters, jackets • closed-toe shoes, boots (cowboy or dress styles only; no work boots or hiking boots)	**Allowed:** • pants, colored jeans (black, white, green), skirts, dresses • shirts, sleeveless shirts, blouses, sweaters, jackets • open-toe sandals, closed-toe shoes, boots (cowboy or dress styles only; no work boots or hiking boots)
Prohibited: • blue jeans • open-toe sandals, flip-flops • shorts • sneakers • T-shirts with words or pictures on them; sleeveless shirts	**Prohibited:** • blue jeans • flip-flops • shorts • sneakers • T-shirts with words or pictures on them

4 **TALK** with a partner. Point to people in the picture in Activity 1, and tell what dress code rules they're breaking.

Example: *A:* She's wearing flip-flops. Flip-flops are prohibited.

B: What kind of shoes can she wear?

A: She can wear open-toe sandals, closed-toe shoes, or boots.

5 **WRITE.** Many employees aren't following the rules, so the boss wrote a memo. Look at the summer dress code in Activity 3 and write sentences in the memo. Use *may* or *may not*.

1. employees / blue jeans
2. employees / sweaters
3. women / open-toe sandals
4. employees / sneakers
5. employees / shorts
6. employees / hiking boots

------------------ MEMO ------------------

REMINDER! Please follow the summer dress code rules.

Employees may not wear blue jeans.

_____

_____

_____

_____

_____

6 **WHAT ABOUT YOU?** Do you have a job? Is there a dress code at your workplace? What can you wear? What can't you wear? Tell your classmates.

Example: You can wear jeans and T-shirts, but you can't wear T-shirts with words on them.

LESSON 3: Listening and Conversation

TCD2, 3–6

1 **LISTEN** to the beginning of a conversation. Then listen for the next best sentence. Fill in the circle for the correct answer. Repeat each item if necessary.

1. Ⓐ Ⓑ Ⓒ   3. Ⓐ Ⓑ Ⓒ

2. Ⓐ Ⓑ Ⓒ   4. Ⓐ Ⓑ Ⓒ

TCD2, 7

2 **LISTEN** to the whole conversation. Check ☑ *True* or *False*.

	True	False
1. Employees can get information about the summer dress code in the employee handbook.	☐	☐
2. The summer dress code is on the bulletin board in the break room.	☐	☐
3. All of the new rules are in the employee handbook.	☐	☐
4. Employees can smoke in an area in front of the building.	☐	☐
5. Employees can never exchange shifts.	☐	☐

TCD2, 8 **Pronunciation:** Reduction and Word Stress: *can* and *can't*

In questions and statements with *can*, the *a* sound is usually reduced. The word *can* is usually unstressed. Listen and repeat the following examples:

> We can listen to the radio.   Can we eat lunch in the cafeteria?

In questions and statements with *can't*, the *a* sound is not usually reduced. The word *can't* is usually stressed. Listen and repeat the following examples:

> We can't listen to the radio.   Can't we eat lunch in the cafeteria?

TCD2, 9
SCD15
A **LISTEN** and write *can* or *can't* in the blanks. Listen again and check.

1. We _____can_____ make personal calls.

2. We _____ send personal e-mails during break.

3. _____ they wear jeans to work?

4. They _____ wear flip-flops to work.

5. _____ employees wear headphones at work?

6. We _____ make personal phone calls at work.

TCD2, 10 **B** **LISTEN** again and repeat the sentences.

Pronounce *can/can't*. • Read and talk about workplace rules.

3 **LISTEN** and read.

TCD2, 11
SCD16

A: What are you reading?

B: Our new employee handbook. There are a lot of new rules.

A: Really?

B: Yes. Listen to this one: Employees may not <u>stand in front of the store during break</u>.

A: You mean we can't <u>take breaks outside</u>?

B: We can, but <u>we have to go in the area behind the building</u>.

A: Oh…I see.

4 **PRACTICE** the conversation in Activity 3 with a partner. Use the information in the chart.

Employees may not...	You mean we can't...	We can, but...
1. make personal calls from store phones	call our families on break	we have to use our cell phones
2. park in the customer parking lot	park our cars in the supermarket lot	we can only park in the parking area behind the building
3. wear sweaters or jackets over our name tags	wear sweaters or jackets when we are cold	we should put our name tags on the sweater so customers can read our names

5 **WHAT ABOUT YOU?** Ask four classmates to name a place they visit and what is allowed or prohibited there. Write their answers in the chart.

Name	Place	What is allowed?	What is prohibited?
Jon	class	drinking water or soda	eating food

6 **TALK.** Tell the class about your classmates' rules in Activity 5.

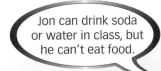

Jon can drink soda or water in class, but he can't eat food.

Unit 4 • Lesson 3 | **59**

LESSON 4: Grammar and Vocabulary

1 GRAMMAR PICTURE DICTIONARY. What are the rules of the apartment building? Listen and read.

TCD2, 12
SCD17

1 Residents <u>must</u> put **garbage** in **Dumpsters**. ✓

2 Residents must park in **assigned spaces** or on the street. ✓

3 Residents must keep their dogs **on leashes** and their cats **indoors**. ✓

4 Residents must not smoke in **common areas**. ✗

5 Residents must not leave **personal belongings** in the laundry room. ✗

6 Residents must not make noise in the **stairwells**. ✗

2 READ the sentences below. Check ☑ the sentence on the right that has a similar meaning.

1. Residents must park in assigned spaces.
   - ☐ Residents have to park in assigned spaces.
   - ☐ Residents may park in assigned spaces.

2. Residents must not smoke in common areas.
   - ☐ Residents don't have to smoke in common areas.
   - ☐ Residents may not smoke in common areas.

3 NOTICE THE GRAMMAR. <u>Underline</u> *must* and *must not* in the rules in Activity 1. What follows *must* and *must not*?

60 | Read and talk about rules for residents. • Use *must* and *have to*.

Must and *Have to* for Requirements

Must and *have to* are similar. *Must* is stronger, and is more common in writing than in conversation.

Subject	*must / have to*	Base Verb
Residents	must / have to	park in assigned spaces.
Employees		wear safety glasses.

Must not and *May not* for Prohibition

Must not means that a person is prohibited from doing something. It is stronger than *can't* and *may not*.

Subject	*must not / may not*	Base Verb
Residents		run in the hallways.
Employees	must not / may not	use company cars on weekends.
Students		talk during the test.

Don't have to for Requirements

Don't have to means *don't need to*.

Subject	*don't / doesn't*	*have to*	Base Verb
I / You / We / They	don't	have to	wear a suit to work.
He / She	doesn't		

4 **COMPLETE** the rules for another apartment building. Use *must* or *must not*.

1. For safety reasons, residents ___*must not*___ run in the hallways or stairwells.

2. Visitors _____ park in visitor parking in front of the building. The assigned spaces in the lot in the back of the building are for residents only.

3. Residents _____ leave anything in the common areas in the building. There should never be any personal belongings in the hallways or stairwells.

4. Residents _____ put garbage in places other than the blue Dumpsters. There are three blue Dumpsters for residents to use next to the building.

5. Residents _____ smoke in the apartments. This is a non-smoking building.

6. Residents _____ keep dogs on leashes in common areas. Leashes must not be over six feet long.

5 **WHAT ABOUT YOU?** Write two things that you have to do and two things that you don't have to do at home, work, or school. Tell your classmates.

I have to _____.

I have to _____.

I don't have to _____.

I don't have to _____.

LESSON 5: Grammar Practice Plus

1 **TALK** about the picture. What do the different illustrations on the sign mean?

Park Rules and Regulations

Fee $20.00

No Hunting

Stay On Trails

Park Hours
8:00 a.m. to
9:00 p.m.

2 **COMPLETE.** Look at the Park Rules and Regulations. Then complete the rules in the park brochure. Use *must, must not, may,* or *may not.*

Park Rules and Regulations

1. Visitors ___*must*___ keep their dogs on a leash.
2. Visitors _____ build fires on the ground.
3. Visitors _____ ride bicycles.
4. Visitors _____ drink alcohol in the park.
5. Visitors _____ pick flowers.
6. Visitors _____ camp in the park.
7. Visitors _____ hunt in the park.
8. Visitors _____ swim in the lake.
9. Visitors _____ leave the park by 9:00 P.M.
10. Visitors _____ fish in the park.

Read signs. • Calculate cost for recreation.

3 **TALK** with a partner. Ask and answer these questions about the Park Rules and Regulations.

1. Do you have to keep your dog on a leash?
2. Can you pick the flowers?
3. Can you ride bikes in the park?
4. Do hikers have to stay on the trails?
5. Can you build a fire in the park?
6. Can you camp in the park?
7. Can you ride horses on the trails?
8. Can you hunt in the park?
9. Do you have to pay to camp in the park?
10. Can you swim in the lake?
11. Do you have to leave the park by 8:00 P.M.?
12. Do you have to enter the park at 8:00 A.M.?
13. Can you fish in the park?

You sometimes means *people in general.*

You can swim in the lake means *Everyone can swim in the lake.*

Do you have to keep your dog on a leash?

Yes, you do.

No, you can't.

Can you pick the flowers?

4 **WRITE.** Think of another place that has rules, such as a museum, a zoo, a childcare center, a swimming pool, or an airport. Write three or more rules in your notebook. Use *must* and *must not*.

5 **TALK.** Tell partner the place you chose in Activity 4 and the rules you wrote.

Math: Calculating Expenses

fishing rod

reel

tackle kit

park ranger

A **READ** the story.

Al wanted to go fishing. He thought this would be fun and a cheap way to get food. So he went to a sporting goods store. He bought a fishing pole for $44.00 and a reel for $59.00. He bought a tackle kit for $26.99. But later that day, a friend gave him an old tackle kit, so he returned his new one to the sporting goods store. Finally, he went fishing. He caught six fish. But while he was leaving the park, a park ranger stopped him. The ranger asked Al for his fishing license. Al didn't have a fishing license. The ranger charged him a $35.00 fine.

B **ANSWER** the questions.

1. How much did Al's six fish cost? _____
2. How much did each fish cost? _____

LESSON 6: Reading

1 **THINK ABOUT IT.** Talk with a partner about citizenship. Are you a United States citizen? If not, are you interested in becoming one? Why or why not?

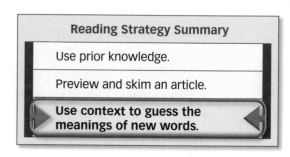
2 **BEFORE YOU READ.** Preview and skim the article on the next page. Talk with your class about the questions below.

1. How are the photos connected to the title?

2. What is the article about?

3 **READ** the article on the next page and underline key words and information.

---

4 **AFTER YOU READ**

A. VOCABULARY. Circle these words in the article on the next page.

government	history	illegal	requirements

READING FOCUS: Use context to guess the meanings of new words

When you don't know the meaning of a word, read the complete sentence with the word in it, and one or two sentences before and after. Then try to guess the meaning.

B. WRITE. Use context to guess the meaning of each word in the box above. Use the words to complete the sentences below.

1. *A:* What are the _____ for a job as a cashier?

   B: You must be 16 years old, and you must know how to use a cash register.

2. *A:* What important events happened in the United States in 1959?

   B: I don't know. I'm not good at U.S. _____.

3. *A:* Let's take this to drink in the car.

   B: No, we can't take that. It's _____ to have open bottles or cans of alcohol in the car.

4. *A:* The _____ should spend more money on public parks and other public areas.

   B: I think it's more important to spend money on education.

C. WRITE answers to these questions about the article.

1. How many years does a person have to live in the United States before applying for citizenship?
2. What can a person with a Permanent Resident Card do?
3. What are two kinds of questions that are on the Citizenship Test?
4. A person who sells illegal drugs does not meet one of the requirements. Which one?
5. What do people promise when they take the Oath of Allegiance?

Citizenship Requirements

All people who are born in the United States are United States citizens. But, generally speaking, a person born in another country must apply to become a citizen of the United States. There is one exception: a person doesn't have to do this when at least one of his or her parents was a United States citizen when he or she was born.

Applicants must meet these requirements:

★ They must live in the United States for five years before they can become citizens. They must also be 18 years old. (There are exceptions to the five-year rule. One exception allows an applicant to apply for citizenship after only three years of residence in the United States if the applicant became a permanent resident based on marriage to a U.S. citizen and continues to be married to and live with the U.S. citizen.)

★ Applicants must have a Permanent Resident Card. This card shows that the United States government allows a person to live and work in the United States all of his or her life. In the past, this card was green, so it was called a Green Card. The card isn't green now, but many people continue to call it a Green Card. With a Permanent Resident Card, a person can leave the United States, for example to visit a family member, and then come back.

GEORGE WASHINGTON
FIRST U.S. PRESIDENT

★ Applicants must also pass a civics test. This is a test about the history and government of the United States. The questions on the history part of the test are about our country's past. The government part of the test includes questions about the jobs of the leaders (presidents) of the United States, and the laws of the United States.

THE U.S. CONSTITUTION

★ Applicants must be able to read, write, and speak simple English. They must also take the Oath of Allegiance. When people take the Oath of Allegiance, they promise to follow the laws of the United States. They must agree to support the Constitution of the United States.

★ Applicants must demonstrate good behavior. This means that a person must not break the law. For example, a person must not buy or sell illegal drugs. It also means that a person must not do things that most people think are bad, for example, always drinking too much alcohol.

TAKING THE OATH OF ALLEGIANCE

For more information about how to become a United States citizen, see the U.S. Citizenship and Immigration Services website at www.uscis.gov.

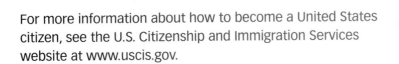

LESSON 7: Writing

1 **THINK ABOUT IT.** Think about when you were a child in school. Then discuss these questions in a group.

1. Was your school a large school or a small school?
2. Did you like school? Why or why not?
3. Who was your favorite teacher? Why?
4. What was your favorite class? Why?
5. What were some rules at your school? What were things students had to do? What were things students couldn't do?
6. Did you ever break any rules? If so, which ones?

The past of *must* and *have to* is *had to*.

The past of *must not* and *can't* is *couldn't*.

2 **BEFORE YOU WRITE.**

A. **READ** the paragraph below about school rules when the writer was a student. Circle the topic sentence. Underline the three supporting sentences. See page 18 in Unit 1 for help, if necessary.

B. **READ** the paragraph again. Draw a rectangle around the past forms of *have to* and *can't*.

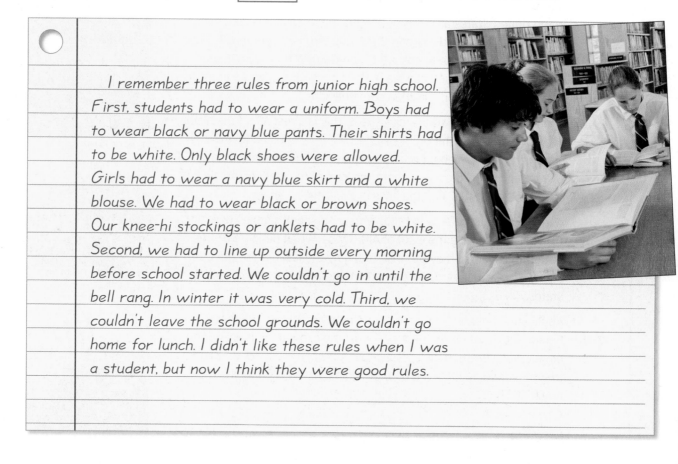

I remember three rules from junior high school. First, students had to wear a uniform. Boys had to wear black or navy blue pants. Their shirts had to be white. Only black shoes were allowed. Girls had to wear a navy blue skirt and a white blouse. We had to wear black or brown shoes. Our knee-hi stockings or anklets had to be white. Second, we had to line up outside every morning before school started. We couldn't go in until the bell rang. In winter it was very cold. Third, we couldn't leave the school grounds. We couldn't go home for lunch. I didn't like these rules when I was a student, but now I think they were good rules.

C. TALK with a partner. Answer the questions about the paragraph in Activity 2A.

1. What three rules does the writer discuss?

2. The writer says that now she thinks these were good rules? Do you agree? Why or why not?

WRITING FOCUS: Avoid run-on sentences

A run-on sentence is an incorrect sentence. It has two or more sentences (or main clauses) that are not separated by a period and are not joined by a connector like *and, but,* or *so*. An easy way to fix a run-on sentence is to make it into two sentences.

Incorrect ✗:

In winter it was very cold we couldn't go in until the bell rang.

In winter it was very cold, we couldn't go in until the bell rang.

Correct ✔:

In winter, it was very cold. We couldn't go in until the bell rang.

D. READ the Writing Focus. Then correct the run-on sentences by rewriting them as two sentences.

1. Incorrect: We couldn't leave the school grounds we couldn't go home for lunch.

   Correct: _____

2. Incorrect: Boys had to wear black or navy blue pants their shirts had to be white.

   Correct: _____

3. Incorrect: We had to clean our classroom, there was no custodian.

   Correct: _____

4. Incorrect: Our teacher didn't allow talking in class we had to be quiet.

   Correct: _____

5. Incorrect: Girls had to wear a navy blue skirt and a white blouse our anklets had to be white.

   Correct: _____

6. Incorrect: We had to line up outside we couldn't go in until the bell rang.

   Correct: _____

 3 **WRITE** a paragraph about rules at your elementary, junior high, or high school.

4 **AFTER YOU WRITE.**

A. EDIT. Look at your paragraph.

1. What rules did you write about?

2. Did you write a topic sentence and two or three supporting sentences?

3. Did you avoid run-on sentences?

4. Did you make any punctuation or spelling errors?

 B. REWRITE your paragraph.

Career Connection

1 **LISTEN** to the conversation. Then practice the conversation with a partner.

TCD2, 13

Manager: Rosa, I need to talk to you about something. Do you have a minute?

Rosa: Yes.

Manager: Yesterday, you brought your daughter to work.

Rosa: Yes. There was a lot of snow, and her school was closed.

Manager: Do you have a copy of the employee handbook? On page 14 it says, "Employees may not bring children to work."

Rosa: I know. But it was an emergency.

Manager: No, a closed school isn't an emergency.

Please find a babysitter to call in the future when your daughter's school is closed.

Rosa: I understand. And I'm sorry about yesterday.

Manager: Don't worry about it. Just remember for the future.

2 **TALK** with a partner. Answer the questions.

1. What is the problem in the conversation?
2. Do you think the rule in the employee handbook is a good rule? Why or why not?
3. Does Rosa's manager believe that Rosa's situation was an emergency?
4. What does the manager want Rosa to do next time her daughter's school is closed?
5. Do you have other ideas about what Rosa can do next time her daughter's school is closed?

3 **WHAT ABOUT YOU?** Talk in a group. Ask and answer questions about rules at your workplaces. What are some things you have to do? What are some things you must not do?

Example: *A:* What do you have to do at work for safety?

B: I have to wear closed-toe shoes at work. I can't wear sandals.

I work in an office. We can't wear jeans.

I'm a nurse. I have to wash my hands before I see a patient.

Check Your Progress!

Skill	Circle the answers.	Is it correct?
A. Use *may* and *can* to talk about what is allowed.	1. Can I **listen** / **listens** / **listened** to music in the break room? 2. No, you **may** / **not** / **may not**. 3. May we **wear** / **wearing** / **wears** shorts? 4. You **may** / **can** / **may not** wear shorts. You must wear pants.	☐ ☐ ☐ ☐
	Number Correct	0 1 2 3 4
B. Use *must, have to,* and *don't have to* for requirements. Use *must not* for prohibition.	5. Do we have to **wear** / **wears** / **to wear** safety glasses? 6. Yes, you **must** / **must not** / **don't have to** wear them at all times. 7. Do I have to **parks** / **parking** / **park** in an assigned space? 8. No, you don't **have to** / **have** / **must** park in an assigned space.	☐ ☐ ☐ ☐
	Number Correct	0 1 2 3 4
C. Understand workplace rules.	9. I can't work tonight. Will you exchange **shifts** / **personal calls** with me? 10. Employees must not **chat with each other** / **wear flip-flops** in the dining area. You may talk in the kitchen. 11. We can't make **personal calls** / **free meals** at work, so I left my cell phone at home. 12. Employees can have one **flip-flop** / **free meal** a day.	☐ ☐ ☐ ☐
	Number Correct	0 1 2 3 4
D. Talk about apartment building rules.	13. Residents' cats must stay **assigned spaces** / **indoors**. 14. Only the residents can park **in common areas** / **in assigned spaces**. 15. Residents must throw trash in **the Dumpsters** / **common areas**. 16. Residents must not make noise **on leashes** / **in stairwells**.	☐ ☐ ☐ ☐
	Number Correct	0 1 2 3 4

COUNT the number of correct answers above. Fill in the bubbles.

Chart Your Success					
Skill	**Need Practice**	**Okay**	**Good**	**Very Good**	**Excellent!**
A. Use *may* and *can* to talk about what is allowed.	⓪	①	②	③	④
B. Use *must, have to,* and *don't have to* for requirements. Use *must not* for prohibition.	⓪	①	②	③	④
C. Understand workplace rules.	⓪	①	②	③	④
D. Talk about apartment building rules.	⓪	①	②	③	④

LESSON 1: Grammar and Vocabulary

 1 **GRAMMAR PICTURE DICTIONARY.** What's the matter with everyone? Listen and read.

TCD2, 14
SCD18

1
A: You have a **cough** and a **runny nose**. You must have a cold!
B: No, I just have terrible **allergies**.

2
A: Are you feeling **out of breath**?
B: Yes, completely.
A: Be careful! You might have **asthma**.

3
A: Your toe is **swollen**!
B: It really hurts. I think it might be infected.
A: Oh, you may need **antibiotics**.

4
A: He has a bad cough and **chest pains**. Do you think it might be the flu?
B: Maybe, or it could be **bronchitis**.

5
A: Your eyes are red. You must have **conjunctivitis**!
B: Is that **pink eye**?
A: Yeah. Your eyes must feel **itchy**, too.

6
A: Can I help you?
B: Yes, I have a **rash**.
A: It could be **eczema**. You might need some medicated lotion.

2 **PRACTICE** the conversations in Activity 1 with a partner.

3 **NOTICE THE GRAMMAR.** Circle *may, might, could,* or *must* in the sentences in Activity 1. Which word/s do we use for something that we think is possible? Which do we use for something we are almost sure or certain about?

Modals of Possibility and Certainty

Use *must* to show that something is almost certain. Use *may*, *might*, and *could* to show that something is possible. The base form of a verb follows a modal.

Subject	Modal		Base Verb + Noun or Adjective
I / You / He / She We / You / They	must	certain	have pink eye. feel itchy.
	may could/might	less certain	have bronchitis. need antibiotics. be infected.

4 **WRITE** sentences. Use *may*, *might*, *could*, or *must* and the word in parentheses.

> **Be Careful!** There is no *to* after modals like *may*, *might*, *could*, or *must*.
>
> **Incorrect** ✗: She must ~~to~~ have the flu.
>
> **Correct** ✔: She must have the flu.
>
> Do not use the *s* form of the verb following the modal in the third person.
>
> **Incorrect** ✗: She must ~~has~~ the flu.
>
> **Correct** ✔: She must have the flu.

1. My ankle is swollen and it really hurts. I'm sure I have a sprained ankle. (must)

   I must have a sprained ankle.

2. Pierre hurt his hand. It's possible he has a broken finger. (might)

   He _____

   _____

3. Lucia and Jose have red eyes. I think it is pink eye. (may)

   They _____

4. You have a runny nose and a headache. I'm sure you have the flu. (must)

   You _____

5. Margarita can't carry heavy things. I'm sure she has a bad back. (must)

   She _____

6. Alex didn't come to work today. Maybe he is sick. (could)

   He _____

5 **TALK.** Work with a partner. Have short conversations using the health words from Activity 1. Use *may*, *might*, *could*, or *must*.

How do you feel today?

I have a runny nose.

You may have allergies.

LESSON 2: Grammar Practice Plus

1 **TALK** about the picture. What problems might these patients have?

2 **LISTEN** to the conversations. Write the number of each conversation in the correct place in the picture.

3 **MATCH** the name of each health care provider with the correct definition.

1. A cardiologist
2. A gynecologist
3. A pediatrician
4. A radiologist
5. A dermatologist
6. A physical therapist

a. _____ reads x-rays.
b. _____ checks your heart.
c. _____ provides health care for women.
d. _____ helps you get better by exercising.
e. _____ provides health care for children.
f. _____ helps with skin problems.

4 **COMPLETE** the chart. Write the words from the box in the correct place in the chart. Match the illnesses with the symptoms.

rash, itchy, eczema, out of breath, red eyes, chest pains, the flu, cough, bronchitis, conjunctivitis, asthma, runny nose, fever

Illness	Symptoms
eczema	rash, itchy

5 **WRITE.** Look at the pictures. Write about each person's symptoms and possible illness. Use the information in the chart.

1 Alexa   2 Pete   3 Alena   4 Rani   5 Anisa

1. _Alexa has a rash. It's itchy. She may have eczema._

2. _____

3. _____

4. _____

5. _____

6 **ROLE-PLAY** Imagine a health problem. Tell your partner your symptoms. Your partner will give you advice about what to do and which doctor to see.

I have itchy skin and a rash.

You might have eczema. You should see a dermatologist.

LESSON 3: Listening and Conversation

TCD2, 16 **Pronunciation:** Stress in Words Ending in *–ologist*, and *–ology*

In words ending in *–ologist* and *–ology*, the syllable with *–ol* has the most stress. Look at the examples. Listen and repeat.

der•ma• ' tol•o•gist   der•ma• ' tol•o•gy

A **LISTEN.** Draw an accent mark before the most stressed syllable in each of the words. Listen and check.

TCD2, 17
SCD19

	Doctor/Scientist	Subject/Medical field
1.	psych•'ol•o•gist	psych•ol•o•gy
2.	bi•ol•o•gist	bi•ol•o•gy
3.	im•mu•nol•o•gist	im•mu•nol•o•gy
4.	gy•ne•col•o•gist	gy•ne•col•gy

TCD2, 18 **B** **LISTEN** and repeat. Then find three more words with these endings. Check their pronunciation in the dictionary.

1 **LISTEN** to the question. Then listen to the conversation between the health care provider and the patient. Then listen to the question again. Fill in the circle for the correct answer. Repeat each item if necessary.

TCD2,
19–21

1. Ⓐ Ⓑ Ⓒ   2. Ⓐ Ⓑ Ⓒ   3. Ⓐ Ⓑ Ⓒ

2 **LISTEN** to the question. Listen to the conversation from Activity 1 again. Listen to the question again. Fill in the circle for the correct answer. Repeat each item if necessary.

TCD2,
22–24

1. Ⓐ Ⓑ Ⓒ   2. Ⓐ Ⓑ Ⓒ   3. Ⓐ Ⓑ Ⓒ

3 **LISTEN** to the conversation. Then read the sentences and check ☑ *True* or *False*.

TCD2, 25

	True	False
1. The patient might have bronchitis.	☐	☐
2. The patient must have a fever.	☐	☐
3. The patient must take an antibiotic.	☐	☐
4. The doctor might do some more tests.	☐	☐
5. The patient must come back in two weeks.	☐	☐

Be careful!

The modal verb *must* has two meanings.

You *must* take this medicine. (necessity; you *need* to take it)

You *must* have the flu. (certainty; you *surely* have it).

4 **READ** sentences 2, 3, and 5 in Activity 3 again. Which use *must* for necessity? Which uses *must* for certainty?

Talk about illnesses and symptoms. • Pronounce endings with *-ologist* and *-ology*.

5 **LISTEN** and read.

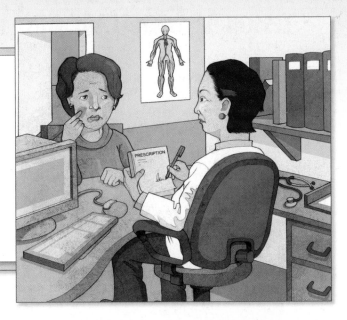

A: Good morning, Doctor Chan.

B: Hello! How are you today?

A: Not so good. I have <u>a bad rash on my face</u>.

B: It might be <u>an allergy</u>. We'll need to do some tests. I'm going to prescribe <u>some lotion</u>.

A: How often do I use <u>it</u>?

B: <u>Use it</u> <u>three times a day for ten days</u>. You must <u>stay out of the sun</u>.

A: Okay. Thank you very much!

6 **PRACTICE** the conversation in Activity 5 with a partner. Use information in the chart.

Symptom	Possible Illness	Medicine	Instructions
1. red itchy eyes	conjunctivitis	eye drops	Use them twice a day, in the morning and at night, for two weeks. / not rub your eyes.
2. a bad cough	bronchitis	an antibiotic	Use two tablets three times a day. / not drink alcohol.
3. chest pains after eating	heartburn	antacid tablets	Take one tablet twice a day before meals. / not eat spicy foods.

7 **TALK** with a partner. What are names of popular over-the-counter medicines? Write them in the chart below. What kinds of illnesses or symptoms do you usually buy them for?

> **Tip**
>
> **Over-the-counter drugs** are common, safe medicines you can buy at the drugstore without a doctor's prescription. Aspirin is an over-the-counter drug.

Medicine	Brand Name	Illness or Symptom
aspirin	*Relief*	*headache*

I usually buy *Relief* aspirin when I have a headache.

LESSON 4: Grammar and Vocabulary

TCD2, 27
SCD21

1 **GRAMMAR PICTURE DICTIONARY.** How is Gita's lifestyle different now? What were her past habits? Listen and read.

1
I <u>used to</u> buy a lot of **frozen dinners** and **desserts**.

2
I used to drink **high-calorie soft drinks**.

3
I used to take the **elevator** at work.

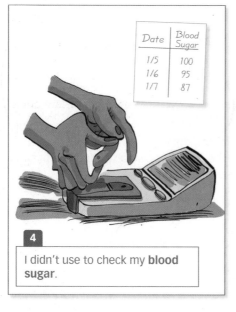

4
I didn't use to check my **blood sugar**.

5
I didn't use to read **food labels**.

6
I didn't use to **work out** at the **gym**.

2 **READ** the sentences in Activity 1 with a partner.

3 **NOTICE THE GRAMMAR.**

A. <u>UNDERLINE</u> *used to* and *didn't use to* in the sentences in Activity 1. Look at the word *use*. How is it different in sentences with *didn't*?

B. What is the meaning of *used to*? Tell your partner.

Discuss lifestyle habits. • Use *used to* for past habits or situations.

Used to for Past Habits or Situations

Use *used to* to talk about past habits or situations that were different in the past than they are now.

Subject	*used to*	Base Verb (+ Object)	Subject	*did not + use to*	Base Verb (+ Object)
I / You / He / She	used to	take the elevator.	I / You / He / She	didn't use to	take the stairs.
We / You / They		buy frozen dinners.	We / You / They		buy fresh food.

4 **READ** the sentences in Activity 1 again and look at the pictures. Check ☑ if the activity is something Gita did before or something she does now.

	Before	**Now**
1. check her blood sugar	○	○
2. take the elevator	○	○
3. drink high-calorie soft drinks	○	○
4. read food labels	○	○
5. work out at the gym	○	○

In the negative form, the word *use* has no *d*, but the pronunciation is the same as the affirmative past form.
I used to smoke.
I didn't use to smoke.

5 **WRITE** the affirmative or negative form of *used to* and the verb in parentheses.

Gita had a blood test and her blood sugar was very high. She doesn't want to get diabetes, so she made some changes in her lifestyle. She (1) ___*didn't use to check*___ (check) her blood sugar, but now she checks it once a week. When she went up to the second floor at work, she (2) _____ (take) the stairs.

She (3) _____ (exercise) only once a month! Now she goes to the gym more often.

When she went to the supermarket, she (4) _____ (buy) junk food, but now she buys a lot of healthy food. She (5) _____ (check) the sugar and fat in her food, but now she reads the food labels on everything. She (6) _____ (eat) frozen dinners every day, but now she cooks more often. She feels much healthier!

 6 **WHAT ABOUT YOU?** Complete the sentences. Tell the class.

I used to _____.

I didn't use to _____.

I used to work out at a gym five times a week.

I didn't use to drive a car.

LESSON 5: Grammar Practice Plus

Math: Interpreting Nutrition Labels

A **READ** the information about nutrition labels.

A **container** is a package, box, bag, or bottle. It can contain one or more servings of food. A **serving** is the amount one person eats or drinks at one time. Each container has a Nutrition Facts label. It tells how many **calories** are in each serving. It also gives the amount of sugar, and the percentage of fat, salt, vitamins, and other nutrients in each serving. The **percentage of daily value** tells what percentage one serving of the food or drink provides of the total a person should get in a day.

oz = ounces   g = grams

B **TALK** with a partner. Look at the apple juice label and answer the questions.

1. How many servings are in this bottle?
2. How many calories are in one serving?
3. How much is in the whole bottle?
4. Sodium is the chemical name for salt. How much salt is in one serving?
5. How much salt is in the whole bottle?
6. Is this product high or low in fat?

Apple Juice

Nutrition Facts

Serving Size 8 fl. oz
Servings Per Container About 2

Amount Per Serving

Calories 110

	% daily value
Total Fat 0g	0%
Sodium 20mg	1%
Total Carbohydrates 28g	9%
Sugars 26g	
Vitamin C	20%

---

1 **COMPLETE** the sentences. In the first sentence, write *used to* or *didn't use to*. Then complete the last sentence with a word or expression from the box.

allergy	diabetes	high blood pressure	diet	vegetarian

1. Rani ___used to___ eat too much salt. Now she always chooses low-sodium soup.

   She could have ___high blood pressure___.

2. Dave _____ eat a lot of sweets.

   Now he always chooses sugar-free products.

   He might have _____.

3. Su-lin _____ care what kind of yogurt she ate.

   Now she always chooses low-fat yogurt.

   She might be on a _____.

4. Pilar _____ like hamburgers.

   Now she eats meat-free burgers.

   She may be a _____.

5. Danny cannot eat cookies with peanuts.

   He must have a peanut _____.

---

2 **WRITE** what each person *used to* do and what each person does *now*.
See page 214 for a list of irregular verb forms.

1. Carlos   **Before:** drank coffee every day   **Now:** drinks tea or juice

   Carlos used to drink coffee every day, but now he drinks juice.
   _____

2. They   **Before:** bought frozen dinners   **Now:** buy fresh food

   _____

3. My sister   **Before:** drove to work every day   **Now:** rides her bike

   _____

4. We   **Before:** didn't play any sports   **Now:** play volleyball once a week

   _____

5. The students   **Before:** didn't read food labels   **Now:** read them all the time

   _____

3 **WHAT ABOUT YOU?** Compare your diet and exercise habits from ten years ago with your habits now.
Complete the chart.

		Ten years ago	Now
Diet	1		
	2		
	3		
Exercise	1		
	2		
	3		

4 **WRITE** six sentences about yourself using information from Activity 3 or other ideas.

Example: *I used to eat junk food every day for a snack, but now I don't. I eat fruit or nuts.*

When the verb is the same in both clauses, you don't have to repeat it in the second clause.

I used to eat meat, but now I don't ~~eat meat~~.

I didn't use to eat low-fat foods, but now I do ~~eat low fat foods~~.

5 **TALK.** Tell a partner about your diet and exercise habits from Activity 4 and ask questions about your partner's habits.

I used to play soccer every weekend.

Why did you stop?

Because I was too busy!

LESSON 6: Reading

1 **THINK ABOUT IT.** What foods can people buy in a vending machine? Which of the foods below are healthy? Which are junk food? Compare your answers with a group.

candy	coffee	cookies
fresh fruit	fruit juice	granola bar
milk	nuts	potato chips
soup	tea	water

Reading Strategy Summary

- Use prior knowledge.
- **Identify arguments for and against.**
- Use context to guess the meanings of new words.

2 **BEFORE YOU READ.** Discuss the questions below with a partner. Share your answers with the class.

1. Why do schools have vending machines?
2. Are vending machines a good idea? Why or why not?

READING FOCUS: Identify arguments for and against

When you read, identify the main issue in the article and look for the arguments for and against the main issue.

3 **READ** the article on the next page. Then choose the best answer to the questions.

1. What is the main issue discussed in this article?
   a. Putting healthy food in school vending machines.
   b. Why students choose unhealthy food.
   c. The problems of overweight children.

2. Which one is an argument *for* healthier food in school vending machines?
   a. It makes money for the school.
   b. Students prefer healthy food.
   c. Students are overweight.

3. Which is an argument *against* healthier food in school vending machines?
   a. Students prefer junk food.
   b. Students need more exercise.
   c. Students want the choice.

4 **AFTER YOU READ.**

A. VOCABULARY. Find and circle these phrases in the article. Use context to guess their meanings. Discuss their meanings with a partner. Check your definitions in the dictionary.

childhood obesity	junk food	mixed feelings	school income

B. COMPLETE the chart with ideas from the article. Work in a group.

Put healthier food in school vending machines	
For	Against

School vending machines get a facelift

1   Lisa Gomez, 16, used to buy soda and candy bars the from school vending machines, but no more. Now she gets bottled water and granola bars. Leong Kim, also 16, used to
5 get candy bars, potato chips, and soft drinks from the machines at school. But now he buys them on his way to school.

    Their school is just one of many schools in the country that are replacing high-fat,
10 high-sugar foods and drinks in their vending machines with healthier choices. Soft drinks, chips, and candy are out. Water, juice, granola bars, and dried fruit are in.

    Why? Because you can't pick up a
15 newspaper or magazine without reading about childhood obesity. About 30 percent of children ages 6 to 19 are overweight or might become overweight.* "We teach students about healthy eating in class, but sell junk
20 food in the hallway," says high school teacher Ali Peshwar. "It must send students the wrong message."

    The students have mixed feelings. "I see the purpose of it—to make sure kids are eating
25 healthier food at school," Lisa says. "But on the other hand, I think we should be able to choose." Leong hates the change. "None of us wants this food," he says. "It's okay to be healthy sometimes, but not all the time."

30   Some groups say that the sale of foods at school is not the problem. A spokesperson for the food industry says that "the best thing schools can do about childhood obesity is to get kids moving in gym class."

35   Another problem is a school's budget. Some schools say they need the money from vending machines to pay for activities such as sports, clubs, and music and art programs. Will students eat the healthier snack foods and drinks so the
40 schools continue to make money?

    School principal Elsa Newman is sure the new program will work. "In 10 years, we will look back and say, 'Can you believe we used to sell that junk to our students?'"

Source: http://www.usatoday.com/news/health/2005–08–21-junk-food-cover_x.htm

Statistics from the Centers for Disease Control and Prevention.

DISCUSSION

1. What do you think?
2. What other suggestions do you have for students?
3. How can they have healthier eating habits?

LESSON 7: Writing

1 **THINK ABOUT IT.** Look at the pictures. Discuss these questions with a partner.

1. What can you say about differences in people's lifestyles today and fifty years ago?
2. Is life healthier now or was it healthier before?

2 **BEFORE YOU WRITE.**

A. READ the paragraph on the next page about people's eating habits 50 years ago and today.

B. TALK in a group about health and diet today compared with health and diet in the past. Use the topics in the box.

home freezers	microwaves	large supermarkets	frozen food	food labels

C. COMPLETE the sentences. Use the information in the paragraph in Activity 2D and your own ideas.

> **WRITING FOCUS: Make a list**
> Make a list to generate ideas for your writing. You can choose the best ideas and organize them afterwards.

Topic: Diet and eating habits fifty years ago and today

People used to _spend more time cooking._ _____

_____

_____

They didn't use to _eat so much fast food._ _____

_____

_____

Now we _____

_____

_____

We don't _____

_____

_____

D. READ the example.

>   Fifty years ago, diet and eating habits were very different. People didn't use to eat so much fast food. They used to spend more time cooking because they didn't have microwaves or pre-made frozen meals. They also didn't use to have large supermarkets, and they couldn't buy so many different kinds of foods.
>
>   Diet and eating habits are different nowadays. People buy fast food and frozen dinners. They cook food in microwaves. It is easier and faster. Supermarkets have more choices, such as low-fat and sugar-free food. Most foods have food labels and we have more information about which foods are safe and healthy. Diet and eating habits are definitely different now!

3   **WRITE.**

A. CHOOSE a topic and make a list of your ideas. Follow the example in Activity 2.

Topics:	**1.** Health and Exercise	**2.** Medicine and Healthcare	**3.** Health and Lifestyle	**4.** Health and Work.

Topic: _____

People used to _____
_____
_____

They didn't use to _____
_____
_____

Now we _____
_____
_____

We don't _____
_____
_____

B. WRITE. Use the information from your chart in Activity 3. Write two paragraphs. The first paragraph should describe the past. The second paragraph should describe the present.

4   **AFTER YOU WRITE.**

A. EDIT your work.

   1. Was the meaning clear?

   2. Did you use the correct verb forms?

B. EXCHANGE your work with a partner. Read each other's work. Then ask and answer questions about your ideas.

Career Connection

1 **LISTEN** to the conversation. Then practice with a partner.

> *Luis:* It's nearly 7 P.M.! I can go home and relax.
>
> *Tina:* You're on your feet all day. You must be really tired.
>
> *Luis:* Yeah, I have to buy some comfortable shoes. But this job is better than my old job.
>
> *Tina:* Why? What did you do before?
>
> *Luis:* I used to work in a bakery. I had to get up at 3:00 every morning, and I ate pastries and cookies all day long. What did you do before?
>
> *Tina:* I used to work in a restaurant. I had to lift heavy trays of food all day. It was bad for my back. This job is a lot better for my health.

2 **WRITE.** Read the conversation again. Write answers to the questions. Compare your answers with a partner.

1. What health problems do you think Luis might have now? Why?

   _____

2. What health problems do you think he had at his old job? Why?

   _____

3. What health problem did Tina use to have at her old job?

   _____

3 **COMPLETE** the chart. Think of possible health problems that people with these jobs might have. Then think of possible causes of these problems.

Job	Possible health problems	Reason
Construction worker	*bad back*	*lifting heavy things*
Cook		
Office worker		
Nurse		
Teacher		

4 **WHAT ABOUT YOU?** Talk in your group. Compare a job or activity that you do now with a job or activity that you used to do. Which is better for your health? Why?

Example: My new job is better for my health. I used to work in a shop. I used to stand in one place all day, and I didn't use to exercise. Now I'm a mail carrier. I have to walk a lot, so I get a lot of exercise every day.

Check Your Progress!

Skill	Circle the answers.	Is it correct?
A. Use modals of possibility and certainty.	1. She has a fever. She might **need** / **needs** / **needing** antibiotics. 2. Mary is very sick with the flu. She **can** / **may** / **must** fell terrible. 3. I'm not sure why his wrist hurts. It **must** / **may** / **can** be broken. 4. I don't know what's wrong with Tim's ankle. It **must** / **will** / **could** be sprained.	☐ ☐ ☐ ☐

| | | Number Correct | 0 | 1 | 2 | 3 | 4 |

Skill	Circle the answers.	Is it correct?
B. Use *used to* for past habits or situations.	5. Before she went on a diet, she didn't **used** / **used to** / **use to** read food labels. 6. I **used** / **use to** / **used to** eat pizza often. Now I only eat healthy foods. 7. She used to **drive** / **drives** / **drove** everywhere. Now she walks. 8. Ed didn't use to **exercise** / **exercises** / **exercised**. Now he exercises every day.	☐ ☐ ☐ ☐

| | | Number Correct | 0 | 1 | 2 | 3 | 4 |

Skill	Circle the answers.	Is it correct?
C. Talk about health problems.	9. Your eyes are red. You might have **allergies** / **antibiotics**. 10. Sam has a rash. It could be **asthma** / **eczema**. 11. **Bronchitis** / **conjunctivitis** gives you chest pains. 12. I feel **itchy** / **out of breath**. I might have asthma.	☐ ☐ ☐ ☐

| | | Number Correct | 0 | 1 | 2 | 3 | 4 |

Skill	Circle the answers.	Is it correct?
D. Understand healthy habits.	13. Don't take the **elevator** / **gym**. It's better to walk. 14. She **reads food labels** / **works out** because she has allergies. 15. I'm on a diet, so I don't **read food labels** / **eat desserts**. 16. I don't **take the elevator** / **work out at the gym**. I exercise at home.	☐ ☐ ☐ ☐

| | | Number Correct | 0 | 1 | 2 | 3 | 4 |

COUNT the number of correct answers above. Fill in the bubbles.

Chart Your Success

Skill	Need Practice	Okay	Good	Very Good	Excellent!
A. Use modals of possibility and certainty.	⓪	①	②	③	④
B. Use *used to* for past habits or situations.	⓪	①	②	③	④
C. Talk about health problems.	⓪	①	②	③	④
D. Understand healthy habits.	⓪	①	②	③	④

LESSON 1: Grammar and Vocabulary

1 **GRAMMAR PICTURE DICTIONARY.** How are these people going to get involved in their community? Listen and read.

TCD2, 29
SCD22

1
A: Do you do any volunteer work?
B: Yes, I volunteer at the youth center. I like **to tutor** teenagers.

2
A: Do you do anything to help other people in your community?
B: Yes. I like **to help out** at the **homeless shelter**.

3
A: Are you involved in your children's education?
B: I help them with homework, and I plan **to join the PTA**.

4
A: Do you have any plans for Saturday afternoon?
B: I want **to donate blood** on Saturday afternoon. There's a **blood drive** at the high school.

5
A: Are you going to take a class at the community center this fall?
B: Yes. I plan **to sign up for** an art class.

6
A: Do you have any personal goals?
B: Yes! I intend **to get in shape** this year. I'm going to join a gym.

2 **PRACTICE** the conversations in Activity 1 with a partner.

3 **NOTICE THE GRAMMAR.** Underline the verbs beginning with *to* in Activity 1. They are infinitives. Then circle the verb before each infinitive.

Infinitives

An infinitive is *to* + the base form of the verb.

Subject	Verb	Infinitive	
I / You	need / don't need		
He / She	intends / doesn't intend	to exercise.	
We / You / They	want / don't want		

Infinitives often follow these verbs.

intend	plan
like	want
need	would like

Infinitives of purpose give a reason why.

Action	Infinitive of Purpose	
I'm going to the library	to return	some books.

For more information about verbs followed by infinitives, see page 204.

4 **COMPLETE** the sentences with the infinitive form of words in the box.

donate	get in shape	sign up	save
join	~~help out~~	volunteer	study

The word *to* can be part of an infinitive, or it can be a preposition telling "where."

I want *to* donate blood. (part of the infinitive *to donate*)

I'm going *to* the clinic. (preposition)

1. I want to volunteer on weekends. I plan _to help out_ at the homeless shelter.

2. I'm interested in art. I plan _____ for an art class at the community center.

3. He joined a gym. He intends _____ this year.

4. He's going to go to the blood drive at the clinic. He wants _____ blood.

5. I'm not going to eat at restaurants this year. I need _____ money.

6. Their children's education is important to them. They plan _____ the PTA.

7. I want _____ at the youth center. I like to tutor teens.

8. I intend _____ English every night this week.

5 **WHAT ABOUT YOU?** Talk in a group. Use the verbs from the box on the left and the infinitive forms of the verbs in the box on the right to make true statements.

(don't) intend	(don't) plan
(don't) like	(don't) want
(don't) need	(don't) like

come	sign up for	work	work out
practice	donate	play	volunteer
get	join	study	
complete	help out	buy	

I plan to finish all my homework assignments.

I don't need to work out every day.

LESSON 2: Grammar Practice Plus

1 **LISTEN.** Where can you do each of the activities in the box? Listen and write the letter in the correct place in the picture.

a. check out books	**d.** join the volunteer fire department	**g.** get in shape	**j.** work with teenagers
b. buy fresh vegetables	**e.** cook meals for homeless people	**h.** help out elderly people	**k.** take a walk on a trail
c. walk dogs	**f.** sign up for art classes	**i.** donate blood	**l.** play basketball

2 **ROLE-PLAY** with a partner. Imagine you see each other while you are going to places in the picture. Make conversations.

Example: *A:* Hi. Where are you going?

　　　　　　B: I'm going to the library.

　　　　　　A: Why?

　　　　　　B: To check out some books.

3 **WRITE.** Imagine you went to places in the picture in Activity 1. Why did you go? Write eight sentences. Use your ideas from Activity 2, or use different ideas.

Example: *I went to the clinic to have a blood test.*

Like to and *would like to* mean different things.

I *like to* volunteer at the library.
(I volunteer at the library, and I *enjoy* it.)
I *would like to* volunteer at the library.
(I don't volunteer at the library, but I *want to* try it.)

4 **TALK** with your classmates. Find someone who would like to do each activity.

Would you like...?	Classmates' names
1. to volunteer at a youth center	
2. to go to the gym every day	
3. to join a study group	
4. to volunteer to walk dogs at an animal shelter	
5. to find a tutor	
6. to donate blood	
7. to join a walking group	
8. to help out at a senior center	
9. to spend time with children	
10. to volunteer at a nature center	
11. to go to a farmer's market	
12. (*your idea*) _____	

5 **TALK.** Report your findings to the class.

6 **WHAT ABOUT YOU?** Talk with a partner. Discuss things in Activity 4 that you would and would not like to do.

I'd like to volunteer to walk dogs at an animal shelter.

Really? I wouldn't like to do that at all.

Why not?

Because I'm afraid of dogs. I don't like to be around them.

LESSON 3: Listening and Conversation

1 **TALK.** Look at the pictures. Check ☑ the holiday you think you will hear about. Tell a partner.

☐ New Year's Day   ☐ Halloween   ☐ Fourth of July   ☐ Thanksgiving

barbecue

ice cream

picnic cooler

fireworks

TCD2,
31–33

2 **LISTEN** to the question. Then listen to each conversation and the question. Fill in the circle for the correct answer. Repeat each item if necessary.

1. Ⓐ Ⓑ Ⓒ
2. Ⓐ Ⓑ Ⓒ
3. Ⓐ Ⓑ Ⓒ

TCD2, 34

3 **LISTEN** to the whole conversation in Activity 2. Answer the questions below.

1. Who is going to make potato salad? _____

2. Who is Paula married to? _____

3. Where is Paula's family going tomorrow? _____

4. What does Dave like to do? _____

5. Who needs to buy chicken? _____

4 **WHAT ABOUT YOU?** Discuss these questions in small groups.

1. What are the most important holidays in your native country?

2. Does your neighborhood have picnics or parties?

3. Do people in your community do anything together to celebrate holidays? What?

4. In your native country, what do people eat at large group picnics or barbecues?

5. Do you attend parades or other events with your friends or family on national holidays?

Talk about holidays. • Calculate entertainment expenses.

5 LISTEN and read.

TCD2, 35
SCD23

A: Hi, Sue. It's Linda.

B: Hi, Linda. What's up?

A: We're having <u>a barbecue at our house</u> on the Fourth. Can you come?

B: <u>I wish I could, but</u> I <u>need to work.</u>

A: Oh, that's too bad. I was hoping you could make it.

B: Sorry. It sounds like fun. Thanks for asking.

A: Sure. Let's try to get together soon.

6 PRACTICE the conversation from Activity 5 with a partner. Use the information in the chart below.

Ways to invite	Ways to decline politely	Ways to give an excuse
1. a party / Thursday night	I'd love to, but	have to go to a PTA meeting
2. a picnic at the beach / Sunday afternoon	I'd really like to, but	need to finish my homework
3. some friends for dinner / Saturday night	Thank you for asking, but	planned to help out at the Youth Center

7 TALK with a partner. Make new conversations. Student A, invite Student B to do something. Student B, decline the invitation. Explain why you can't accept. Use infinitives to explain.

Math: Budgeting

A READ the information about Sandy's entertainment budget.

Every month, Sandy budgets $85.00 for fun and entertainment. Look at her fun and entertainment expenses for June, July, and August.

June	July	August
Park fee $6.00	Boat rental at park $6.00	Dinner with friends $35.00
2 movies $18.00	Parking fee at park $5.00	Drinks with friends $16.00
DVD rentals $10.00	Food for picnic at park $23.67	Movie $9.00
Lunch with friends $12.00	Coffees at coffee shop $5.95	Fast food $7.39
Pizza with friends $13.00	Beach fee $12.00	Music festival $22.00
Fast food $9.35	DVD rentals $10.00	Magazines $13.79

B CALCULATE Sandy's total fun and entertainment expenses for each month.

How much was she over or under her budget each month?

June	July	August
Total:	Total:	Total:
Over/Under Budget:	Over/Under Budget:	Over/Under Budget:

LESSON 4: Grammar and Vocabulary

TCD2, 36
SCD24

1 GRAMMAR PICTURE DICTIONARY. What does everyone want to do? Listen and read.

1

A: Do you want <u>to go</u> to the mall with me on Sunday?

B: No, thanks. I don't need <u>to buy</u> anything, and I don't really like (window shopping).

2

A: Would you like to go to the beach with me this weekend?

B: No, thanks. I don't enjoy **hanging out** at the beach.

3

A: Do you want to go to a movie with me this Sunday?

B: I'd love to see you, but I hate **wasting money** at movie theaters. Movies are so expensive these days!

4

A: Would your family like to go to the **music festival** this Saturday?

B: Sorry. We enjoy going to music festivals, but my son has a baseball game this Saturday.

5

A: I'm going **hiking** in the state park this Sunday. Do you want to come?

B: Thanks for asking. I love hiking, but I'm afraid I'm busy this Sunday.

6

A: I plan to go to a party for the homeless shelter Friday. Why don't you come?

B: Sorry. I would, but I can't stand **making small talk** with **strangers**.

2 READ the conversations in Activity 1 with a partner.

3 NOTICE THE GRAMMAR. <u>Underline</u> the infinitives in Activity 1. Then (circle) the words after *enjoy, like, love, can't stand, don't like,* and *hate.* They end in *–ing.* They are gerunds.

Learn about invitations and refusals. • Use gerunds as objects.

Gerunds as Objects

A gerund is a noun. A gerund looks like the *–ing* form of a verb, but it takes the place of a noun in a sentence. Gerunds are always singular.

Affirmative

Subject	Verb	Gerund
I / You	like	hiking.
He / She	hates	

Negative

Subject	Verb	Gerund
I / You	don't like	hiking.
He / She	doesn't hate	

Questions

Do	Subject	Verb	Gerund
Do	you	enjoy	hiking?
Does	he / she		

Answers

Affirmative	Negative
Yes, I do.	No, I don't.
Yes, he / she does.	No, he / she doesn't.

A gerund often follows these verbs: *dislike, enjoy,* and *finish.*

An infinitive *or* a gerund can follow these verbs: *like, can't stand, love, hate,* and *prefer.*

For more information on verbs followed by gerunds, see page 206.

 4 **WHAT ABOUT YOU?** Complete the sentences with words from the box.

love	like/enjoy	don't like / dislike / don't enjoy	can't stand/hate

1. I _____ window shopping.

2. I _____ to hang out on the beach.

3. I _____ wasting money.

4. I _____ hiking.

5. I _____ making small talk with strangers.

6. I _____ to go to music festivals.

5 **TALK** with a partner. Ask and answer questions about the items in Activity 4.

Do you like hiking on nature trails?

Yes, I love hiking.

 6 **WHAT ABOUT YOU?** Play a chain game. Talk about activities you like and don't like.

Example: *Sue:* I hate to drive in heavy traffic.

Tom: Sue hates to drive in heavy traffic. I enjoy hiking.

Jim: Sue hates to drive in heavy traffic. Tom enjoys hiking. I love going to the beach.

LESSON 5: Grammar Practice Plus

1 COMPLETE the paragraph with the gerund form of the words in the box.

attend	hang out	visit	waste
~~go~~	shop	walk	window shop

I live in a small town north of New York City, and I enjoy

(1) _____*going*_____ to the city on weekends and holidays. I take the train

when I go. The ride takes about an hour. I hate (2) _____

time, so I always bring a book to read on the train. In the city, I enjoy

(3) _____ concerts or just (4) _____

at a coffee shop with my friends. I don't go to department stores because

I can't stand (5) _____ in big, crowded stores. But I

do enjoy (6) _____ when I walk past the stores on

Fifth Avenue. I also enjoy (7) _____ museums, and

I love (8) _____ on the trails in Central Park.

TCD2, 37 🎧 **Pronunciation:** Sentence Stress and Meaning

When we ask if someone likes something, the object of the verb *like* has the most stress because it is the focus of the sentence. If the object of *like* is more than one word, important words, like nouns and verbs, are stressed.

Do you like <u>reading</u>?   Do you like <u>hanging out</u> with your <u>friends</u>?

When we answer the question with *love* or *hate,* to express a stronger emotion, the verbs usually receive the most stress. Look at the examples. Listen and repeat.

A: Do you like <u>exercising</u>?
B: I <u>hate</u> exercising.
A: Do you like <u>window shopping</u>?
B: I <u>love</u> window shopping.

TCD2, 38 **A** **LISTEN.** <u>Underline</u> the stressed word or words in the sentences below. Then listen and check.
SCD25

1. *A:* Do you like hiking?
   B: I love hiking.
2. *A:* Do you like making small talk?
   B: I hate making small talk.
3. Do you like shopping?
4. I love shopping, but I hate wasting money.

TCD2, 39 **B** **LISTEN** again and repeat. Then practice with a partner.

Practice sentence stress and meaning. • Talk about likes and dislikes.

2 **COMPLETE** the conversation with the gerund or infinitive form of the verb.

> **Habib:** What do you usually do in your free time, Antonio?
>
> **Antonio:** I don't have free time. I have two children! They enjoy (1) _____ (play) at the park, so we go there a lot. How about you? Do you have family here?
>
> **Habib:** No. I usually just hang out with my friends. But I'd like (2) _____ (meet) some new people, so I want (3) _____ (volunteer) somewhere.
>
> **Antonio:** Are you interested in (4) _____ (work) with young people?
>
> **Habib:** Actually, I prefer working with old people.
>
> **Antonio:** Maybe you should think about (5) _____ (help out) at the senior center.

> We often use gerunds after *interested in* and *think about*.
>
> He's *interested in* going to the festival.
>
> She's *thinking about* volunteering at the shelter.

3 **LISTEN** to the conversation in Activity 2 and check your answers. Then practice the conversation with a partner.

TCD2, 40

4 **WRITE** these sentences using a gerund instead of an infinitive.

Example: I like to listen to classical music.

I like listening to classical music.

1. I love to get up early in the morning.

   _____

2. I like to exercise.

   _____

3. I hate to go to the supermarket.

   _____

4. I like to take tests.

   _____

5. I hate to go to the dentist.

   _____

6. I like to spend money on clothes.

   _____

5 **WHAT ABOUT YOU?** Write *T* (True) or *F* (False) to indicate whether each sentence in Activity 4 is true for you. Tell a partner.

Example: *I like to listen to classical music. F*

6 **WRITE.** Look at your false statements from Activity 5. Rewrite them as negative statements. Use gerunds.

Example: *I don't like listening to classical music.*

LESSON 6: Reading

1 **THINK ABOUT IT.** Talk in a group about these questions.

1. Do you have a pet? If not, would you like to have one?
2. Do most people in your native country like pets? If so, what kind?
3. Do you know anyone who lives or works in a nursing home?

Reading Strategy Summary

Use prior knowledge.
Preview and skim an article.
▶ Distinguish between fact and opinion. ◀

2 **BEFORE YOU READ.** Look at the Web article on the next page. Preview and skim the article. What is it about?

3 **READ** the article on the next page. Would you be interested in this volunteer job?

4 **AFTER YOU READ**

A. TALK. Answer these questions with a partner.

1. What does Mary Kelly, the volunteer, do?
2. What is the dog's name?
3. What day of the week does Mary work?
4. What rules does she describe?
5. How many volunteers take dogs to other nursing homes?

READING FOCUS: Distinguish between fact and opinion

A fact is something that is true. You can prove it.

Three shelter volunteers take dogs to nursing homes.

An opinion is a person's feeling or idea about something. There is no proof that it is true, and other people do not always agree.

Everyone should do volunteer work.

B. WRITE *F* (Fact) or *O* (Opinion) next to these sentences from the article.

1. _____ Dogs are wonderful animals.
2. _____ The dog's name is Sid.
3. _____ Wednesday is Sid's favorite day of the week.
4. _____ Two other volunteers take shelter dogs to other nursing homes.
5. _____ You'll love being involved in such a great program.

C. DISCUSS the questions with your class.

1. What should you do if you want to find out more about volunteering?
2. Do you know people in your neighborhood that volunteer? How often do they do their volunteer work?
3. What other ways can you volunteer in your community?

New Tricks Program

1   When I moved to my town, I wanted to become involved in my community. I thought about signing up to be a tutor at the library, but I was helping my children with homework every night, and I wanted to do something different. I used to have a dog when I was a child, and I remembered how much I loved

5   walking him. I decided to find out about volunteering at the animal shelter. I found information and a volunteer application on the shelter's website. I applied, and started taking a dog to visit residents at a nursing home.[1] That was five years ago, and I'm still volunteering once a week. Volunteering at an animal shelter is a very rewarding and enjoyable experience.

10   My dog's name is Sid. He's a large brown dog. He's very intelligent. Wednesday is Sid's favorite day of the week. He loves seeing me, he loves riding in the car, and he loves going to the nursing home.

And the residents really love Sid! I enjoy seeing them become more cheerful as soon as they see Sid. They love talking to him and petting[2] him. They also love

15   feeding[3] him—and this is a problem! One man used to keep food from his lunch for Sid—every day. But Sid and I only come once a week! Now there's a new rule for residents: Residents must not feed the dogs.

Of course Sid and I have to follow some rules, too. I have to keep Sid on a leash. Sid can't jump up on residents' beds. We have to find out if new residents

20   like dogs before we go near them. I usually ask them, "Would you like to meet the dog?" Usually, they are reaching out to pet him even before they say yes.

I love my volunteer work, and I plan to continue doing it for a long time. Two other volunteers take shelter dogs to other nursing homes. Taking a dog to visit a nursing home is the best thing you can do for the residents. And it's

25   the second best thing you can do for a shelter dog. (The best thing would be taking the dog home with you to keep as your pet!) And it's a wonderful thing to do for yourself. You'll love being involved in such a great program. If you are interested in becoming a volunteer, please <u>click here</u>. To find out about donating money to this great program, <u>click here</u>. Or call 218-555-0623.

— *Mary Kelly*

[1] *nursing home*: a home for elderly people who need special care
[2] *petting*: touching an animal with your hand in a friendly way
[3] *feeding*: giving food to a person or an animal

LESSON 7: Writing

1 **THINK ABOUT IT.** Below are common forms. Check ☑ the forms you have seen in English. Talk in a group about where you saw them and what they are for.

1. ☐ a job application
2. ☐ a class registration
3. ☐ a community service program application

4. ☐ a driver's license application
5. ☐ (other) _____
6. ☐ (other) _____

2 **BEFORE YOU WRITE.**

A. **TALK** in a group. What information do you usually find on an application? Make a list.

    Examples: *name*
                  date of birth

B. **READ** this section of an application for volunteer work at an animal shelter. <u>Underline</u> the infinitives. (Circle) the gerunds.

> **Tip**
>
> Sometimes an application asks you to write about yourself. For example:
> - **job application**: Describe your previous work experience.
> - **school application**: Why do you want to go to this school?
> - **volunteer work application**: Why do you want to be a volunteer?

Animal Shelter   Application for Volunteers

1. How did you hear about our volunteer programs?

> *A friend told me about them.*

2. Which program would you like to volunteer for? Why would you like to volunteer?

> *I'd like <u>to volunteer</u> for the New Tricks program. I want to work with elderly people. I enjoy (spending time) and making small talk with them. I don't have a pet now, but I used to have dogs and cats and other pets. I love being around animals. I look forward to taking a dog to a nursing home. But I could help out at the shelter in other ways, too. I am also interested in talking with you about other programs.*

3. When and how often can you volunteer?

> *I can volunteer once a week. I can work any day, but I prefer to work mornings.*

WRITING FOCUS: Use parallel structure

It is important to use parallel structure in writing. We don't mix gerunds and infinitives in a sequence of activities.

Incorrect ✗: I like <u>to work</u> with animals, <u>driving</u>, and <u>to talk</u> with elderly people.

Correct ✔: I like <u>working</u> with animals, <u>driving</u>, and <u>talking</u> with elderly people.

C. (CIRCLE) the sentence in Activity 2B that provides an example of parallel structure using two gerunds.

D. **FIND** the mistakes in the sentences below. Write the sentences correctly.

1. I love to spend time outdoors and working with animals.
2. I can't stand to go to malls and window shopping.
3. I like working with my hands and to fix things.

3 WRITE. Complete this part of an application for volunteers. Follow these two steps.

1. Write the name of a volunteer job you might like. _____
2. Complete the application below. Use pencil so you can edit.

1. How did you hear about our volunteer programs?

2. Which program would you like to volunteer for? Why would you like to volunteer?

3. When and how often can you volunteer?

4 AFTER YOU WRITE.

A. **EDIT.** Look at your application.

1. Did you explain why you would like the volunteer job?
2. Did you use gerunds and infinitives correctly?
3. Did you use parallel structure?

B. **TALK.** Exchange applications with a partner. Do you understand why your partner wants to volunteer? Why or why not? Discuss with your partner.

Career Connection

1 **LISTEN** to the conversation. Then practice with a partner.

> *Luz:* Do you plan to go to the holiday party this year?
>
> *Vera:* I don't know. I'm not planning to go. How about you? Are you going?
>
> *Luz:* Of course. It'll be fun. And it'll be a good chance to talk with people in other departments.
>
> *Vera:* I don't like making small talk with people I don't know. Can we bring our husbands?
>
> *Luz:* Yes. My husband wants to come.
>
> *Vera:* Oh, all right. What are you going to wear?
>
> *Luz:* I have no idea. I need to buy something.

2 **TALK** with a partner. Ask and answer the questions.

1. Who would prefer not to go to the party? Why?
2. Who will Vera and Luz have a chance to talk with at the party?
3. Can employees' husbands and wives attend the party?
4. Whose husband wants to attend?
5. What does Luz need to buy?

3 **DISCUSS.** Write *T* (True) or *F* (False) about work parties in your culture. Then discuss your answers in a group.

1. _____ Employers or co-workers often have parties.
2. _____ Husbands/Wives usually go to work parties.
3. _____ Most people drink alcohol at work parties.
4. _____ Parties are important for business and for work relationships.
5. _____ People have to pay to go to work parties.
6. _____ Work parties are often in people's homes.

4 **ROLE-PLAY.** Imagine that you are invited to a year-end party at your workplace or at a friend's home. Do you know the answers to these questions? Check ☑ *I know.* or *I don't know.*

	I know.	I don't know.
1. Should you bring your husband or wife?	☐	☐
2. Can you bring your friends or family members?	☐	☐
3. What should you wear?	☐	☐
4. Will you have to pay to attend?	☐	☐
5. Is it okay not to attend?	☐	☐
6. Should you bring something to eat or drink?	☐	☐
7. Is it okay to drink alcohol at the party?	☐	☐

5 **TALK.** Think about a party that you went to recently. Talk about the party with a group.

Check Your Progress!

Skill	Circle the answers	Is it correct?
A. Use infinitives.	1. I joined a gym. I need **get / getting / to get** in shape. 2. He likes dancing. He wants **to take / to takes / taking** a dance class. 3. My sister plans **sign up / to sign up / signing up** for a class. 4. I want **to donate / donates / donating** blood.	☐ ☐ ☐ ☐
	Number Correct	0 1 2 3 4
B. Use gerunds as objects.	5. She can't stand **drive / driving / drove** to work. 6. I love **cooking / cook / cooks** on weekends. 7. Do you like **working / works / worked** at the hospital? 8. Does Emily enjoy **to shop / shopping / shop** with her friends?	☐ ☐ ☐ ☐
	Number Correct	0 1 2 3 4
C. Talk about plans for free time.	9. Did you join the **shelter / PTA** at your son's school? 10. After school, Miguel **donates / tutors** students who have problems with math. 11. I love to draw. I plan to **sign up for / donate** an art class. 12. I plan to **join / help out at** the hospital.	☐ ☐ ☐ ☐
	Number Correct	0 1 2 3 4
D. Express likes and dislikes.	13. I make my own coffee at home. I don't like **wasting / donating** money. 14. Sue doesn't like **joining / making small talk** with strangers. 15. After school, I like hanging **up / out** with friends. 16. I go to the mall a lot. I like **hiking / window shopping**.	☐ ☐ ☐ ☐
	Number Correct	0 1 2 3 4

COUNT the number of correct answers above. Fill in the bubbles.

Chart Your Success					
Skill	Need Practice	Okay	Good	Very Good	Excellent!
A. Use infinitives.	⓪	①	②	③	④
B. Use gerunds as objects.	⓪	①	②	③	④
C. Talk about plans for free time.	⓪	①	②	③	④
D. Express likes and dislikes.	⓪	①	②	③	④

LESSON 1: Grammar and Vocabulary

1 GRAMMAR PICTURE DICTIONARY. What problems do you see in this town? Listen and read.

TCD3, 2
SCD26

1
A: There is too much traffic.
B: I know! And there aren't enough sidewalks.

2
A: There is too much **air pollution**.
B: That's for sure. And there aren't enough trees or parks.

WATCH STEP

3
A: Is there enough **public transportation** in your town?
B: No, there isn't. There are too many people!

BEEP
BEEP
BEEP

4
A: There is too much **crime** in our neighborhood.
B: And there aren't enough police officers.

2 BR
APTS
For Rent
$2500/Mo

5
A: There isn't enough **affordable housing**.
B: That's true. And there are too many expensive apartments.

6
A: Are there enough **trash collection services** in your town?
B: Yes, but there aren't enough **garbage cans**.

2 PRACTICE the conversations in Activity 1 with a partner.

3 NOTICE THE GRAMMAR.

A. CIRCLE the words or phrases that follow *too much, too many,* and *enough* in the sentences In Activity 1.

B. **COMPLETE.** Use one picture from Activity 1 to complete each sentence below.

1. There is too much _____.

2. There are too many _____.

3. There aren't enough _____.

> **Remember:**
> Count nouns have plurals.
> 3 cat**s**, 4 **people**
> Non-count nouns don't have plurals.
> pollution, housing

Count and Non-count Nouns with *too many*, *too much*, and *(not) enough*

Use *too* to say there is more than a good or normal amount. Use *enough* to say you have as much as you need, and *not enough* to say you don't have as much as you need.

Statements with *too many* and *too much*
Use *too many* before a count noun and *too much* before a non-count noun.

	Quantifier	Count Noun
There are	too many	old cars.
		people.

	Quantifier	Non-count Noun
There is	too much	crime.
		pollution.

Statements with *(not) enough*
Use *enough* or *not enough* before both count and non-count nouns.

	Quantifier	Count Noun
There are (not)	enough	trees.
		sidewalks.

	Quantifier	Non-count Noun
There is (not)	enough	housing.
		space.

Questions with Count Nouns

	Quantifier	Count Noun
Are there	too many	cars?
	enough	trees?

Questions with Non-count Nouns

	Quantifier	Non-count Noun
Is there	too much	pollution?
	enough	housing?

---

4 **COMPLETE** the chart. Write the nouns from the box in the correct column.

accident	car	fresh air	garbage	job	money	people	rain	supermarket	work

Count nouns	Non-count nouns
job	money

5 **WRITE** sentences with *too many* or *too much* and the word in parentheses.

1. (cars)   There ___*are too many cars.*___

2. (supermarkets)   There _____

3. (jobs)   There _____

4. (crime)   There _____

5. (public transportation)   There _____

 6 **WHAT ABOUT YOU?** Tell a group about a problem with traffic, crime, or pollution in your neighborhood.

LESSON 2: Grammar Practice Plus

1 TALK about the picture with a partner.

There's too much traffic in this town.

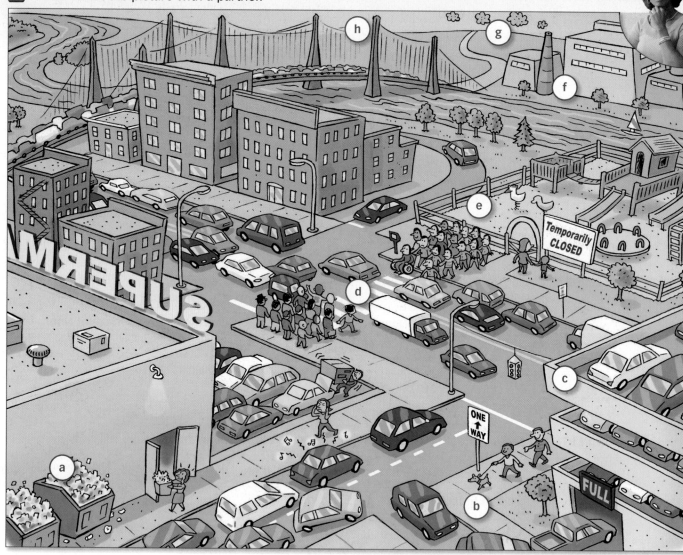

2 MATCH the letters in the picture with the correct words below.

1. __c__ parking garage
2. _____ playground
3. _____ factory
4. _____ smoke
5. _____ bridge
6. _____ crosswalk
7. _____ Dumpster
8. _____ sidewalk

3 TALK. Look at the picture in Activity 1. Ask and answer questions with *too many*, *too much*, *enough*, or *not enough*. Use nouns from the box.

bridges	factories	playgrounds	smoke	trash
cars	parking spaces	pollution	traffic	Dumpsters

Example: *A:* Are there enough parking spaces?
　　　　　　B: No, there aren't.

Too and (not) enough with Adjectives

Too comes before an adjective: too + adjective. Enough comes after an adjective: (not) + adjective + enough.

Statements with too

Subject	be	too + Adjective
The neighborhood	is (not)	too crowded.
The roads	are (not)	too busy.

Statements with (not) enough

Subject	be	Adjective + enough
The river	is (not)	clean enough.
The sidewalks	are (not)	wide enough.

4 **WRITE** sentences with the same meaning as the sentences below. Use *too* or *not enough* and the adjective in parentheses.

Don't use *too much* before an adjective.
The roads are too ~~much~~ crowded.

1. The room is too dark. (light)
   The room isn't light enough.

2. The sidewalks are too narrow. (wide)
   _____

3. The restaurant isn't clean enough. (dirty) _____

4. The classroom isn't quiet enough. (loud) _____

5. The exam is too easy. (hard) _____

6. The library is too far away. (close) _____

7. The park isn't safe enough. (dangerous) _____

8. The instructions are too confusing. (clear) _____

5 **WRITE.** Look at the picture in Activity 1. Write five sentences. Use *too* or *not enough* and an adjective in the box.

Example: *The box is too big to fit in the car.*

big	busy	clean	crowded	dirty	heavy	large	narrow	small	wide

6 **WHAT ABOUT YOU?** Work in a small group. Talk about places in your neighborhood. Use the places in the box for ideas.

Places				
bank	grocery store	library	parking garage	school
Laundromat	health clinic	park	playground	shopping mall

Example: A: There's a grocery store in my neighborhood.
B: Do you like it?
A: No, it's not great. It's too small, and there isn't enough fresh fruit.

7 **WRITE** five sentences about places in your neighborhood. Use the information from your conversation in Activity 6.

Example: *The grocery store in my neighborhood is too small.*

LESSON 3: Listening and Conversation

TCD3, 3–5

1 **LISTEN** to the question. Then listen to the conversation. Listen to the question again and fill in the circle for the correct answer. Repeat each item if necessary.

1. Ⓐ Ⓑ Ⓒ
2. Ⓐ Ⓑ Ⓒ
3. Ⓐ Ⓑ Ⓒ

TCD3, 6–8

2 **LISTEN** to the question. Then listen to the conversation. Listen to the question again and fill in the circle for the correct answer. Repeat each item if necessary.

1. Ⓐ Ⓑ Ⓒ
2. Ⓐ Ⓑ Ⓒ
3. Ⓐ Ⓑ Ⓒ

3 **READ** Danny's electric bill. Answer the questions. Compare answers with a partner.

1. How much electricity did Danny use in July?
2. How much did he use in June?
3. How much money does he have to pay?
4. How much did he pay last month?
5. When does he have to pay by?
6. Do you think this bill is high or low (compared to your own electricity bill)? Discuss some reasons why.

☀HOME ENERGY SERVICES

RS-1   001   Residential Service

Service address:
Daniel Rodriguez
1469 West Route Blvd.,
Orlando, Florida 32802

Bill date: 08/05/2008
Due date: 08/20/2008
Billing Period: 07/01/2008 to 07/31/2008

Previous balance	$44.95
Payment – Thank you	-44.95
Customer charge	11.67
Fuel charge	25.12
Distribution charge	16.18
Tax	11.05
TOTAL CURRENT BILL	**$64.02**

Use History

Month	kWh*
July	314
June	137
May	121
Apr	158
Mar	243
Feb	250
Jan	259

*A *kilowatt* is a unit of electric power. The short form of *kilowatt per hour* is kWh.

TCD3, 9 **Pronunciation:** Word Linking

When the vowel sounds /u/ and /o/ come before a word that starts with a vowel sound, we add a /w/ sound in natural speech to link the words together. Look at the examples. Listen and repeat.

The bill is too /w/ expensive.   There are two /w/ errors.   There is no /w/ air pollution.

TCD3, 10
SCD27
A **LISTEN.** Find the linking /w/ sounds in these sentences. Draw a line to show the link. Then listen and check your answers.

1. It's so expensive.
2. We have two air conditioners.
3. I have no idea.
4. It's two o'clock.

TCD3, 11 **B** **LISTEN** and repeat.

Read a utility bill. • Link words with vowel sounds.

TCD3, 12
SCD28

4 **LISTEN** and read.

> *A:* Excuse me…
>
> *B:* Yes, may I help you?
>
> *A:* Yes, <u>I think there's a mistake on my bill</u>. <u>It's too high. I see some extra charges</u>.
>
> *B:* <u>Oh, I'm so sorry</u>. I'll <u>check it for you</u>.
>
> *B:* Thank you very much. I appreciate it.
>
> *A:* No problem. Please let me know if you need anything else.

5 **PRACTICE** the conversation in Activity 4 with a partner. Use the information in the chart.

Problem	Apology	Solution
1. My room is too noisy. I can't sleep.	I apologize about that.	…find another room for you.
2. It's cold and I don't have enough blankets in my room.	I'm terribly sorry.	…send some up right now.
3. My room is too hot. The air conditioner isn't working.	I'm sorry for the inconvenience.	…send someone up to fix it.

6 **WHAT ABOUT YOU?** Have you ever made a complaint? What did you complain about? Describe the situation to your partner.

Example: *A:* I complained in a restaurant.

              B: What was the problem?

              A: The service was too slow.

7 **ROLE-PLAY.** Work with a partner. Write two conversations with complaints. Then perform your conversations for the class.

May I help you?

Yes. I ordered 45 minutes ago. I don't have enough time to wait.

LESSON 4: Grammar and Vocabulary

 TCD3, 13 SCD29

1 **GRAMMAR PICTURE DICTIONARY.** What are ways to save energy and help the environment? Listen and read.

1

Unplugging your home appliances **saves** energy.

2

Wrapping your hot water **pipes** in insulation saves on your heating bill.

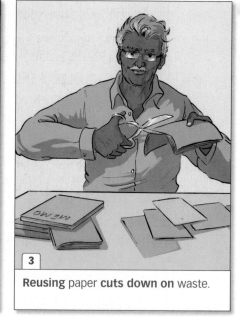

3

Reusing paper **cuts down on** waste.

4

Turning down your **thermostat** in winter **lowers** your heating bills.

5

Recycling plastic and glass **reduces** trash.

6

Weatherproofing your home **keeps** it warm in winter.

2 **READ** the sentences in Activity 1 with a partner.

3 **NOTICE THE GRAMMAR.** Underline the subject in each sentence in Activity 1. Circle the verb that goes with the subject. Are the verbs in the singular or plural form?

Learn ways to save energy. • Use gerunds as subjects.

Gerunds as Subjects

A gerund can be the object or the subject of a verb. When the gerund is the subject, always use the third person singular form of the verb.

Gerund as Subject

Subject	Verb	Adjective
Recycling	is	good.
Exercising		healthy.

Gerund as Object

Subject	Verb	Object
I	like	recycling.
We		exercising.

A gerund can also have its own object.

Subject		
Gerund	**Object of Gerund**	**Verb + Object**
Recycling	plastic	reduces trash.

4 **WRITE** sentences. Use the verbs in parentheses as gerunds.

1. (weatherproof) your doors / save energy

   Weatherproofing your doors saves energy.

2. (reuse) plastic bags / reduce waste

   _____

3. (turn off) your computer at night / save energy

   _____

4. (unplug) your TV / save electricity

   _____

5. (insulate) your home / lower your heating bills

   _____

6. (recycle) old appliances / help the environment

   _____

7. (pay) your bills online / save paper

   _____

Be Careful!

A gerund can have a plural object, but the verb is still third person singular.

Insulating **pipes** saves energy.

 5 **WHAT ABOUT YOU?** Talk in small groups. Which of the solutions in Activity 1 do you want to try?

Unplugging my appliances sounds like a good idea. I want to try that.

LESSON 5: Grammar Practice Plus

1 MATCH. Write the correct number of the item in the circles in the picture.

1. roof
2. fireplace
3. thermostat
4. faucet
5. washing machine
6. hot water tank

2 LISTEN to the radio show about energy-saving tips for your home. Then match the verbs with the objects. Write the object on the line.

1. reducing _____*air leaks*_____   **a.** the roof
2. insulating _____   **b.** air leaks
3. taking _____   **c.** the hot water tank
4. fixing _____   **d.** the washing machine
5. wrapping _____   **e.** shorter showers
6. closing _____   **f.** leaky faucets
7. using cold water in _____   **g.** the lights
8. turning off _____   **h.** the refrigerator door

3 COMPLETE the sentences with the gerund form of the verbs in the box.

fix	insulate	reduce	run	save	take	wrap

1. ___*Reducing*___ air leaks and _____ your roof will lower your energy bills.

2. _____ shorter showers and _____ leaky faucets will cut down on water use.

3. _____ your hot water tank in an insulation blanket will reduce heat loss.

4. _____ your washing machine only when it is full will save electricity.

5. _____ energy will save you money, too!

Negative Gerunds

To form the negative of a gerund, add *not* before the gerund.

Negative Gerund	Object of the Gerund	Verb + Object
Not using	your dishwasher every day	saves energy.

4 **COMPLETE** the sentences. Use the affirmative or negative form of the gerund.

1. (leave)_____*Leaving*_____ the lights on when you go out wastes electricity.

2. (unplug) _____ your TV at night wastes energy.

3. (fix) _____ leaky faucets wastes water.

4. (run) _____ the faucet while you brush your teeth saves water.

5. (put) _____ too much water in the kettle wastes electricity.

6. (use) _____ your dishwasher when it is half empty wastes energy.

5 **WHAT ABOUT YOU?** Talk in a group. Discuss each of the topics below. Write one sentence about each idea.

Example: *Buying a smaller car is a good idea because it will save gas, but it won't be big enough for a family camping trip.*

1. Buying a smaller car
2. Carpooling to work
3. Paying your utility bills online
4. Using a microwave instead of an oven

6 **TALK.** Tell a partner about one thing you do that uses too much energy, water, or gas. Give each other some suggestions.

My heating bills are too high in winter. Do you have any advice?

How about weatherproofing your windows?

Math: Calculate Energy Cost

A **kilowatt** is a unit of electric power. The short form of kilowatt is kW.

A **READ** the problem.

> A window air conditioner uses 3 kW per hour.
> Your electricity costs 8 cents per kW. How much does it cost to run the air conditioner 7 hours a day for one week?

B **CALCULATE.** Multiply the units.

1. 3 kW/hr × 7 hrs = ____*21 kW*____

2. 21 kW/hr × 8 cents = _____

3. $_____ × 7 days = _____

LESSON 6: Reading

1 **THINK ABOUT IT.** Talk in a small group. What days do they collect trash in your neighborhood? What are the rules for recycling in your city or town?

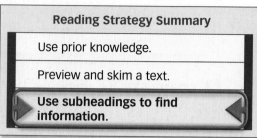

Reading Strategy Summary

Use prior knowledge.

Preview and skim a text.

Use subheadings to find information.

> **READING FOCUS: Use subheadings to find information**
> Subheadings can help you skim and scan the text to find the information you need.

2 **BEFORE YOU READ.** Preview and skim the brochure on City Trash Collection Services. Then read the questions below. Next, scan to find the sections with answers to the questions. Write the subheading with the correct answer in the spaces below.

1. How do I recycle small appliances?   **a.** _____

2. What can I do with waste from my garden?   **b.** _____

3. What can I do with old paint?   **c.** _____

3 **READ.**

A. **READ** the brochure. Answer the questions above with a partner.

B. **WRITE** answers to the questions below. Write complete sentences.

1. Jan has an old refrigerator. What should she do with it?

    She should call the City Recycling Center for a pick-up date.

2. Jungho has a new cell phone. What should she do with the old one?

    _____

3. Hector has some empty glass bottles. What should he do with them?

    _____

4. Khaled has some old cooking pans. What should he do with them?

    _____

4 **AFTER YOU READ.** Find and circle these words in the text. Then match them with their meanings.

curbside	exceeding	refuse	hazardous	beverage

1. more than _____

2. on the sidewalk _____

3. dangerous _____

4. drink _____

5. trash _____

CITY TRASH COLLECTION SERVICES

1 The city provides trash and recycling collection once each week. Your trash day is **THURSDAY**. Please place trash containers and bags at curbside by 7 A.M., but not before 6 P.M. the previous evening.

Preparing Items for Collection ☞ [This is a subheading.]

ALL refuse must be in plastic bags or containers not exceeding 35 gallons in size or 35 pounds in weight.
5 For safety reasons, do not place broken glass or sharp objects in plastic bags.

Recycling Collection Services

Recycling saves money for the city. We don't have enough space for all the city's trash. Collecting and sorting your metal, glass, plastic and paper helps the environment. Please recycle!

10 Recycling collection is the same day as the trash collection. The recycling program uses two bins: a green bin for paper items and a blue bin for plastic, metal, and glass containers. The following items are recyclable:

- **Paper.** Newspapers and magazines, tied together with string. No pizza boxes or any boxes with food in them.
15 - **Metal.** Aluminum cans. Small metal items, for example, pots and pans, wire hangers, irons, and metal toasters. For items that are too big for the blue bin, such as stoves or refrigerators, please call the City Recycling Center to make an appointment for collection.
- **Plastic.** Clean plastic bottles with numbers 1 or 2. No plastic bags.
20 - **Glass.** Green, clear, and brown food and beverage containers. No window glass.
- **Yard Waste.** The city offers yard waste collection from April to November. Yard waste includes leaves, grass, and branches up to 3 inches wide. Put all yard waste in brown paper bags clearly labeled "yard waste." There is a limit of 20 bags
25 of yard waste per collection. Do not mix trash with your yard waste.

Prohibited Items

- **Hazardous materials** such as paint, gasoline, and old batteries. These items are too dangerous for regular trash collection. Please contact City Trash Collection Services for information.
- **Electronic waste** includes computers, printers, scanners, televisions, laptops, fax machines,
30 CD and DVD players, VCRs, and cell phones. Bring your electronic waste to the City Recycling Center weekdays from 8:30 A.M. −4:30 P.M.
- **Clothing.** Put your clothing and other textiles in the clothing collection container at the City Recycling Center.

DISCUSSION

1. Do people in your neighborhood follow the trash collection rules?
2. Do they recycle? Why or why not?
3. Is the situation better in your home country? Discuss with your class.

LESSON 7: Writing

1 **THINK ABOUT IT.** Look at the pictures. Discuss the problems you see with your class. What can you do to solve these problems?

1. Saving energy at home

2. Cutting down on trash

3. Reducing city traffic

2 **BEFORE YOU WRITE.**

> **WRITING FOCUS: Use a graphic organizer**
>
> A word-web is a type of graphic organizer. It is a way to organize your ideas before you start writing. Use a word-web to organize your main ideas.

A. TALK. Denise chose the topic: Saving Energy at Home. She used a word-web to organize her ideas before writing. Read the information in her word-web. Do you agree with her ideas? Can you add any more ideas? Talk with a partner.

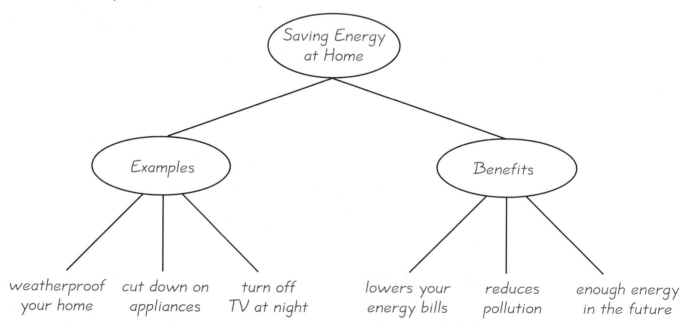

B. READ Denise's paragraphs. Draw a wavy line under the topic sentences. Underline the supporting sentences. Circle the connecting words.

Saving Energy at Home

There are many ways of saving energy at home. First, you can weatherproof your doors and windows. Weatherproofing will keep your home warm in winter. Second, you can cut down on the number of electrical appliances you have in your home. Using too many appliances, such as air conditioners and dishwashers, uses a lot of energy. Third, you can turn off appliances when they are not in use. Leaving your TV or computer on at night wastes electricity.

Saving energy at home has many benefits. The main advantage is that you will lower your energy bills. You can spend money on other things like food or clothes. In addition, you will reduce pollution. Producing gas and electricity causes air and water pollution. Using less energy helps save the environment. Finally, saving energy today means there will be enough energy for everyone in the future.

 3 **WRITE.** Choose one topic from Activity 1. Write two paragraphs about it in your notebook. First, write the topic in the top circle of the word-web. Then write examples in one part of the diagram and benefits in the other part. Use the examples in your first paragraph and the benefits in your second.

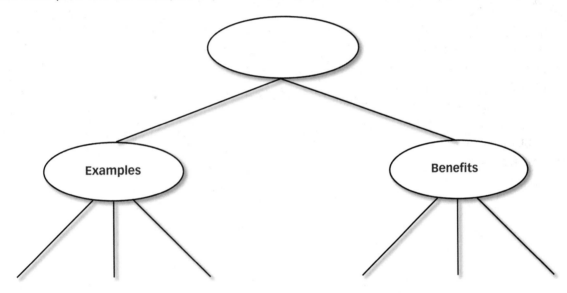

4 **AFTER YOU WRITE.**

A. EDIT. Exchange papers with a partner and check the following.
1. Did the first paragraph have examples?
2. Did the second paragraph talk about benefits?
3. Was there a topic sentence in each paragraph?
4. Were connecting words used?
5. Were gerunds, *too*, and (*not*) *enough* used correctly?

 B. REWRITE. Discuss anything your partner marked on your paper. Then rewrite your paper.

1 **LISTEN** to the conversation. Then practice with a partner.

> *Supervisor:* Do we need any supplies?
>
> *Custodian:* Yes, we do. There isn't enough packing tape in the supply cabinet. We need to order some more.
>
> *Supervisor:* Okay, I'll write it on the supply list. Anything else?
>
> *Custodian:* Well, we have a small problem with the trash collection. There are too many cardboard boxes. We don't have enough recycling bins to hold them. I think we need more bins.
>
> *Supervisor:* Getting more recycling bins is a great idea. How many do we need?

2 **TALK** with a partner. Answer the questions.

1. What supplies are needed?
2. Who is going to write the supply list?
3. Why do they need more recycling bins?

3 **COMPLETE** the chart. Write problems in your workplace or a workplace you know. Write possible solutions.

Problem	Solution
The break room is too small.	Change the break room, or add another break room.

4 **WHAT ABOUT YOU?** Talk in small groups.

1. Describe working conditions at your job or in a workplace that you know. (Is there enough space? Is the trash a problem? Is there enough storage? Is it clean?)
2. Make some suggestions for improving any problems.
3. Present your ideas to the class.

Check Your Progress!

Skill	Circle the answers	Is it correct?
A. Use count and non-count nouns with *too many, too much,* and *(not) enough*.	1. I like the city, but there is **too much / enough / too many** air pollution. 2. There were **too much / enough / too many** people at the store, so David left. 3. There aren't **enough moneys / enough money / too much money**. 4. Karen can't finish the test. There **isn't enough / aren't enough / is enough** time.	☐ ☐ ☐ ☐

		Number Correct	0	1	2	3	4

Skill	Circle the answers	Is it correct?
B. Use gerunds as subjects.	5. **Installing / Install / Installs** insulation keeps your house warm. 6. **Turning / Turn / Turns** off your appliances saves energy. 7. Wearing warm clothes **cut / cuts / cutting** down on heating bills. 8. Leaving the faucet on **waste / wastes / wasting** water.	☐ ☐ ☐ ☐

		Number Correct	0	1	2	3	4

Skill	Circle the answers	Is it correct?
C. Talk about the community.	9. This street is not safe for walking. We need more **sidewalks / traffic**. 10. I don't need a car. I use **public transportation / affordable housing**. 11. Her city isn't safe. There's too much **crime / air pollution**. 12. **Trash collection / air pollution** keeps garbage off the streets.	☐ ☐ ☐ ☐

		Number Correct	0	1	2	3	4

Skill	Circle the answers	Is it correct?
D. Talk about ways to save energy.	13. Insulating your **water pipes / thermostat** lowers your energy bill. 14. **Weatherproofing / Unplugging** your home keeps it warmer inside. 15. Turning off lights **keeps / saves** electricity. 16. **Reducing / Reusing** paper cuts down on waste.	☐ ☐ ☐ ☐

		Number Correct	0	1	2	3	4

COUNT the number of correct answers above. Fill in the bubbles.

Chart Your Success

Skill	Need Practice	Okay	Good	Very Good	Excellent!
A. Use count and non-count nouns with *too many, too much,* and *(not) enough*.	⓪	①	②	③	④
B. Use gerunds as subjects.	⓪	①	②	③	④
C. Talk about the community.	⓪	①	②	③	④
D. Talk about ways to save energy.	⓪	①	②	③	④

LESSON 1: Grammar and Vocabulary

TCD3, 16
SCD30

1 **GRAMMAR PICTURE DICTIONARY.** People are talking to newcomers about services in their community. Listen and read.

1

A: Our library has some good **programs** for kids.
B: I know. I've already **enrolled** my children in the reading program.

2

A: You can get help with **tax preparation** at the library.
B: I know. We've already **contacted** someone to help us.

3

A: The Community Center has inexpensive **fitness classes**.
B: I know. I've already **registered** for a yoga class.

4

A: Have you **received** a brochure for **career advancement** classes yet?
B: Yes, I got it from the Employment Center.

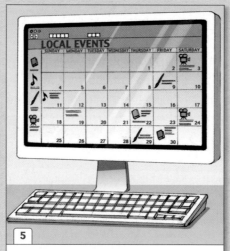

5

A: Have you **checked out** the city website yet? There's a great calendar of **local events**.
B: Yes, I have. It's great.

6

A: Have you **subscribed** to the local newspaper yet?
B: Yes, I have. I have an online **subscription**.

2 **PRACTICE** the conversations with a partner.

3 **NOTICE THE GRAMMAR.** Underline *have* (or the contraction *'ve*) or *haven't* and the verb that it goes with. Circle *already* and *yet*.

Present Perfect with *yet* and *already*

Many verbs are irregular. You'll learn some irregular past participles in Lesson 2.

Use the present perfect to talk about completed past actions when the exact time of the action is either not important or not known.

Statements with *already*

Use the present perfect with *already* to talk about actions that have happened before now.

Subject	*have*	*already*	Past Participle	
I / You	have			
He / She	has	already	registered	for the class.
We / You / They	have			

Contractions

I have = I've
You have = You've
He has = He's
She has = She's
We have = We've
They have = They've

Statements with *yet*

Use the present perfect with *yet* in negative statements to say that something is still expected to happen.

Subject	*have + not*	Past Participle		*yet*
I / You	haven't			
He / She	hasn't	registered	for the class	yet.
We / You / They	haven't			

Questions and Answers

Use *yet* in questions. We don't usually use *already* in questions.

Have	Subject	Past Participle	*yet*
Have	you	registered	yet?
Has	he / she		

Yes / No	Subject	*have (not)*
Yes,	I	have.
No,	he / she	hasn't.

4 **COMPLETE** the questions with the present perfect and *yet*. Then point to pictures in Activity 1, and ask and answer the questions with a partner.

1. ___*Has*___ he ___*checked out*___ (check out) the city website ___*yet*___?

2. _____ they _____ (subscribe) to a local newspaper _____?

3. _____ she _____ (enroll) her children in the reading program _____?

4. _____ she _____ (register) for a fitness class _____?

5. _____ she _____ (contact) anyone about tax preparation help _____?

6. _____ he _____ (receive) a career advancement class brochure _____?

5 **ROLE-PLAY** with a partner. Student B has moved to a new city. Student A is an old friend who already lives in the city. Student A asks Student B questions.

Have you enrolled in an English class yet?

No, I haven't. But I want to.

LESSON 2: Grammar Practice Plus

1 **LISTEN.** Write the names of the Johnson family members in the correct space in the picture.

1. Mrs. Johnson	**2.** Mr. Johnson	**3.** Evan	**4.** Max and Lily	**5.** Bingo

a. _____

b. _____

c. _____

d. _____

e. _____

2 **TALK** with a partner about what the Johnsons have already done and what they haven't done yet. Use the information in the box below. Use the present perfect.

Example: They've already licensed their dog.

1. license / their dog	**5.** subscribe / an Internet service
2. enroll / their children in the summer reading program	**6.** receive / brochure for career advancement classes
3. receive / tax preparation assistance	**7.** contact / neighborhood watch group
4. subscribe / local newspaper	**8.** check out / fitness classes at the community center

3 PRACTICE. Read the past and past participle forms of these irregular verbs. Practice saying them with your class. *See page 214 for a list of common irregular verbs.*

Irregular Verbs		
Base Form	**Simple Past**	**Past Participle**
buy	bought	bought
do	did	done
find	found	found
get	got	gotten
go	went	gone
have	had	had
take	took	taken

4 COMPLETE the paragraph about Ed. Use the present perfect.

I moved to this city last month. I am living with my brother and his family

because I (1) _____ *haven't found* _____ (**not find**) an apartment yet. But I

(2) _____ (**find**) a job already, and I (3) _____ (**open**)

a checking account. I (4) _____ (**not get**) my driver's license yet, but I

(5) _____ (**buy**) a car. After I get my driver's license, I intend to enroll in

a night class. There are some free career advancement classes at the local Employment

Center. I (6) _____ (**not go**) to the library yet, but I need to go there

to check out their services. Of course, I (7) _____ (**not subscribe**) to a

newspaper yet, but I will when I find a place to live!

5 WHAT ABOUT YOU? Think of three interesting things to do in your town, city, or state. Has your partner done them yet? Ask and answer questions.

Tip

So have I. and **I have, too.** mean that you have had the same experience.

Neither have I. and **I haven't either.** mean that you also have not had the experience.

Have you gone to the new library yet?

Yes, I have.

Have you gone to the free movies in the park?

No, I haven't.

I have, too.

Neither have I.

LESSON 3: Listening and Conversation

1 **LISTEN** to the question. Then listen to the conversation. Listen to the question again. Fill in the circle for the correct answer. Repeat each item if necessary.

1. Ⓐ Ⓑ Ⓒ   2. Ⓐ Ⓑ Ⓒ   3. Ⓐ Ⓑ Ⓒ

Math: Understanding Sliding Payment Scales

A TCD3, 21 **LISTEN** and write each person's salary and the amount of his or her medical bill.

1. Joe makes $ __13,400__ a year, and his medical bill is $ __150__ .

2. Maria makes $ _____ a year, and her medical bill is $ _____ .

3. Raul makes $ _____ a year, and his medical bill is $ _____ .

4. Gina makes $ _____ a year, and her medical bill is $ _____ .

B **READ** the chart and write the amount each person in Activity A has to pay.

Sliding Scale for Single Patients with No Dependents			
Income	Percent You Pay	Income	Percent You Pay
$0.00 – $9,570.00	0	$14,355.01 – $15,312.00	60
$9,570.01 – $10,527.00	10	$15,312.01 – $17,704.50	70
$10,527.01 – $11,484.00	20	$17,704.51 – $19,140.00	80
$11,484.01 – $12,441.00	30	$19,140.01 – $23,925.00	90
$12,441.01 – $13,398.00	40	$23,925.01 – $999,999.99	100
$13,398.01 – $14,355.00	50		

1. Joe has to pay __$75__ .   3. Raul has to pay _____ .

2. Maria has to pay _____ .   4. Gina has to pay _____ .

Percentages

Joe must pay 50% of his $150 medical bill.
To find the percentage:

1. Multiply the number by the percent. (150.00 × 50 = 7500.00)

2. Divide the answer by 100. (7500.00 ÷ 100 = 75.00)

   Note: When you divide by 100, you are just moving the decimal two places to the left.

---

2 **LISTEN** and read.

TCD3, 22
SCD31

A: Hi, Alice. Are you and your family enjoying life in San Diego?

B: Yes, we are. Thanks.

A: Have you enrolled the kids in school yet?

B: Yes. But I need to find a <u>math tutor for Bart</u>.

A: The <u>library</u> has <u>a tutoring program</u>. Have you heard about it?

B: No, I'll <u>check out their website</u>. Thanks.

A: Sure. Good luck. Nice running into you.

B: Yeah, nice seeing you again. Bye.

3 **PRACTICE** the conversation in Activity 2 with a partner. Use the information in the chart.

Activity	Location of service	Community program or service offered	Intention
1. a business writing class for myself	community center	career advancement program for adults	contact their office
2. a part-time job for Bob	city website	link to a listing of local jobs	check out the link
3. an after-school program for Julie	youth center	teen leadership program	call and ask for a brochure

Present Perfect: *Have you ever*...?

We use *ever* with the present perfect to ask whether someone experienced something at any point up to the present time.

Have	Subject	*ever*	Past Participle	
Have	you	ever	taken	the bus?
Has	he / she			

Affirmative	Negative
Yes, I have.	No, I haven't.
Yes, he / she has.	No, he/she hasn't.

 4 **WHAT ABOUT YOU?** Read the questions and write two more. Ask and answer them with a partner.

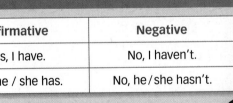 We use *never* in negative present perfect statements.

I've *never* taken the bus.
He's *never* taken the train.

1. Have you ever checked out your city or town website?

2. Have you ever subscribed to a newspaper or magazine?

3. Have you ever helped out with any local events?

4. Have you ever bought a new car?

5. Have you ever found a job or an apartment in the newspaper or online?

6. _____ ?

7. _____ ?

LESSON 4: Grammar and Vocabulary

 1 **GRAMMAR PICTURE DICTIONARY.** What services do these people use? Listen and read.

TCD3, 23
SCD32

1

A: How long have the **senior shuttle** drivers been **on strike**?
B: Since Monday. My mother needs to find transportation soon!

2

A: How long have you been **without electricity**?
B: For six hours. I've been **on hold** for an hour!

3

A: How long have you been **out of work**?
B: For three months. The employment center is helping me a lot though.

4

A: How long has our **Internet service** been **down**?
B: Since 11:00 this morning. I've called the cable company already.

5

A: How long has he been **retired**?
B: Since last year. He keeps busy at the senior center, though.

6

A: How long has she been **diabetic**?
B: For about six years. She exercises at the gym regularly and gets advice at the health clinic.

2 **PRACTICE** the conversations with a partner.

3 **NOTICE THE GRAMMAR.** Underline the present perfect. Circle *how long, for,* and *since.*

Learn about useful community services. • Use present perfect with *for* or *since.*

Present Perfect with *for* or *since*

Use the present perfect with *for* or *since* to describe situations or states that started in the past and continue to the present (and may continue into the future).

- Use *for* with a length of time (*one month, three hours, a long time, two weeks*).
- Use *since* with a specific past time (*yesterday, last week, 2:30, my birthday*).

Statements

Subject	*have*	Past Participle		*for/since* + time
I / You	have		retired	*for* six months.
He / She	has	been		
We / You / They	have		out of work	*since* last year.

Questions with *How long...?*

Use *How long* and the present perfect to ask about the length of time.

How long	*have*	Subject	Past Participle		Short Answers
	have	I / you		retired?	*For* six months.
How long	has	he / she	been		
	have	we / you / they		out of work?	*Since* last year.

---

4 **COMPLETE** the paragraph about Paul and his family. Use *for* or *since*.

Paul has problems. His mother has been diabetic (1) _____ twenty years, and recently, her health has gotten worse. She has been seriously ill (2) _____ over a year now. Paul's father retired last year, and he's been a little bored (3) _____ then. Paul has been out of work (4) _____ two months. He subscribes to the local newspaper online so that he can check out the employment ads. But there was a storm last night, and his Internet service has been down (5) _____ early this morning. His family has also been without electricity (6) _____ three hours. Paul needs some help!

5 **WRITE** questions about Paul's problems. Use *How long*. Then ask and answer the questions with a partner.

Example: Paul's mother / be diabetic *How long has Paul's mother been diabetic?*

1. Paul's father / be retired _____

2. Paul / be out of work _____

3. Paul's Internet service / be down _____

4. His family / be without electricity _____

6 **WHAT ABOUT YOU?** Talk in a group. Have you ever had any of the problems Paul's family has had? Which ones? What did you do? Tell your group.

LESSON 5: Grammar Practice Plus

🎧 **Pronunciation:** Blending with *has* and *have*

In spoken English, we often blend subject pronouns with *has* and *have*. Sometimes it is hard to hear the *'s* or *'ve*. Look at the examples of simple past and present perfect. Listen and repeat.

Simple Past	**Present Perfect**
He worked here for a year.	He has (He*'s*) worked here for a year.
They lived in Miami for ten years.	They have (They*'ve*) lived in Miami for ten years.

When speaking, we also blend nouns with *has* and *have*. Listen to these examples.

Simple Past	**Present Perfect**
John worked here for a year.	John has (*John's*) worked here for a year.
The men finished the work.	The men have (*men've*) finished the work.

TCD3, 25
SCD33 **A** **LISTEN.** Check which form you hear, the simple past or the present perfect.

Simple Past		**Present Perfect**	
1. They bought tickets.	☐	They have bought tickets.	☐
2. He read the book.	☐	He has read the book.	☐
3. Jan received the letter.	☐	Jan has received the letter.	☐
4. Li and Su enrolled in the class.	☐	Li and Su have enrolled in the class.	☐

TCD3, 26 **B** **LISTEN** and repeat both forms of all the sentences.

🎧 **1** **LISTEN.** Write the reasons the people need help.
TCD3, 27

Person	Reason the person needs help	Place the person will contact for help
1. Dan	*bored and lonely on weekends*	
2. Julia's son		
3. Alisa		
4. Marco's daughter		

2 **LISTEN** again and write the place the person will contact.

3 **WRITE** sentences about the people and their problems in Activity 1. Use the present perfect.

1. Dan _has been bored and lonely on the weekends for six months._

2. Julia's son _____

3. Alisa _____

4. Marco's daughter _____

4 **TALK** in a group. Look at the chart in Activity 1 and answer the questions.

1. What were the solutions to the problems?
2. What other questions or problems might new people in a community have?
3. What are some organizations, agencies, or services in your community? What services do they provide?

How long... Questions with the Present Perfect

Present Perfect with *be* + Noun

How long	have	Subject	be	Noun	Short Answer
How long	have	you	been	a volunteer?	For five years.
	has	he		a diabetic?	

Present Perfect with Verbs other than *be*

How long	have	Subject	Past Participle		Short Answer
How long	have	you	lived	in Miami?	Since last year.
	has	she	had	diabetes?	

5 **WRITE** five questions to ask a partner using the present perfect. Then ask a partner your questions and take notes on the answers.

Example: *How long have you lived in this city?*

1. _____

2. _____

3. _____

4. _____

5. _____

6 **TALK.** Tell your classmates information about your partner from Activity 5. Ask questions about your classmates.

Example: *Student A:* Elena has lived in this city for three years.

Student B: Elena, where did you live before?

Elena: I lived in Panama.

LESSON 6: Reading

1 **THINK ABOUT IT.** Talk in a group.

    1. What do you think makes a happy marriage?

    2. Do you know a happily married couple?

    3. How long have they been married? Why have they been successful?

> **Reading Strategy Summary**
>
> Use prior knowledge.
>
> Preview and skim an article.
>
> **Identify examples to clarify meaning.**

2 **BEFORE YOU READ.** Preview and skim the interview on the next page. Where do you think you might see this kind of interview? Predict two things the couple might talk about.

    1. _____

    _____

    2. _____

    _____

3 **READ.**

    A. READ the questions. Then read the interview to find the answers.

        1. Where are Mr. and Mrs. Cruz from?

        2. What are they celebrating this month?

        3. How long have they been married?

        4. How long have they lived in their town?

        5. What does Mrs. Cruz want to do tomorrow?

> **READING FOCUS: Identify examples to clarify meaning**
>
> Identifying examples can help you understand the meaning of specific words.

    B. DISCUSS the answers with a partner.

4 **AFTER YOU READ.** Read the sentences below. Write examples from the interview that help you understand the words in bold and the meaning of the sentences they are in.

    1. And we've always tried to schedule some **leisure activities** together.

    Examples (of leisure activities): _____

    _____

    _____

    2. What are some things that you've done together that you are **proud of?**

    Examples (of things they're proud of): _____

    _____

    _____

    3. But we've supported each other during some **hard times,** too.

    Examples (of hard times): _____

    _____

    _____

Celebrating 50 Years

Today, our Neighbors reporter, Jason Hogen, talks with Simon and Anita Cruz of New Hope County, who celebrated their 50th wedding anniversary last week.

JASON: You two have been married 50 years. And you look happy together. What marriage tips can you give young couples? How do people stay happily married for half a century?

SIMON: Well, first, they need to know that they won't always feel happy. We've had many problems and disagreements[1] over the years. But we've tried to learn from them and laugh about them. It's important to have a sense of humor[2].

ANITA: And we've always tried to schedule a few **leisure activities** together. We used to go to movies every Friday. Now we golf, and we go to the senior center for activities and events. We went dancing last weekend.

SIMON: We've always had good friends, too. We've been in this town for 25 years and our friends and neighbors have been very important to us.

JASON: What are some things you've done together that you are **proud of?**

ANITA: Well, we've always supported the community—we've been involved in food and clothing drives, for example. We've helped out at the schools and we've volunteered at the youth center for over 40 years. A few years ago, we donated time and money to help clean up the river—and now you can fish in the river again. I'm very proud of these things. But of course I'm proudest of raising our children[3]. We raised five children, and so far they've given us 13 grandchildren and three great-grandchildren.

SIMON: We've had a good life. But we've supported each other during some hard times, too. We've experienced two floods[4], a tornado[5]—

ANITA: And a fire…

SIMON: And a fire. And I've been unemployed twice.

ANITA: But all of that is in the past. We're really very happy now. Our children all have good jobs and great families. We're healthy. I still work in the garden, and Simon takes a walk with a neighbor every day.

JASON: Did your family give you anything special for your anniversary?

SIMON: We got a computer for our anniversary. Anita is excited, because we haven't had a computer before—this is our first one. She wants to contact an Internet service tomorrow so that she can start sending messages to all our children and grandchildren and to all her friends.

---

[1]*disagreement*: a situation in which two people have different views and each one thinks he or she is right

[2]*sense of humor*: ability to see that things are funny; ability to laugh at things

[3]*raising (children)*: taking care of the children who live with you and helping them become adults

[4]*floods*: situations in which water covers areas where water should not be, such as streets, homes, etc. Too much rain usually is the reason for floods.

[5]*tornado*: a violent storm in which the wind spins or whirls in circles

LESSON 7: Writing

1 **THINK ABOUT IT.** Write five important events from your life. Then tell a group.

I came to this country

_____

_____

_____

_____

_____

2 **BEFORE YOU WRITE.**

A. READ. Look at the timeline and read the paragraph about Ashur's life. Then find a sentence in the paragraph to support each date on the timeline.

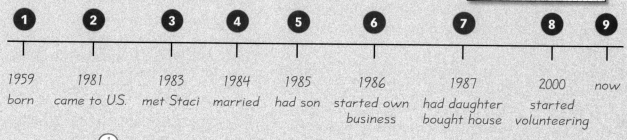

1959 born
1981 came to U.S.
1983 met Staci
1984 married
1985 had son
1986 started own business
1987 had daughter bought house
2000 started volunteering
now

① I was born in Syria in 1959, but I've lived in the United States for many years.

I met my wife, Staci, two years after I arrived in this country. A year later, in 1984,

we got married. We had a son in 1985, and in 1986, we started our own flower shop.

We had a daughter in 1987 and we bought our house that year, too. In 2000, my wife

and I started volunteering at different organizations in town. We have tutored adults

at the community center for almost five years now. I've been very happy here.

B. WRITE answers to the questions. Use *for*.

1. How long has Ashur lived in the United States? _____

2. How long has he been married? _____

3. How long has he had his own flower shop? _____

4. How long has he been a parent? _____

5. How long has he lived in his house? _____

C. MAKE A TIMELINE of important events in your life.

- Write the year you were born at the left end of your timeline.

- Write other dates and events on your timeline. Use events like those in Activity A, or use other events.

WRITING FOCUS: Make a timeline

You can make a timeline to help you organize events in your life, or events in history, into chronological order.

19____
born

20____
now

3 **WRITE** a paragraph about your life. Use the five events on your timeline in Activity 2C. Use Ashur's paragraph in Activity 2A as an example. Include at least four dates (different years).

4 **AFTER YOU WRITE.**

A. **READ** your paragraph to a partner. Listen to your partner read his or her paragraph. Ask each other questions about the events in your lives.

B. **TALK.** Work with another pair. Look at your partner's paragraph and tell the other pair information about your partner.

Example: Jana has been married for eight years. He has lived in the United States for three years. He has been a father for six months.

C. **EDIT** your work.

1. Did you write about important events in your life?

2. Did you include all the important information from your timeline?

3. Did you include five dates (years)?

Career Connection

TCD3, 28

1 **LISTEN** to the conversation. Then practice with a partner.

Tami: Hi, Judy. What brings you here?

Judy: Oh, hi, Tami. I came in to look at city job listings. But I don't have my college degree yet.

Tami: You might find something. The city needs maintenance workers, park and recreation workers, custodians, people to help in the offices…

Judy: I didn't see anything today.

Tami: Well, the jobs change every week. And if you don't want to come back, you can check them out on the city website.

Judy: Thanks!

Tami: And have you tried the Board of Education?

Judy: No, not yet. But I'll check listings there, too. Maybe I could get a part-time job as a cook or a teacher's aide.

2 **WRITE** answers to the questions.

1. Where is Judy looking for a job? _____

2. Can she apply for a job working for the city today? _____

3. Where else will she check listings? _____

4. What kinds of jobs does she think she could get there? _____

3 **TALK** in a group. Discuss these questions to complete the word-webs: What other jobs can people get with their city or with their Board of Education?

Board of Education Jobs — teacher

City Jobs — street cleaner

4 **TALK** in a group. Look at the jobs in Activity 3. Which ones do you think require a college degree? What skills or training do you think the others require?

5 **WHAT ABOUT YOU?** Are you interested in any of the jobs in Activity 3? Do you think you would be qualified for any of the jobs? Why or why not?

Check Your Progress!

Skill	Circle the answers	Is it correct?
A. Use the present perfect with *yet* and *already*.	1. Have you **do / did / done** your homework yet? 2. No, I **have / haven't / hasn't**. I'm going to do it tomorrow. 3. **Has / Haven't / Have** your English class started yet? 4. Yes, it has already **starts / start / started**.	☐ ☐ ☐ ☐
	Number Correct 0 1 2 3 4	
B. Use the present perfect with *for* or *since*.	5. I've been there **since / for** three weeks. 6. How long has he been gone? **Since / For** yesterday. 7. I've been without electricity **since / for** Saturday. 8. My Internet service has been down **since / for** three days.	☐ ☐ ☐ ☐
	Number Correct 0 1 2 3 4	
C. Talk about community services.	9. Have you **subscribed / registered** to the local newspaper, yet? 10. I've **contacted / enrolled** the landlord. The apartment isn't ready. 11. Have you **registered / received** your textbooks yet? 12. I need help with my tax **advancement / preparation**.	☐ ☐ ☐ ☐
	Number Correct 0 1 2 3 4	
D. Talk about obtaining services.	13. I need a job. I've been **out of work / down** for a year. 14. My Internet connection has been **without electricity / down** since 6:00 A.M. 15. I've been **on strike / on hold** with the cable company for an hour. 16. He's been **registered / retired** for a year. He keeps busy at the senior center.	☐ ☐ ☐ ☐
	Number Correct 0 1 2 3 4	

COUNT the number of correct answers above. Fill in the bubbles.

Chart Your Success					
Skill	Need Practice	Okay	Good	Very Good	Excellent!
A. Use the present perfect with *yet* and *already*.	⓪	①	②	③	④
B. Use the present perfect with *for* or *since*.	⓪	①	②	③	④
C. Talk about community services.	⓪	①	②	③	④
D. Talk about obtaining services.	⓪	①	②	③	④

LESSON 1: Grammar and Vocabulary

TCD3, 29 SCD34

1 GRAMMAR PICTURE DICTIONARY. What have these people been doing? Listen and read.

1

Luca <u>has been</u> (weeding) the garden.

2

Terry has been **handing out flyers.**

3

Alicia has been **translating documents.**

4

Michael has been **organizing** his **work tools.**

5

Li has been **baking** cookies.

6

Peter and Lilia have been **picking** tomatoes.

2 READ the sentences in Activity 1 with a partner.

3 NOTICE THE GRAMMAR.

A. (CIRCLE) the main verbs. <u>Underline</u> the two helping verbs (*have*/*has* + *be*) before each main verb.

B. **TALK.** What do you notice about the activities in the pictures? Did they start in the past? Have they already finished? Could they continue? Discuss with your class.

Present Perfect Continuous

Use the present perfect continuous to talk about actions or states that started in the past, continue into the present, and may continue in the future.

Affirmative and Negative Statements

Subject	*have (not)*	*been*	Verb+*ing*
I / You / We / They	have (not)	been	weeding.
He / She	has (not)		

You can use contractions with *have* and *has*.

She has been weeding. → She's been weeding.

They have been weeding. → They've been weeding.

Yes/No Questions

Have	Subject	*been*	Verb+*ing*
Have	I / you / we / they	been	weeding?
Has	he / she		
Have	we / you / they		

Short Answers

Affirmative	Negative
Yes, I / you have.	No, I / you haven't.
Yes, he / she has.	No, he / she hasn't.
Yes, we / you / they have.	No, we / you / they haven't.

Wh- Questions

Wh- Question Word	*have*	Subject	*been*	Verb+*ing*
What	have	I / you / we / they	been	doing?
Where	has	he / she		working?

4 **COMPLETE** the sentences. Use the present perfect continuous.

1. Vera looks tired. She _____*has been working*_____ (work) hard.

2. Mario has several dictionaries open on his desk. He _____ (translate) something.

3. Stan and Lucia look sick. They _____ (not feel) well.

4. There's a nice smell in Linda's kitchen. She _____ (bake) cookies.

5. Sam is cold and tired. He _____ (hand out) flyers all day.

6. Your garden is full of weeds. You _____ (not weed).

7. Jan and Tom have many boxes. They _____ (organize) their documents.

8. Your hands are red. _____ you _____ (wash) dishes?

9. Maria's face is red. She _____ (exercise).

10. Lee and Frankie have sore backs. They _____ (pick) fruit all day.

5 **TALK** with a partner. Look again at the pictures in Activity 1. Ask questions about what each person has been doing.

Has Luca been picking tomatoes?

No, he hasn't. He's been weeding the garden.

LESSON 2: Grammar Practice Plus

1 **TALK** about the picture. What have these people been doing today?

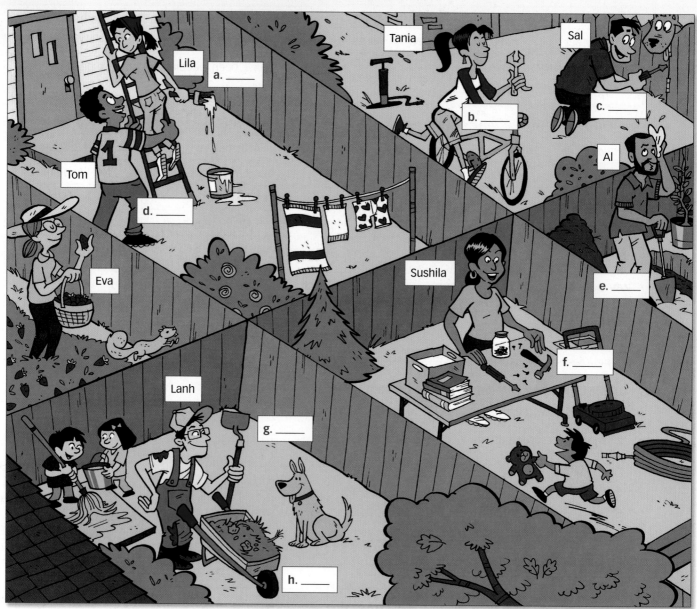

2 **MATCH.** Write the number next to the correct tool in the picture.

1. hammer   3. hoe   5. screwdriver   7. wheelbarrow

2. ladder   4. paintbrush   6. shovel   8. wrench

3 **WRITE** sentences about five people in the picture. What have these people been doing today? Use the words in the box. What tools have they been using?

fixing a fence	painting	digging a hole	weeding	fixing her bike

Example: *Lanh has been weeding. He's been using a hoe and a wheelbarrow.*

Talk about repeat actions in the recent past. • Use present perfect continuous.

4 **TALK** with a partner. Ask and answer questions about the picture in Activity 1. Use the answers in the box.

Example: *A:* Why have Lila and Tom been painting?

B: Because they want to <u>sell their house</u>.

~~sell their house~~	make strawberry jam	keep the neighbor's dog out	plant vegetables	ride her bike to work

Present Perfect Continuous for Repeated Actions in the Recent Past

Use the present perfect continuous to tell about actions repeated over a period of time up to the present. We often use an adverb, such as *recently* or *lately*, to tell what we've been doing in the recent past.

Subject	Present Perfect Continuous	Object	Adverb
I / You	have been playing	soccer	recently.
He / She	hasn't been baking	cakes	lately.
We / You / They	have been taking	a cooking class	recently.

5 **MATCH** the people's actions with the reasons for them.

_b_ **1.** Jasmina has been studying Portuguese.   **a.** They want to become chefs.

___ **2.** Lilia has not been weeding the garden.   **b.** She wants to translate some documents.

___ **3.** Pietro has been organizing his class notes.   **c.** He wants a new career.

___ **4.** Tran and Phun have been taking cooking classes.   **d.** She has a backache.

___ **5.** Shu and Kris have been handing out flyers.   **e.** He's going to take an exam.

___ **6.** Leo has been reading job ads in the newspaper.   **f.** They want to tell people about a neighborhood meeting.

6 **WRITE** about the recent activities of each person in Activity 5. Use *recently* or *lately* and *because* to join the sentences.

Example: *Jasmina has been studying Portuguese recently because she wants to translate some documents.*

7 **WHAT ABOUT YOU?** Work in a small group. Tell about three things you've been doing recently. Explain why.

I've been riding my bike to work lately because I want to lose weight.

LESSON 3: Listening and Conversation

1 **PREDICT.** Look at the pictures. What jobs do you see? What are the people doing?

TCD3,
30–33

2 **LISTEN** to the question. Then listen to the conversation. Listen to the question again. Fill in the circle for the correct answer. Repeat each item if necessary.

1. Ⓐ Ⓑ Ⓒ   3. Ⓐ Ⓑ Ⓒ

2. Ⓐ Ⓑ Ⓒ   4. Ⓐ Ⓑ Ⓒ

TCD3, 34

3 **LISTEN** again to the conversations and complete the chart.

Problem	Solution
1. *She hasn't been filing documents.*	
2.	
3.	
4.	

TCD3, 35 **Pronunciation:** Blending *Wh-* Question Words with *has* + *he/she/it*

Native speakers usually blend the contractions of *Wh-* question words + *has* with *he* or *she*. It's sometimes difficult to hear the difference between *he* and *she*. Look at the examples. Listen and repeat.

     1. What's she been doing?   3. Where's she been living?

     2. What's he been doing?   4. Where's he been living?

TCD3, 36 **A** **LISTEN** and complete the sentences with the full form of each word.
SCD35

     1. Where _____ _____ been eating?   3. What _____ _____ been weeding?

     2. What _____ _____ been baking?   4. Where _____ _____ been studying?

TCD3, 37 **B** **LISTEN** again and repeat.

4 **LISTEN** and read.

A: You're working as <u>a front desk clerk</u>, right?

B: Yes, that's right.

A: How do you like it so far?

B: I like it very much.

B: That's wonderful! And what have you been doing to improve your work skills?

A: I've been <u>taking a class in business English</u>.

B: <u>That sounds great</u>.

5 **PRACTICE** the conversation from Activity 4 with a partner. Use the information in the chart.

Position	Recent activity	Ways to encourage others
1. an auto mechanic	researching online about new types of car engines	Good for you.
2. an office assistant	organizing the office filing system	Sounds like you're on the right track.
3. a nurse's assistant	reading about new health rules and regulations	Well, that sounds like a great idea.

6 **WHAT ABOUT YOU?** What have you been doing to improve your English skills? Tell a partner. Take notes in the chart about your partner.

Example: A: What have you been doing to improve your listening skills?

B: I've been listening to the news in English every day.

Listening	
Speaking	
Reading	
Writing	

7 **TALK.** Tell your class about one of your partner's answers from Activity 6.

Tomo has been listening to the news to improve his listening skills.

LESSON 4: Grammar Picture Dictionary

1 GRAMMAR PICTURE DICTIONARY. What have these people been doing at their jobs? Listen and read.

TCD3, 39
SCD37

1

Marcia and Tony have been **raising money** for over two months. They have raised over $3,000.

2

Tim has been **coaching** soccer since 2003. His team has **won** five **championships**.

3

Frank and Stella have been **designing** homes for 20 years. They have designed over 200 homes.

4

Tony has been **directing movies** for a few years. His films have won several **awards**.

5

Rani has been designing **websites** since she graduated from college. She has **created** more than 50 websites.

6

Sandy has been **signing** books today since 1:00 P.M. So far, she has signed about 50 books.

2 READ the sentences in Activity 1 with a partner.

3 NOTICE THE GRAMMAR. Circle *for* and *since* in the conversations above. Underline the words or phrases that describe a past time (for example, *1:00, last week*). Put a rectangle around the words or phrases that describe a period of time (for example, *three days, ten years*.)

Use present perfect continuous to talk about job experience.

Present Perfect Continuous with *How long...*, *for*, and *since*

Use the present perfect continuous with *for* or *since* to talk about how long something has been happening. Use it to focus on the *ongoing* situation.

Questions with *How long...*

How long	have	Subject	been	Verb + *ing*	Object
How long	have	I / you	been	designing	homes?
	has	he / she			
	have	we / you / they			

Answers and Statements with *for* and *since*

Subject	have	been	Verb + *ing*	Object	for... / since...
I / You	have	been	designing	homes	for ten years. since 1998.
He / She	has				
We / You / They	have				

Present Perfect or Present Perfect Continuous?

We often use the **present perfect** to talk about quantity, or the number of times an action has happened. (She **has written** three books. I **have sent** five e-mails today.)

We use the **present continuous** to talk about continuing actions. We don't use it to talk about quantity or number of times an action has happened.

---

4 **WRITE** the present perfect or the present perfect continuous. Circle *since* or *for*.

1. Rita _____*has written*_____ (write) ten books. She _____*has been writing*_____ (write) books **since /** **(for)** 20 years.

2. Fabian _____ (raise) money **since / for** two years. His organization _____ (build) homes for 30 families so far .

3. I _____ (design) websites **since / for** 2001. I _____ (create) 12 websites in that time.

4. Sue _____ (direct) three movies in her career. She _____ (make) films **since / for** she was a college student.

5. We _____ (play) soccer **since / for** five years, but we _____ (not win) a single game.

5 **TALK** with a partner. Ask and answer questions about the people in Activity 1. Use *since* or *for*.

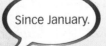

How long have Marica and Tony been raising money?

Since January.

You can give a short answer for these *How long...* questions.
How long has she been working?
Since 9:00 A.M.
For three hours.

LESSON 5: Grammar Practice Plus

1 **WHAT ABOUT YOU?** Work in a group or walk around the class. Ask and answer present perfect or present perfect continuous questions with *Have you…?* or *How long have you….* Complete the chart.

Find someone who…	Name
1. has been studying English for less than two years.	
2. has studied more than two languages.	
3. has been playing the same sport for more than five years.	
4. has played or watched more than ten sports games this year.	
5. has been reading the same book for more than one month.	
6. has read more than three books in the last year.	
7. has been working in the same job for more than a year.	
8. has applied for more than three different jobs this year.	

2 **TALK** about a student in your class. Use the information in your chart.

Example: Rudy has been studying English for almost two years. He has also studied German and Russian. He says Russian is the most difficult language.

3 **COMPLETE** the story about Dave. Circle the present perfect continuous or the present perfect form of the verb.

Dave joined the Riviera Soccer Club two years ago. His team (1) **has won** / **has been winning** two championships since he joined. He is their star player! Recently, he (2) **has coached** / **has been coaching** high school soccer teams. To raise money for high school soccer programs, he (3) **has designed** / **has been designing** a T-shirt with his picture on it. His fans (4) **have bought** / **have been buying** over 300 T-shirts. So far he (5) **has raised** / **has been raising** $1,000. He (6) **has signed** / **has been signing** T-shirts for his fans since 9 A.M. this morning.

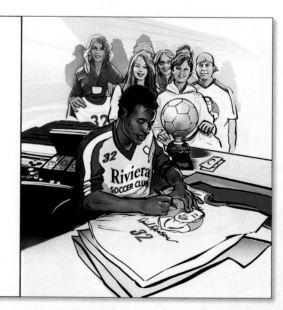

4 **READ** the flyer. What questions could you ask Elsa about her life and experience? Tell a partner.

INTRODUCING

Elsa Martinez

Motivational Speaker,
Author, and Businessperson

Starting Your Own Business

Tuesday, May 17 • 3:30 P.M.–5:00 P.M.

Washington Community College
303 Main Street, East Springfield

For more information or to register call:
1-800-555-6903

Call now. Seating is limited!

5 **LISTEN.** First read the questions. Then listen and answer them.

TCD3, 40

1. How long has Elsa had her own business? _____ *For twenty years*

2. How long has she been retired? _____

3. How long has Elsa been giving motivational speeches? _____

4. Who has she been trying to help? _____

5. What has she been raising money for? _____

6. What has she written a book about? _____

6 **WHAT ABOUT YOU?** Write one of your goals on a piece of paper. What have you been doing recently to achieve your goal? Ask and answer questions with a partner about your goals. Take notes.

Example: *My goal is to work as a nurse. I've been taking classes and doing research on the Internet.*

7 **WRITE** an introduction about your partner like the one you heard in Activity 5. Describe what your partner has been doing recently to achieve a goal. Then introduce your partner to the class.

Example: *Good afternoon and welcome. Today I'd like to introduce Maria. Maria is going to talk to us today about how she… To achieve her goal, she has been…*

Math: Calculate work time

A **READ** the problems below.

1. Bernie has to answer 150 e-mails. It takes two minutes to answer each e-mail. He's been answering e-mails for two hours.

2. Sonya has to make 40 sandwiches. It takes six minutes to make each sandwich. She's been making sandwiches for half an hour.

B **CALCULATE.** How much more time will Bernie and Sonya need to finish their jobs?

LESSON 6: Reading

1 **THINK ABOUT IT.** Talk in a small group. What kinds of behavior make a good employee? What kinds of behavior cause an employee to lose his or her job? Make two lists.

2 **BEFORE YOU READ.** Preview and skim the article. Underline the correct topic of the article.

1. How to find a job quickly.

2. How to get along with your co-workers.

3. How to get a better job.

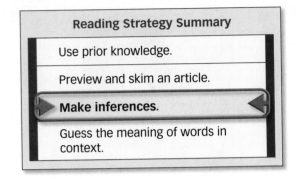

Reading Strategy Summary

Use prior knowledge.
Preview and skim an article.
Make inferences.
Guess the meaning of words in context.

3 **READ** the article and underline one idea you feel is useful. Then tell your partner.

4 **AFTER YOU READ.**

A. WRITE. Underline the statement that is an inference.

1. Marta
   a. Marta wants to learn more about nursing.
   b. Marta cooks food for the senior residents.
   c. Marta reads about health issues.

2. Boris
   a. Boris drives delivery trucks.
   b. Boris likes his job.
   c. Boris likes to solve problems.

3. Chuan
   a. Chuan started his job six months ago.
   b. Chuan is good at talking about computers.
   c. Chuan will have a job evaluation.

> **READING FOCUS: Make inferences**
>
> Sometimes a text does not state information directly. When you *make an inference*, you make a guess about something, using information in the text.
>
> **Stated in text:**
> Suzanna was often late to work. She lost her job.
>
> **Inference:**
> It was important to Suzanna's boss that employees arrive on time.

B. VOCABULARY. Find and circle these phrases in the text. Guess their meanings from context. Then complete each sentence below with the correct phrase.

keep your job	keep up to date	keeps him busy	keeps a record

1. She _____ of her job duties every day.

2. His homework _____ in the evenings.

3. I need to use the Internet to _____ with the news.

4. You have to work hard if you want to _____.

| HOME | CAREERS | CASE STUDIES | CAREER LINKS |

MOVING UP THE JOB LADDER

Getting a job is just the first step on the job ladder, but how can you climb higher? Being on time and having a positive attitude may be enough to keep your job, but will you get promoted? "You can't always expect your boss to notice your hard work," says Jim Caulfield of the Business Ladder Institute. Today's employees need to create their own promotion opportunities. Here are three strategies from our career experts on ways to get promoted.

JOB LADDER
President
Vice President
Manager
Assistant Manager
Administrative Assistant
Receptionist

Strategy 1: Learn new skills

Case study: Marta

Marta has been working as a health aide for five years. She works in a senior care center. Her main job duties are personal care of the residents, preparing meals, and giving medication. She's interested in medicine and has been watching the nurses to learn about their work. She asks questions to make sure she is giving the correct medication. She also reads a monthly health journal to keep up to date with recent research. Recently, there were some opportunities for job training, and the care center offered to pay her tuition.

Strategy 2: Solve problems

Case study: Boris

Boris has been driving delivery trucks for about two years. He likes his job because the hours are flexible and the pay is good. But many of his coworkers have been complaining that the manager does not organize the schedules effectively. They have to wait too long between deliveries. So Boris suggested a new way to organize the schedules. Now Boris is in charge of schedules. He has more responsibility and he earns more money, too.

Strategy 3: Keep a record of your successes

Case study: Chuan

Chuan has been working as a computer salesperson for six months. Since he started this job, he has sold 25 laptops and 12 desktop computers. Although his job keeps him busy, he has been learning about new computer programs in his spare time. He has helped over 35 customers with their computer problems. He keeps a record of all his successes. He'll show it to his manager at his job evaluation.

DISCUSSION

1. Are any of these case studies similar to your work experience or the experience of someone you know?

2. What other kinds of advice can you suggest to people who want to climb the job ladder?

3. In your opinion, why do people usually get promoted in your workplace or a workplace that you know?

LESSON 7: Writing

1 **THINK ABOUT IT.** Answer the questions with your class.

1. How do you find a job? Where do you look?

2. What are some different ways you can apply for a job?

3. What are some things you might need to write?

> **WRITING FOCUS: Write a cover letter**
>
> When you apply for a job by mail or by e-mail, you should send your résumé and a cover letter. The cover letter explains why you want the job. It is also a chance to tell the employer why he or she should read your résumé and why you are the right person for the job.

2 **BEFORE YOU WRITE.**

A. READ the details about the cover letter on the next page. Look at the greeting and the closing. Have you learned other ways to begin and end a formal or informal letter? Complete the chart with your ideas.

	Formal	Informal
Greeting	*Dear Mr. Rose:*	
Closing	*Sincerely,*	

B. READ the cover letter. Why is Jo-An a good match for this job? What skills does she have?

3 **WRITE.** Follow these steps.

1. Write three jobs you are interested in.

   a. _____

   b. _____

   c. _____

2. Talk with a partner about what skills you need for each job.

3. Choose the job you are most interested in.

4. Write a cover letter.

930 South Street
Baltimore, MD 21201

1. your contact information

November 15, 2008

2. today's date

Mr. David Rose
Manager of Human Resources
Arcadia Hotel
193 Coleman Avenue
Baltimore, MD 21201

3. employer's contact information: name of contact, position, company name, address

Dear Mr. Rose:

4. greeting: common way to begin a letter

I am applying for the position of front desk clerk, which was advertised in the Weekly Post on November 14.

5. first paragraph: What job are you applying for? Where did you find the job listing?

I have been working as a hotel front desk clerk for the last three years. I work with customers from different countries, making reservations and answering the phone. Recently, I have been taking computer and business communications courses. I speak Spanish fluently, and I have good computer and math skills.

6. middle paragraph: Why are you the right person for the job?

I would be very happy to meet with you for an interview. Please call me at (443) 555-2468 or e-mail me at japetersen@email.com. I would be happy to give you references. My résumé is enclosed.

7. final paragraph: Suggest an interview, give your phone number and/or e-mail address. Mention references.

Thank you for your consideration.

Sincerely,

8. closing

Jo-An Petersen

9. signature: Sign a letter sent by mail. You don't need a signature in an e-mail

Jo-An Petersen

10. typed name

> **Note**
>
> In a letter, write:
> *My résumé is enclosed.*
>
> In an e-mail, write:
> *My résumé is attached.*

---

4 **AFTER YOU WRITE.**

A. **EDIT.** Exchange letters with your partner and check the following.

1. Did your partner include all the parts of a cover letter? Mark it.
2. Did the letter say why your partner is the right person for the job?
3. Did your partner use the present perfect and the present perfect continuous correctly?

 B. **REWRITE.** Discuss anything your partner marked or wrote on your letter. Then rewrite your letter.

Career Connection

1 **LISTEN** to the conversation. Then practice the conversation with a partner.

TCD3, 41

Manager:	Pete, have you been filling out a report form every day?
Pete:	Yes, I have, but I haven't filled one out yet today.
Manager:	Please don't forget to fill out a form immediately after you finish your deliveries, okay?
Pete:	Sure. I'll remember from now on.
Manager:	It's important to keep our records up to date and accurate. We need to show them to our supervisor whenever he comes in.
Pete:	Yes. I understand. I'll keep that in mind.

2 **CHECK** ☑ *True* or *False*.

	True	False
1. The manager wants to know if Pete has been filling out the forms.	☐	☐
2. Pete has not been filling out the report forms.	☐	☐
3. Pete is going to fill out a form today.	☐	☐
4. The manager explains why Pete needs to fill out the forms immediately.	☐	☐
5. Pete apologizes for not filling out a form.	☐	☐

3 **DISCUSS** in a group. What are some different ways of responding to criticism at work? Have short conversations using these expressions.

Criticism	Responding to criticism
You've been coming in late often.	I know. I'm sorry. It won't happen again.
You've been spending too much time on personal calls.	Have I? I'm sorry. I won't do it again.
You haven't been using the right tools.	I didn't realize that. Thanks for telling me.
You haven't been wearing your safety helmet.	Sorry about that. I'll remember next time. Thanks for reminding me.

4 **WHAT ABOUT YOU?** Have you ever been criticized by a boss or a teacher? Tell a group about a mistake you've made at work or at school. Then role-play a conversation.

You didn't tell me you were going to take time off to go to the doctor..

I'm sorry. I'll be sure to tell you in advance next time.

148 | Respond to criticism.

Check Your Progress!

Skill	Circle the answers	Is it correct?
A. Use the present perfect continuous.	1. Have you **baking** / **been baking** / **baked** since this morning? 2. No, I **have** / **haven't** / **hasn't**. I just started. 3. We have **been waiting** / **waited** / **waiting** for two hours! 4. Has he been handing out the flyers? Yes, he **have** / **has** / **have been**.	☐ ☐ ☐ ☐

| | | Number Correct | 0 | 1 | 2 | 3 | 4 |

Skill	Circle the answers	Is it correct?
B. Use the present perfect continuous with *How long...*, *for*, and *since*.	5. How long have you **been studying** / **studying** / **study** English? 6. I've been studying English **since** / **for** three years. 7. He's been raising money for the organization **since** / **for** 2004. 8. How long have you been waiting? We've been waiting **since** / **for** 10:00 A.M.	☐ ☐ ☐ ☐

| | | Number Correct | 0 | 1 | 2 | 3 | 4 |

Skill	Circle the answers	Is it correct?
C. Talk about recent activities.	9. Have you been **picking** / **weeding** the garden? 10. I've been **baking** / **picking** cookies for the party. 11. I've been **organizing** / **handing out flyers** at the supermarket since noon. 12. Have you **organized** / **translated** this letter yet?	☐ ☐ ☐ ☐

| | | Number Correct | 0 | 1 | 2 | 3 | 4 |

Skill	Circle the answers	Is it correct?
D. Talk about jobs.	13. Tom has been **coaching** / **directing** movies for 20 years. 14. My movie won two **awards** / **championships**. 15. They've been **raising** / **designing** a new website for the organization. 16. How long has he been **signing** / **coaching** pictures for his fans?	☐ ☐ ☐ ☐

| | | Number Correct | 0 | 1 | 2 | 3 | 4 |

COUNT the number of correct answers above. Fill in the bubbles.

Chart Your Success

Skill	Need Practice	Okay	Good	Very Good	Excellent!
A. Use the present perfect continuous.	⓪	①	②	③	④
B. Use the present perfect continuous with *How long...*, *for*, and *since*.	⓪	①	②	③	④
C. Talk about recent activities.	⓪	①	②	③	④
D. Talk about jobs.	⓪	①	②	③	④

LESSON 1: Grammar and Vocabulary

1 GRAMMAR PICTURE DICTIONARY. These employees are learning about office equipment. Listen and read.

TCD4, 2
SCD38

1

A: What do I do if <u>I need</u> to use the **fax machine**?

B: It's easy. First you **dial** the fax number, and then press "Start."

2

A: What do I do if paper **gets stuck** in the **printer**?

B: If the paper **jams,** turn off the power and open this door.

3

A: What do I do if I want to **make an outside call**?

B: Press 9, then **dial** the number you want.

4

A: What do I do if I want to **save** a file on this **laptop**?

B: If you want to save your file, you have to **click** "Save."

5

A: What do I do if the **photocopier runs out of** paper?

B: If it runs out of paper, put more paper in this drawer.

6

A: What do I do if the **scanner** doesn't start?

B: First, **make sure** the power is on.

2 PRACTICE the conversations in Activity 1 with a partner.

3 NOTICE THE GRAMMAR. <u>Underline</u> the subject and main verb after *if* in the conversations in Activity 1. What form are the verbs?

Present Real Conditional

Sentences with *if* have two clauses. The *if* clause gives a possible situation or condition. Use the simple present. The main clause can tell you what usually happens or what you should usually do in this situation.

Statements

if Clause		Main Clause	
If + Subject	**Verb**	**Subject**	**Verb Phrase**
If the paper	gets stuck,	—	turn off the power. (imperative)
		you	turn off the power. (simple present)
		you	should turn off the power. (modal)

The *if*-clause can also be the last clause of the sentence. Do not use a comma in this case.

Main clause	if Clause
Turn off the power	if the paper gets stuck.

Wh- Questions

Wh- question word	Auxiliary	Subject	Verb	if + Simple Present
What	do	I	do	if the paper gets stuck?

---

4 **MATCH** the information below. Then ask and answer questions with a partner.

Example: *A:* What do I do if <u>I need more paper</u>?

   B: Get some from the supply room.

1. I need more paper? _____
2. the photocopier doesn't start? _____
3. the paper gets stuck? _____
4. the printer breaks down? _____
5. I want to send a file? _____
6. I want to make an outside call? _____

a. make sure the power is on
b. get some from the supply room
c. first dial 9
d. call a technician
e. turn off the power and open the door
f. click "Send"

5 **WRITE** sentences. Use the information in Activity 4.

Example: *If you need more paper, you should get it from the supply room.*

6 **WHAT ABOUT YOU?** Which of the machines in Activity 1 do you use? What other machines do you use at home, at school, or at work? Discuss with a partner.

I use a computer at home every day.

LESSON 2: Grammar Practice Plus

1 **TALK** about the picture. Find these things. Write the number of each item below in the correct place in the picture.

1. emergency exit
2. fire alarm
3. first aid kit

4. smoke detector
5. flashlight
6. warning sign

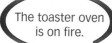

The toaster oven is on fire.

2 **TALK.** Ask and answer questions about the problems in the picture with a classmate.

Example: A: What should you do if the toaster oven catches fire?
   B: You should unplug it right away.

1. the toaster is on fire / unplug it	4. you cut your hand / find the first aid kit
2. you hear a fire alarm / go to the emergency exit	5. the light doesn't work / get a flashlight
3. the photocopier doesn't stop / turn off the power	6. there is water on the floor / make a warning sign

We use *in case* when we need to prepare for a possible future situation.

You should take an umbrella in case it rains.
(It may rain later.)

You should have a first aid kit in case you get hurt.
(You may get hurt sometime later.)

3 **WRITE.** Look at the first aid kit. Why do you need each item in the kit? Tell a partner. Then write five sentences in your notebook.

Example: *A:* Why do you need bandages?

B: In case you get a cut on your hand.

You need bandages in case you get a cut.

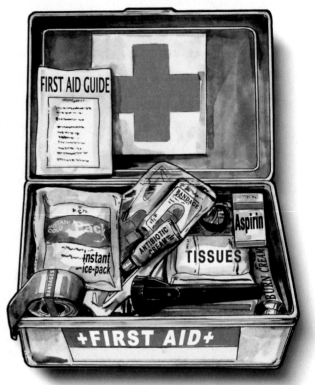

TCD4, 3 **4** **LISTEN** to the office manager talking to employees about the office first aid kit. Listen and match. Were your answers in Activity 3 similar?

1. _____ swelling
2. _____ emergency
3. _____ fever / pain
4. _____ a cut
5. _____ a minor burn

a. bandages
b. aspirin
c. burn cream
d. cold pack
e. call 911

5 **WHAT ABOUT YOU?** What kinds of emergencies could happen at your place of work, at your school, or at home? What should you do if these things happen? Write sentences.

Example: *If you hear a fire alarm, you should leave the building immediately.*

1. _____

2. _____

3. _____

4. _____

5. _____

LESSON 3: Listening and Conversation

 1 **LISTEN.** Complete the sentences with words from the box. Then listen and check your answers.

TCD4, 4

directory	delete	leave	pound	save

1. If you want to hear the message again later, you have to _____ it.

2. If you call someone who isn't there, you can _____ a message.

3. Do you want to _____ the message, or do you want to hear it again?

4. At the end of a message, you sometimes have to press the _____ (#) sign.

5. If you don't know someone's phone number, you can often find it in a _____.

 2 **LISTEN** to the four callers. Then listen to the question. Fill in the circle for the correct answer. Repeat each item if necessary.

TCD4, 5–8

1. Ⓐ Ⓑ Ⓒ   3. Ⓐ Ⓑ Ⓒ

2. Ⓐ Ⓑ Ⓒ   4. Ⓐ Ⓑ Ⓒ

TCD4, 9 **Pronunciation:** Intonation with *yes/no* and *wh-* questions

When asking *yes/no* questions, voices usually rise at the end. Voices usually fall when asking *wh-* questions. Look at the examples. Listen and repeat.

1. If I want to make a copy, do I press this button?

2. If I want to make a copy, what do I do?

A **LISTEN** and check ☑ if the intonation rises or falls.

TCD4, 10
SCD39

1. ☐ Rises   ☐ Falls

2. ☐ Rises   ☐ Falls

3. ☐ Rises   ☐ Falls

4. ☐ Rises   ☐ Falls

B **LISTEN** again and repeat.

TCD4, 11

Use a ticket machine. • Use proper intonation and questions.

LISTEN and read.

TCD4, 12
SCD40

A: Excuse me. Can you please show me how to buy a bus ticket?

B: Yes, of course. First choose the ticket type. One way or round trip?

A: One-way.

B: Okay. Next, select your payment type. Cash or credit?

A: I'll use my credit card.

B: Okay, press "Credit." Then swipe your card right here. Your ticket will come out of this slot.

A: Great! Thanks. But if I make a mistake, what do I do?

B: If you make a mistake, press "Cancel" and just start again.

4 **TALK.** Work with a partner. Explain how to use the ticket machine. Use the words *first*, *next*, and *then*.

5 **TALK.** Work with a partner. Student A, look at picture A. Student B, look at picture B. Put the instructions next to your picture in the correct order. Then ask and tell how to use the machine.

Example: A: Excuse me. Can you show me how to use this _____, please?

B: Yes, of course! First…

Student A	
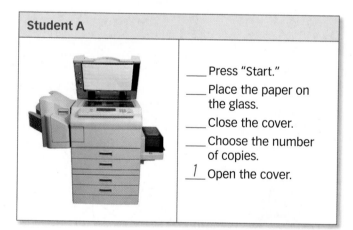	____ Press "Start." ____ Place the paper on the glass. ____ Close the cover. ____ Choose the number of copies. _1_ Open the cover.

Student B	
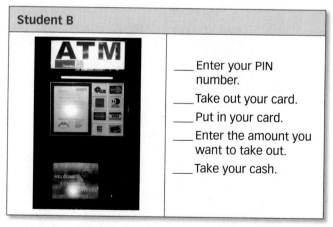	____ Enter your PIN number. ____ Take out your card. ____ Put in your card. ____ Enter the amount you want to take out. ____ Take your cash.

6 **WHAT ABOUT YOU?** Tell your partner how to use a machine at home, at school, or at work.

Example: My laptop is very easy. First, open the cover. Next, push the "On" button. Wait a minute and then enter your user name and password.

LESSON 4: Grammar and Vocabulary

1 GRAMMAR PICTURE DICTIONARY. Lucia is looking at the notice board. What is she thinking? Listen and read.

TCD4, 13
SCD41

2 READ the sentences with a partner.

3 NOTICE THE GRAMMAR. Underline the verb in the main clause of each sentence in Activity 1. Circle the verb in each *if* clause. What form is the verb in each clause?

Future Real Conditional

Use *if* + simple present and a main clause with *will* to talk about things that are probable in the future under a certain condition.

Statements

If Clause	Main Clause
If + Subject + Simple Present	Subject + Future
If I don't keep fit,	I will gain weight.

We can also put the *if* clause in the second part of the sentence. There is no comma when the *if* clause comes second.

Main Clause	*if* Clause
I won't gain weight	if I keep fit.

Wh- Questions

If Clause	*wh-* Question
If you lose your job,	what will you do?

Wh- Question	*if* Clause
What will you do	if you lose your job?

4 **COMPLETE** the paragraph. Use the present or future in the affirmative or negative form.

There are many ways I can improve my life. If I (1) ___*get up*___ (get up) earlier, I (2) _____ (not / be) late for work. I want to study more, but I always get home too late. If I (3) _____ (finish) work on time, I (4) _____ (get) home earlier and I (5) _____ (have) more time to study. I want to lose some weight, but I am very hungry at lunchtime and I eat a lot. I (6) _____ (not / feel) so hungry if I (7) _____ (eat) a healthy snack at 11 A.M. I want to save some money. If I (8) _____ (study) at home and (9) _____ (not / go) shopping this weekend, I (10) _____ (not / spend) too much money.

5 **ROLE-PLAY.** Work with a partner. Look at the sentences in Activity 1. Role-play Lucia and a friend. Ask and answer questions.

1. work the early shift
2. take a computer class
3. work closer to home
4. take a fitness class
5. invest money

6 **WHAT ABOUT YOU?** Ask the questions in Activity 5 again with a new partner. Answer with your own ideas.

Should I work the early shift?

If you work the early shift, you'll get home earlier.

LESSON 5: Grammar Practice Plus

1 **MATCH** the information below to make complete sentences. Explain the meaning of the words in bold.

1. If you don't feel well, _____
2. I usually **take a day off** _____
3. If you are late for work too often, _____
4. If there is a lot of work, _____

a. you could **get fired**.
b. you should **call in sick**.
c. we have to **work overtime**.
d. if my family visits.

2 **COMPLETE** the sentences with the correct form of the verbs in the box.

be	stay	keep	take

1. Sarah: I have called in sick a lot, and if I _____ another sick day, my boss will get angry. What should I do?

2. Maria: We often have to do overtime at work. If I don't _____ late, I'll lose my job. What should I do?

3. Leon: I'm often late for work because my car breaks down. If I _____ late again, I'll get fired. What should I do?

4. Phuong: I have to sit at a desk all day and I don't get any exercise. If I _____ fit, I'll gain weight. What should I do?

3 **WRITE** sentences with possible solutions for the people in Activity 2.

1. Sarah / talk to her boss / understand the problem

   If Sarah talks to her boss, he will understand the problem.

2. Maria / start work earlier / not have to stay late

   _____

3. Leon / ask his coworkers / give him a ride to work

   _____

4. Phuong / go for a walk at lunchtime / get exercise

   _____

Give someone advice. • Talk about goals. • Calculate elapsed time.

4 LISTEN to Alex talk about his goals to improve his life. Complete the chart with Alex's information.

TCD4, 14

Example: | take math classes at night | ➡ | will get a better job |

1. [ ] ➡ [ ]

2. [ ] ➡ [ ]

3. [ ] ➡ [ ]

5 WHAT ABOUT YOU? Write three ways you want to improve your health, education, or work. Then write the probable outcomes of each action.

Example: | eat healthier food | ➡ | will feel better |

1. [ ] ➡ [ ]

2. [ ] ➡ [ ]

3. [ ] ➡ [ ]

6 TALK with a partner about the ideas in your chart in Activity 5.

Example: *A:* I want to eat healthier food.
B: Why do you want to eat healthier food?
A: If I do, I'll feel better.
B: What if you don't eat healthier food?
A: If I don't, I'll feel tired.

7 WRITE three sentences about possible ways to improve your health, education, or work. Use the chart in Activity 5.

Example: *If I eat healthier food, I'll feel better.*

Math: Calculate time

A READ the problems.

1. Leon has trouble getting to work on time. He starts work at 9:00 a.m. It takes him 15 minutes to get dressed, 15 minutes to take a shower, 20 minutes to eat breakfast, and 35 minutes to walk to work. If he gets up at 7:30 a.m., what time will he get to work?

_____

2. Maria has trouble finishing her work on time. Today she has to write twenty reports. Each report takes twenty minutes. If she starts at 1:00 p.m., what time will she finish?

_____

B CALCULATE the time. Write the answers.

LESSON 6: Reading

1 **THINK ABOUT IT.** What types of emergencies are in the pictures?

2 **BEFORE YOU READ.** Skim each paragraph in the reading on the next page. After you skim each paragraph, write the number of the paragraph next to the question it answers.

1. _____ Why do I need to give my name and address?

2. _____ What happens if I make a mistake?

3. _____ What should I say first?

4. ___1___ What is 911?

5. _____ What will the operator ask me?

6. _____ Why should I talk with my family about 911?

> **READING FOCUS: Identify the main idea of a paragraph**
>
> It is helpful to skim a text to identify the main ideas. Read the first sentence of each paragraph to determine the main idea of the paragraph. Getting a picture of the main ideas first will help you to understand the details later.

> **Reading Strategy Summary**
>
> Use prior knowledge.
>
> **Identify the main idea of a paragraph**
>
> Guess the meaning of words in context.

3 **READ** the article. Match the sentence parts. Read the article again and check your answers.

1. If you need medical help immediately, ___d___

2. If you speak too fast, _____

3. If you call from a cell phone, _____

4. If you call 911 accidentally, _____

5. If you don't give your phone number, _____

6. If you talk about emergency situations, _____

a. they will not be able to contact you.

b. you should say the name of the city first.

c. you'll know when to call 911.

d. you should call 911.

e. the operator may not understand you.

f. you should stay on the line and explain.

4 **AFTER YOU READ.** Look at the *italicized* words in the article. They have similar meanings to the words in parentheses below. Write the word from the article in each space below.

1. My son is hurt. Please send an ambulance ___immediately___ (very soon).

2. Can you tell me your _____ (address)?

3. I am _____ (not understanding clearly) about which number to call.

4. I called the wrong number _____ (by mistake).

5. My mother is having _____ (difficulty) breathing.

6. Please don't _____ (end the call).

What happens if you call 911?

911 is a special emergency phone number that you can use to get help fast.

You should only call 911 for a medical, fire, or police emergency and only if you need help *immediately*. First, tell the operator what kind of emergency it is. For example, if someone suddenly has *trouble* speaking or breathing, that is a medical emergency. If a house is on fire or you see smoke from a neighbor's window, that is a fire emergency. If you see a crime—for example, if you see someone breaking into a house or a store—that is a police emergency. When you call 911, you can start by saying: "This is a...(police) emergency. I want to report a...(robbery)."

Next, the operator will ask you for the *location* of the emergency. This will help the emergency services get to the scene. If you are calling from a cell phone, say the name of the city first. Make sure to include the street name, building number, and other helpful information, such as the name of the nearest cross street.

> Some cities have a 24-hour non-emergency number. You can call this number, for example, if someone steals your car. The non-emergency number keeps 911 available for true emergencies.

After that, the operator may ask you questions such as: What is the emergency? or What happened? Where are you? or Where do you live? Who needs help? or Who is with you? Remember to speak slowly and clearly. If you talk too fast, the operator may have trouble understanding what is wrong and what kind of help you need. Emergency services may need your name, address, and phone number in case they need to contact you later for more information. Do not *hang up*. Listen carefully to any instructions and advice.

If you dial 911 *accidentally*, do not hang up. Stay on the line and tell the operator that everything is all right. If you don't, a police officer might be sent anyway.

Sometimes people are *confused* about when to call 911. It is a good idea to talk with your family or with your coworkers about situations when you should, or shouldn't, call 911.

POLICE • FIRE • MEDICAL • EMERGENCY
24 hours/7 days a week

DISCUSSION

1. What should you do if someone is sick, but it is not an emergency?
2. Why do you need to say the name of the city first if you use a cell phone?
3. How can we stop people from calling 911 accidentally?

LESSON 7: Writing

1 **THINK ABOUT IT.** Discuss these problems in a group. Think of two solutions to each problem.

What can you do if...?

1. you don't understand the homework assignment.
2. your daughter or son is not getting good grades at school.
3. you do not get along with a coworker.
4. you don't like your new schedule at work.
5. you don't understand the rules about vacations and sick days at work.

2 **BEFORE YOU WRITE.**

A. READ about Nabil's problem.

> *I have a problem at school. I study very hard and listen carefully to the teacher, but I don't always understand the homework assignments. The teacher speaks very fast and she doesn't write the assignments on the board. I often make a mistake, or I don't understand what to write. If I don't finish the assignments on time, I'll get a bad grade. What should I do?*

WRITING FOCUS: Use a chart to plan your writing

Using a chart can help you organize your ideas. Brainstorm and list ideas first, and then go back and order them from best idea to worst.

B. READ the chart. How many solutions are there? Do you agree with the order of the solutions? Number the solutions from 1 (best) to 3 (worst).

Problem:	Solutions:
I don't understand the homework assignment.	☐ Ask a classmate for help.
	☐ Ask for extra help from a counselor or tutor.
	☐ Ask the teacher to explain.

C. READ Nabil's paragraph based on his chart. Did you order the solutions as Nabil did?

> If you don't understand your homework assignment at school, there are different ways of solving the problem. First, you should talk to your teacher. If you ask, your teacher will explain the assignment again. If you still don't understand, or if your teacher is too busy, you can ask another classmate to help you. If your classmate doesn't understand the assignment, ask for help from a counselor or a tutor at your school. Finally, if you often have problems with your homework, the class may be too difficult for you and it might be a good idea to think about moving to an easier class.

3 WRITE.

A. WRITE. Think of another problem at work or at school, or choose a problem from Activity 1. Write a paragraph about this problem on a piece of paper. Use Nabil's paragraph in Activity 2A as an example.

B. COMPLETE the chart. Read a partner's problem. Think of some possible solutions to your partner's problem. Write the problem and these solutions in the chart below. Then read the solutions again and order them.

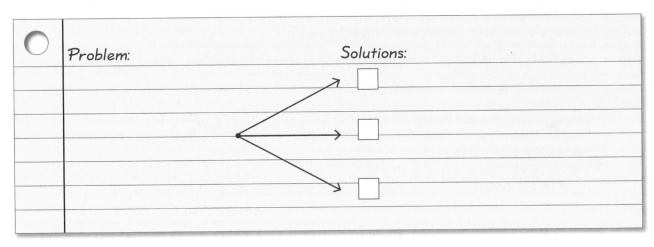

C. WRITE a paragraph describing your solutions. Use Nabil's paragraph in Activity 2C as a guide. Remember to choose the best order for your ideas.

D. DISCUSS. Read the paragraph your partner wrote. Discuss the solutions.

4 AFTER YOU WRITE.

A. EDIT your work.

1. Was the problem clear?
2. Did you write two or three solutions?
3. Were they in a logical sequence?
4. Did you include a topic sentence?
5. Did you include a concluding sentence?
6. Did you use *if* clauses correctly?

B. REWRITE your paragraph with corrections.

Career Connection

1 LISTEN and read the conversation. Then practice with a partner.

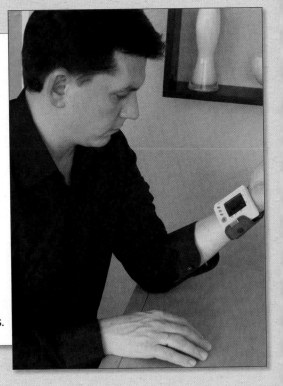

Tony: Every time I use this home blood pressure monitor I get a different reading. I think I'm doing it wrong. Can you show me to use it correctly?

Lisa: Yes, of course. First you have to put the strap around your arm.

Tony: Like this? Am I doing this correctly?

Lisa: That looks a little too tight.

Tony: Oh, how about now?

Lisa: Now it looks a bit too loose. If it's too tight or too loose, you'll get an incorrect reading.

Tony: Oh, okay. What do I do next?

Lisa: Then turn it on. You shouldn't move or speak.

Tony: Oh, I didn't realize that.

Lisa: You should see your blood pressure on the screen in a few moments.

2 TALK with a partner. Answer the questions.

1. Why did Tony think he was doing something wrong?

2. What do you think Tony was doing incorrectly?

3. What does Tony say or do that gives you a clue about what he was doing wrong?

3 WRITE. Think of a machine or tool that you know how to use. (You can use the machine you talked about in Lesson 3.) Write the steps for using it. Then write 2 or 3 problems that you think a person might have if they didn't know how to use it.

Steps	Possible Problems
	Make sure that…?

4 TALK. Work in a group. Take turns telling your group how to use the item that you wrote about in Activity 3. Explain the possible problems they should watch out for.

Example: Make sure the strap isn't too tight or too loose.

5 WHAT ABOUT YOU? In a group, discuss recent situations when you asked a coworker, family member, neighbor, or classmate for help.

Last week, I asked my neighbor to help me carry a heavy box into my apartment.

Check Your Progress!

Skill	Circle the answers	Is it correct?
A. Use present real conditionals.	1. If the printer doesn't work, **make** / **making** / **makes** sure the power is on. 2. If my cell phone rings, you should **answer** / **answering** / **answers** it. 3. What do I if I **wants** / **want** / **wanted** to make a copy? 4. What should I do if Mr. Chan **call** / **calls** / **called**?	☐ ☐ ☐ ☐
	Number Correct 0 1 2 3 4	
B. Use future real conditionals.	5. If I **work** / **will work** / **working** at home, I'll spend less on gas. 6. What will you do if you **lose** / **lost** / **will lose** your job? 7. If I **will exercise** / **exercise** / **exercising** more, I won't be so tired. 8. If you cook for the party, what **do** / **will** / **did** you make?	☐ ☐ ☐ ☐
	Number Correct 0 1 2 3 4	
C. Talk about workplace problems and solutions.	9. If paper **jams** / **clicks** in the printer, you can call me for help. 10. How do I save a document on the **laptop** / **photocopier**? 11. First, dial the phone number on the **fax machine** / **scanner**. 12. Make sure there is paper in the **printer** / **laptop**.	☐ ☐ ☐ ☐
	Number Correct 0 1 2 3 4	
D. Talk about cause and effect.	13. If I **invest** / **improve** money now, I will have enough to retire. 14. If I **commute** / **keep fit**, I'll be healthier when I'm older. 15. If she works **the day shift** / **overtime** she'll get more sleep. 16. If I **improve** / **invest** my English skills, I will get a better job.	☐ ☐ ☐ ☐
	Number Correct 0 1 2 3 4	

COUNT the number of correct answers above. Fill in the bubbles.

Chart Your Success					
Skill	Need Practice	Okay	Good	Very Good	Excellent!
A. Use present real conditionals.	⓪	①	②	③	④
B. Use future real conditionals.	⓪	①	②	③	④
C. Talk about workplace problems and solutions.	⓪	①	②	③	④
D. Talk about cause and effect.	⓪	①	②	③	④

LESSON 1: Grammar and Vocabulary

1 GRAMMAR PICTURE DICTIONARY. This husband and wife are moving. Listen and read.

TCD4, 16
SCD42

1

A: Did you **look over** the **lease** yesterday?

B: Yes, I looked it over. It looks okay.

2

B: Did you **drop off** the **security deposit** this morning?

A: Yes. I dropped it off on the way to work.

3

B: Did you **fill out** a **change-of-address form** today?

A: Yes. I filled it out at the post office on my lunch break.

4

B: Did you **figure out** how to get the **furniture** through the doorway?

A: No. My brother is going to come and help us figure it out tomorrow.

5

A: Did you **pick out** the **curtains** for the kitchen this morning?

B: No. You can help me pick them out right now.

6

A: Did you **turn in** the keys to our old apartment today?

B: No. I'll turn them in tomorrow.

2 PRACTICE the conversations with a partner.

3 NOTICE THE GRAMMAR. Underline the two-word verb in each question. Circle the word that comes between the two-word verb in each response.

Separable Phrasal Verbs

Phrasal verbs are two-word verbs. They have a verb and a particle (a small word such as *on, in, off, out, over, out, into*). A particle changes the meaning of a verb.

Common Phrasal Verbs

drop off	figure out	pick out	put on	turn in	turn on
fill out	look over	pick up	take off	turn off	wake up

Some phrasal verbs are separable. This means an object can come after the phrasal verb or between the verb and the particle.

Subject	Phrasal Verb (Verb + Particle)	Object
He	filled out	the form.

Subject	Verb	Object	Particle
He	filled	the form / it	out.

When the object is a pronoun, it *must* go *between* the verb and particle.

I dropped off **the security deposit**.

Incorrect ✗:
I dropped off **it** this morning.
Correct ✔:
I dropped **it** off this morning.

---

4 WRITE. Answer the questions about the people in Activity 1. Use the underlined phrasal verb and *it* or *them*.

1. Has she picked out the curtains?

   No, she hasn't _picked them out._

2. Has she looked over the lease?

   Yes, she's _____

3. Has he figured out how to get the furniture in the apartment?

   No, he hasn't _____

4. Has he filled out a change-of-address form?

   Yes, he's _____

5. Has she turned in the keys?

   No, she hasn't _____

6. Has he dropped off the security deposit?

   Yes, he's _____

5 WHAT ABOUT YOU? Write three sentences about things you *dropped off, figured out, filled out, looked over, picked out,* or *turned in* recently. Then read your sentences in a group and give additional information.

Example: _I turned my homework in on Tuesday._
I dropped my children off at school this morning.

1. _____

2. _____

3. _____

LESSON 2: Grammar Practice Plus

1 **TALK.** Look at the picture and the phrases in the box. Which tasks has Eva finished? Which tasks does she still need to do? Ask and answer questions in a group.

drop off mail at the post office	put together the new lamp
fill out change-of-address form	put up the curtains
hook up the computer	set up the aquarium
put away the dishes	take out the trash
put in the ceiling fan	take down the old wallpaper

Example: *A:* Has Eva dropped off her mail at the post office?

B: No, she hasn't dropped it off yet.

2 **WRITE** five sentences about what Eva needs to do. Put the object between the two words of the phrasal verb.

Example: *Eva needs to drop her mail off at the post office.*

Inseparable Phrasal Verbs

Some phrasal verbs are *inseparable*. This means the object always comes after the particle. It never comes <u>between</u> the verb and the particle.

Common Inseparable Phrasal Verbs

come over	get on	run into
get off	get up	grow up

Subject	Phrasal Verb	Object
I	ran into	my old teacher.
He	got off	the bus.

3 **COMPLETE** the conversation with the words in the box.

come over	drop him off	figure them out	put it together

Tom: Hi. How are you doing?

Jamal: Not great. I bought a new bookshelf, and I can't

(1) _____*put it together*_____. I've been trying all day.

Tom: Were there any instructions?

Jamal: Yes, but I can't (2) _____. Hey, can

you (3) _____and help me tonight?

I'll order pizza.

Tom: Sorry. I'm busy this evening. I have to take my friend Jack

to the airport.

Jamal: What about after you (4) _____?

Would that be too late?

Tom: No, that would be okay.

Jamal: Great!

Tom: Okay. See you later.

4 **LISTEN.** Were your answers correct?

TCD4, 17

5 **READ** the conversation in Activity 3 again. Then write a phrasal verb to match each meaning.

Phrasal Verb	Meaning
1. *figure out*	solve a problem
2.	assemble
3.	visit someone's house
4.	deliver

6 **WRITE.** Work with a partner. Write four sentences. Use each phrasal verb in Activity 5.

LESSON 3: Listening and Conversation

1 **WHAT ABOUT YOU?** How did you find your house or apartment? Was it easy or difficult? Did anyone help you? Discuss with a partner.

2 **LISTEN** to the question. Listen to Jill talk to her father about an ad for an apartment. Listen to the question again. Fill in the circle for the correct answer. Repeat each item if necessary.

TCD4, 18–21

1. Ⓐ Ⓑ Ⓒ   3. Ⓐ Ⓑ Ⓒ

2. Ⓐ Ⓑ Ⓒ   4. Ⓐ Ⓑ Ⓒ

3 **LISTEN** again. Each conversation has one phrasal verb. Check ☑ the four phrasal verbs you hear.

TCD4, 22

☐ check out   ☐ find out

☐ drop off   ☐ move out

☐ fill out   ☐ put away

☐ look over   ☐ stop by

4 **LISTEN** again. What advice does Jill's father give her? Take notes. Then discuss with a partner. Use the questions below.

1. What rooms should Jill look at?

2. What should she do if the landlord wants her to sign a lease?

3. What utilities should she ask about?

4. What else should she ask about?

TCD4, 23 🎧 **Pronunciation:** Reductions of *have to, want to, going to*

In conversation, we often pronounce *have to, want to*, and *going to* as *hafta, wanna,* and *gonna*. Look at these examples. Listen and repeat. You will hear the careful pronunciation and then the reduction.

    1. I have to sign a lease.   I *hafta* sign the lease.

    2. I want to paint the kitchen.   I *wanna* paint the kitchen.

    3. I'm going to move.   I'm *gonna* move.

TCD4, 24 **A** **LISTEN.** Circle the words you hear.
SCD43

1. *A:* Let's paint the kitchen tomorrow.
   B: I told you I don't want to paint the kitchen this week.   want to   *wanna*

2. *A:* Don't forget to pick up milk when you go to the store.
   B: I'm not going to go to the store.   going to   *gonna*

3. *A:* Let's go to a movie tonight.
   B: Sorry, I can't. I have to study for a test.   have to   *hafta*

TCD4, 25 **B** **LISTEN** again and repeat.

Inquire about a rental unit. • Make polite requests.

5 **LISTEN** and read.

A: I'd like to rent the apartment. Is it available now?

B: No, not yet. I'm going to paint the kitchen, and I want to put in <u>some new kitchen cabinets</u>.

A: If I rent the apartment, can I pick out the color of the paint for the kitchen?

B: Sorry. I always use white paint. If you want another color, you can repaint it after you move in.

A: Okay. <u>Can I drop some things off</u> this weekend?

B: Well, okay. But first could you please <u>sign the lease</u>?

A: No problem. I can do that right now.

6 **PRACTICE** the conversations with a partner. Use information in the chart.

Landlord plans	Polite requests	Tenant must do
1. a ceiling fan	Do you mind if I set up my phone and Internet service	fill out some forms
2. a new bathroom sink	Would you mind if I drop off some boxes	call to let me know you're when you're coming
3. a few smoke detectors	Is it all right if I come over and figure out where to put furniture	give me your deposit

7 **WHAT ABOUT YOU?** Imagine you are looking for a house or apartment. Which things would be the most important? Write numbers 1–6, with 1 as the most important and 6 as the least. Then discuss with a group.

_____ low rent or house payments   _____ a big apartment or house

_____ a safe neighborhood   _____ an attractive place

_____ good schools in the area   _____ a quiet building

I need a big apartment. My family plans to visit a lot.

I need a safe neighborhood because my children walk to school every day.

LESSON 4: Grammar and Vocabulary

TCD4, 27
SCD45

1 **GRAMMAR PICTURE DICTIONARY.** What did people ask Stan, the maintenance supervisor, to do last week? Listen and read.

1
Ms. Baker asked him **to install** an **air conditioner**.

2
Mrs. Hagen asked him **to replace** a **showerhead**.

3
His boss told him **to inspect** all the **fire extinguishers** and smoke detectors.

4
Mrs. Madari asked him **not to spray extermination chemicals** in her apartment.

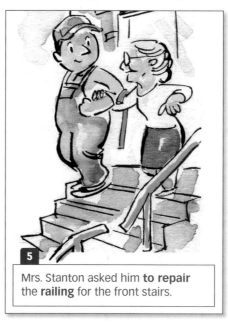

5
Mrs. Stanton asked him **to repair** the **railing** for the front stairs.

6
Mr. Ross asked him **to remove** a **light fixture**.

2 **READ** the sentences with a partner.

3 **NOTICE THE GRAMMAR.** Circle the first verb in each sentence. Draw a square around *him*. Underline what the people want him to do.

Reported speech: *asked... to... / told... to...*

Use reported speech to tell what someone asked or told another person to do. Asking someone to do something is more polite than telling. *Asking* is a request. *Telling* someone to do something is a command.

Statements

Subject	Simple Past Verb	Object	Reported Information
She	asked	you / him / her	(not) to remove a light fixture.
I	told	him	(not) to replace the showerhead.

Who questions

Who	Simple Past Verb	Object	Reported Information
Who	asked	them	(not) to remove the light fixture?
	told	you	(not) to replace the showerhead?

4 **TALK.** Look at the pictures in Activity 1. Ask and answer questions with a partner.

Examples: *A:* Who asked Stan to remove a light fixture?
B: Mr. Ross did.

> Use quotation marks to write a person's exact words.
> He said, "Repair the ceiling."
> Don't use quotation marks with reported speech.
> He told me to repair the ceiling.

5 **WRITE** what the people in Activity 1 asked Stan to do to solve these problems.

1. Her apartment was too hot.

   Ms. Baker asked Stan to install an air conditioner.

2. Going down the stairs was dangerous for her.

   _____

3. She didn't want dangerous chemicals in the apartment.

   _____

4. He wanted to make sure the emergency and safety equipment worked.

   _____

5. The ceiling light was broken.

   _____

6 **WHAT ABOUT YOU?** What have people asked or told you to do or not to do recently? Tell a group.

> Our teacher told us not to talk during the test this morning.

> My husband asked me to pick up some milk at the supermarket today.

LESSON 5: Grammar Practice Plus

TCD4, 28

1 LISTEN. Listen to the phone messages that apartment residents left for their landlord. Check ☑ the requests you hear.

☐ paint the bathroom   ☐ clean the laundry room   ☐ install new carpet

☐ install a ceiling fan   ☐ replace a stove   ☐ inspect the fire extinguisher

☐ check the wiring   ☐ remove some shelves   ☐ repair the toilet

☐ choose some cabinets   ☐ remove a closet door   ☐ replace the locks on the door

2 MATCH the verbs on the left with verbs that have the same meaning on the right.

1. _____ install   **a.** check out

2. _____ inspect   **b.** change

3. _____ remove   **c.** put in

4. _____ replace   **d.** pick out

5. _____ repair   **e.** take down (or take out)

6. _____ choose   **f.** fix

3 WRITE about the residents' requests. Use verbs from Activity 2.

1. _A resident asked the landlord to install a ceiling fan._

2. _____

3. _____

4. _____

4 **MATCH.** Look at Margaret's requests. Who is she talking to? Match each request to a person from the box.

her husband	the exterminator	the cable company	the painter	her old landlord	the electrician

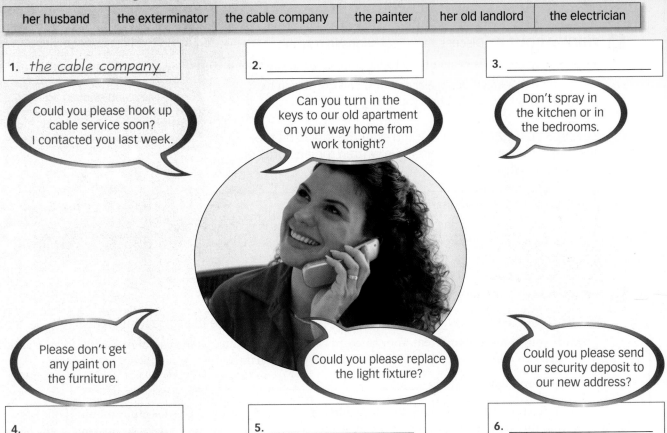

1. _the cable company_

> Could you please hook up cable service soon? I contacted you last week.

2. _____

> Can you turn in the keys to our old apartment on your way home from work tonight?

3. _____

> Don't spray in the kitchen or in the bedrooms.

4. _____

> Please don't get any paint on the furniture.

5. _____

> Could you please replace the light fixture?

6. _____

> Could you please send our security deposit to our new address?

5 **WRITE** sentences about what Margaret said. Use reported speech. Use *asked…to* for requests and *told…to* for commands.

Example: *Margaret asked the cable company to hook up service soon.*

 6 **WHAT ABOUT YOU?** Work in a group. Discuss the questions.

1. Has a friend or relative ever asked you to help with work in their house or yard?
2. Has a friend or relative recently asked you to do something that you did not want to do?

Math: Determining the cost of moving

A **READ** the problem.
Yun is saving money to move to a new apartment. She is looking for a place that costs about $1,000 per month. She will need to pay a one-month deposit and the first and last months' rent when she signs her lease. Hooking up the phone will cost $64. Internet and cable set-up will cost $89. Yun's friends will come over and help her clean and move, but she will need to rent a truck. The truck will cost $35 for the day, plus $25 for gas and $15 for insurance.

B **CALCULATE.** How much does Yun have to save? _____

LESSON 6: Reading

1 **THINK ABOUT IT.** Discuss these questions in a group.

1. Do you know any laws about what a landlord can and can't do?
2. Do you rent a house or an apartment? If you do, do you have a lease? What are some things your lease says?

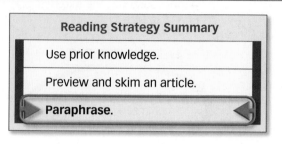

2 **BEFORE YOU READ.** Preview and skim the article on the next page. Do you think the article is written for landlords or for tenants? Why?

> **READING FOCUS: Parapharase**
>
> As you read, stop often and try to repeat the writer's ideas in your own words, by saying them (silently, to yourself, or out loud) or writing them. This will help you understand and remember the information.

3 **READ** the article. Then complete the activities below.

A. READ the items below. Which sections are paraphrased? Write the correct subheading of the section.

1. If you do not pay your rent, your landlord can get a legal notice telling you to move out. If your landlord gives you this notice, you have to move out of your apartment by a specific time.

   Section subhead _____

2. You pay extra money when you move into a house or an apartment. Usually the amount is one or two months' rent. If you stay until the end of your lease, and if you don't damage the apartment, the landlord returns your deposit in full when you move.

   Section subhead _____

B. WRITE. Choose one of the other sections of the article. Paraphrase it.

_____

_____

_____

_____

_____

C. READ a partner's paragraph. Tell which section your partner paraphrased.

4 **AFTER YOU READ.** Answer the questions in a group.

1. What is a lease?
2. Can a landlord refuse to rent to you because you are from another country?
3. Can a landlord come into your apartment any time he or she wants to?
4. What are some tenant responsibilities, according to the law?

What You Should Know Before You Rent

1. **The following information may be useful to you if you are a first-time renter.**

The Lease

Your lease is a legal agreement with your landlord. Read it carefully before you sign it. It should give the date the lease begins and the date it ends. A lease is usually for one year. It should
5. describe the house or apartment and give the address. It should include the name and address of the landlord, the cost of the rent, and when the rent must be paid. It says who is responsible for paying utilities such as phone, electricity, gas, and water. The lease should also include the landlord's rules and information about the security deposit.

The Security Deposit

10. The amount of the security deposit is usually the same as one or two months' rent. Usually, you get your deposit back when you move out. The landlord may keep some of the money if you break or damage anything. The landlord can also keep some or all of your deposit if you don't stay for the complete term of your lease.

Moving

15. Without a lease, you usually have to tell the landlord 30 days before you move out, or the landlord can keep your security deposit. If you have a lease and you move before the lease ends, the landlord may charge you for future rent payments and also keep your deposit.

Eviction

If you don't pay your rent, the landlord can get an eviction notice. The eviction notice is a legal
20. paper telling a tenant to move out by a specific date. The landlord cannot remove things from your apartment or house without giving you an eviction notice and time to move.

Entry

Your landlord can go into your house or apartment to make repairs or to show it to possible future tenants. But the landlord cannot
25. just stop by and enter without telling you. The landlord must tell you before entering your apartment.

Discrimination

The landlord cannot refuse to rent to you because of your race, national origin, religion, sex, family status, or disability.

30. ### Tenant Responsibilities

You must pay your rent on time. You must keep the property clean and safe. You must not disturb neighbors. You must not damage or remove any of the landlord's property. You must throw away garbage. You must not keep pets without permission. Follow the
35. landlord's rules and the rules of your lease.

LESSON 7: Writing

1 **THINK ABOUT IT.** Discuss these questions in a group.

1. Have you ever written a letter to complain about something or to ask someone to do something about a problem? If so, what was the problem?

2. Who did you send your letter to? How did the person respond?

2 **BEFORE YOU WRITE.**

> **WRITING FOCUS: Identify your audience**
>
> When you write a letter, it is important to think about your reader. Who are you writing to? What is your relationship? What do you want from the reader? Might anyone else read your letter? When you write a letter of complaint to someone you do not know very well, you should be polite, but you should also be very direct with your request.

A. READ the letter Consuela Inez wrote. Who is she writing to? Why? Is she polite? Is she direct?

Alex Cheaply
8 Farmington Road
Croton, NY 10520

December 30, 2007

Dear Mr. Cheaply,

I am writing to ask you to repair my stove.

I called you on December 13 to ask you to fix my stove. You didn't answer the phone, but I left a message. I dropped by your apartment on December 18 to talk to you, but you were not home. I left a note on your door.

Now I am writing. I know you are very busy, but my stove has been broken for over two weeks. My microwave isn't big enough to cook all the food for my family. We haven't eaten a hot meal at home in fifteen days.

Please call me <u>today</u> to tell me when someone will come to my apartment to repair my stove. Thank you for your help.

Sincerely,

Consuela Inez

Consuela Inez
Tel: (914) 555-8652
ciz@yahaaa.com

Tip

In a letter of complaint, be sure to:

- include the date and your contact information;
- include reasons for your complaint and important details, but don't be rude;
- keep a copy of the letter in case the person you write to does not respond. If you don't get a reply, you will have the copy.

B. **UNDERLINE** the places in the letter where the writer did the following:

1. described the problem and made a request
2. gave details about the problem
3. made the request again and asked for specific action
4. thanked the landlord
5. gave her phone number and e-mail address

3 **WRITE** a letter of complaint. Follow the steps below. Use the letter in Activity 2 to help you.

1. Think of a complaint to write about.
2. Write the name and address of the person you are writing to on the top left of your paper.
3. Write the date under the name and address.
4. Use the greeting, "Dear (Mr. or Mrs. or Ms.) _____,"
5. Say what the problem is, and request help. Remember to think about the best way to talk to the person you are writing to.
6. Include any important reasons for or details about the problem.
7. Request help again, asking for specific action.
8. Thank the person.
9. Write your own contact information.

4 **AFTER YOU WRITE.**

A. **EDIT.**

1. Did you follow the steps in Activity 3?
2. Were you polite? Were you direct? Were you careful not to be rude?

B. **ROLE-PLAY.** Exchange your letter with a partner. Imagine you are the person your partner wrote to. Role-play a phone call responding to his or her letter.

Career Connection

1 **LISTEN** and read the conversation. Then practice with a partner.

> *Sid:* Hi, Hugo. I need some help replacing some light fixtures in the restaurant this afternoon. Can you help?
>
> *Hugo:* I'd like to, but Melissa told me to replace showerheads in a few guestrooms after lunch.
>
> *Sid:* I'll talk to her. I can't put in the new light fixtures without help.
>
> *Hugo:* I think she wants the new showerheads installed before guests check in later today. But you can ask her.

2 **TALK** with a partner. Answer the questions.

1. Where do the people work?
2. Who needs help? What does he need help with?
3. What did Hugo plan to do this afternoon?
4. Who is Melissa? How do you know?

3 **WORK** in a group. Read the situation and discuss the questions. Can you think of ways to solve everyone's problems?

> Sid asks Melissa if Hugo can help him this afternoon. Melissa says no. Her manager is going to be in town this evening, and he told Melissa to replace the showerheads six months ago. She needs Hugo's help. She tells Sid that one of the waiters can help him.

> Sid isn't happy. He has to connect wiring in the ceiling. He thinks an electrician should do this work, but he hoped Hugo would know how to help him. He is afraid to say anything to Melissa because he just started this job three weeks ago. He thinks maybe he should explain his problem to Hugo, but he isn't sure. He doesn't know if Hugo would be angry or complain to Melissa.

> Hugo would like to help Sid. But the old showerheads don't work well, and guests have complained. If he doesn't put in the new showerheads and guests complain again, they will be allowed to change rooms. Then the housekeepers and the front desk clerks will have more work, and they will be angry with Hugo. And if guests complain and there are no other rooms for them, the hotel will have to give them their money back.

4 **WHAT ABOUT YOU?** Work in a group. Discuss the questions.

1. Do you ever have problems at work or school?
2. Who helps you solve your problems?
3. Do you help other people solve problems? If so, who?

Check Your Progress!

Skill	Circle the answers	Is it correct?
A. Use separable phrasal verbs.	1. Have you figured **out** / **up** / **on** how to unlock the door yet? 2. I'll **look over it** / **look it over** / **look over** tomorrow. 3. Did you pick **over** / **out** / **on** the curtains yet? 4. Will you **turn it in** / **turn in it** / **turn it out** for me?	☐ ☐ ☐ ☐

		Number Correct	0	1	2	3	4

Skill	Circle the answers	Is it correct?
B. Use reported speech: *asked... / told... to....*	5. She asked him **to inspect** / **to inspecting** / **inspect** the alarm. 6. Who asked them **remove** / **removes** / **to remove** the light fixture? 7. I told **him to get** / **him get** / **he to get** a new refrigerator. 8. I told her **don't** / **not** / **not to** replace the old sofa.	☐ ☐ ☐ ☐

		Number Correct	0	1	2	3	4

Skill	Circle the answers	Is it correct?
C. Talk about moving.	9. The **change-of-address form** / **lease** for the house is for one year. 10. I moved yesterday. I need to get a **change of address form** / **security deposit** at the post office. 11. He needs to **take off** / **drop off** the keys at his landlord's house. 12. Do you need a pen to **fill out** / **turn in** the form?	☐ ☐ ☐ ☐

		Number Correct	0	1	2	3	4

Skill	Circle the answers	Is it correct?
D. Talk about building maintenance and problems.	13. Please **inspect** / **remove** the smoke detectors to make sure they work. 14. It's too dark in here. We need to add a **showerhead** / **light fixture**. 15. Please don't **spray** / **repair** extermination chemicals in our garden. 16. The **fire extinguisher** / **railing** on my grandmother's stairs is broken.	☐ ☐ ☐ ☐

		Number Correct	0	1	2	3	4

COUNT the number of correct answers above. Fill in the bubbles.

Chart Your Success					
Skill	Need Practice	Okay	Good	Very Good	Excellent!
A. Use separable phrasal verbs.	⓪	①	②	③	④
B. Use reported speech: *asked... to... /told... to...*	⓪	①	②	③	④
C. Talk about moving.	⓪	①	②	③	④
D. Talk about building maintenance and problems.	⓪	①	②	③	④

LESSON 1: Grammar and Vocabulary

1 **GRAMMAR PICTURE DICTIONARY.** What happened to change these people's lives? Listen and read.

TCD4, 30
SCD46

1

Marietta
<u>Before</u> I got my driver's license, I commuted by bus every day. The buses were often late because of the traffic. I was always **in a bad mood**. I **took out a loan** to buy a car <u>as soon as</u> I passed my driving test. Now I drive to work every day. It's faster and it's more convenient, but it costs more.

2

Angelo
Before I got promoted, I shared a workspace with my coworkers. It was crowded and noisy. I got my own office when I became an **associate manager**. My new office is quieter, but my coworkers don't **socialize** with me so much anymore.

3

Huong and Joseph
We used to **eat out** every week before we had our baby. After we became parents, we stopped going out. It was too **difficult** to find a babysitter. We were usually **exhausted** by 8 P.M. anyway!

2 **DISCUSS** the events in Activity 1. How were the people's lives better before these events? How were they better after?

3 **NOTICE THE GRAMMAR.** <u>Underline</u> *after, before, when,* and *as soon as* in the sentences in Activity 1. Where do these words appear in the sentences?

Past Time Clauses with *after, when, as soon as,* and *before*

Use *after, when, as soon as,* or *before* to tell when something happened in relation to something else. These words can connect two clauses and make a sentence.

After, when, and *as soon as* introduce an event that happened before another event. When you use *as soon as* or *when,* the second event is often very soon after the first event.

Time Clause (1st event)	Main Clause (2nd event)
After they had a baby,	they didn't go out anymore.
When I got a promotion,	I got my own office.
As soon as she got her license,	she bought a car.

Use *before* to introduce an event that happened <u>after</u> another event.

Time Clause (2nd event)	Main Clause (1st event)
Before I got my driver's license,	I went to work by bus.

It is also possible to put the main clause first.

Main Clause	Time Clause
They didn't go out anymore	*after* they had a baby.

Wh- Questions

What did she do	*before* she got the job?
How did you feel	*when* you got promoted?

We use the words *just* and *right* with *before* and *after* to mean that two events happen at almost the same time.

I got a job right after I graduated. (I didn't have to wait a long time.)

Just before I got home, Bob called. (I missed his call. I came home a short time later.)

---

4 **WRITE.** Combine the two sentences using a time clause and the word in parentheses.

1. He was often late for work. He got his driver's license. (before)

Before he got his driver's license, he was often late for work.

2. She bought a car. She started to drive to work. (as soon as)

_____

3. He didn't have an office. He got promoted. (before)

_____

4. He got his own office. His coworkers didn't socialize with him. (when)

_____

5. They had a baby. They didn't eat out very often. (after)

_____

6. It was difficult to find time to socialize. They became parents. (after)

_____

5 **TALK** with a partner. Ask and answer questions about the people in Activity 1. Use time clauses.

Example: *A:* What did Marietta do before she got her driver's license?
　　　　　　 B: She commuted to work by bus.

LESSON 2: Grammar Practice Plus

1 **LISTEN.** Look at the milestones in Antonio's life. Listen to his story. Write the dates in the picture as you listen. Then listen again and check your answers.

TCD4, 31

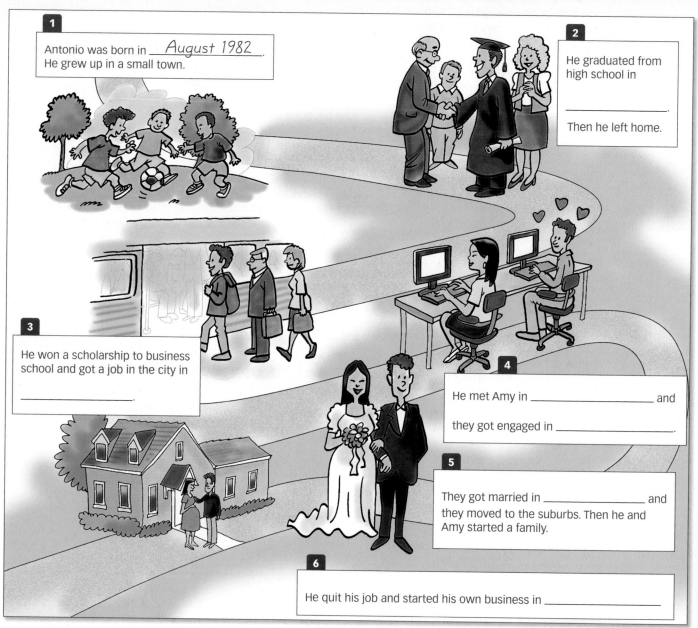

1

Antonio was born in ___August 1982___.
He grew up in a small town.

2

He graduated from high school in

_____.

Then he left home.

3

He won a scholarship to business school and got a job in the city in

_____.

4

He met Amy in _____ and

they got engaged in _____.

5

They got married in _____ and they moved to the suburbs. Then he and Amy started a family.

6

He quit his job and started his own business in _____

2 **MATCH** the phrases with their meanings.

1. _____ to *spend your childhood* in

2. _____ to *receive money for education*

3. _____ to *promise to marry someone*

4. _____ to *set up a company*

5. _____ to *leave your job*

a. to get engaged

b. to quit

c. to start a business

d. to grow up in

e. to get a scholarship

Listen for specific information. • Check meaning. • Use gerunds with time words.

Gerunds with *before* and *after*

A gerund can follow *before* or *after* if the subject of the main clause and the time clause are the same.

In these examples, *he* is the subject of both the main clause and the time clause. When this is the case, the subject (*he*) + verb (*moved*) can become a gerund (*moving*).

Main Clause	Time Clause
He lived in a small town	before **moving** to the city. (before *he* **moved** to the city.)

Wh- Question	Time Clause
What did *he* do	after **getting** engaged?) (after *he* **got** engaged?)

3 **REWRITE** the questions and sentences using gerunds. Then ask and answer the questions with a partner.

1. Before he graduated from high school, he lived in a small town.

   Before graduating from high school, he lived in a small town.

2. He moved to the city after he left home.

   _____

3. What did Antonio do after he got a scholarship to business school?

   _____

4. He got engaged to Amy before he graduated from business school.

   _____

5. What did Antonio do before he quit his job?

   _____

6. After they had a baby, they were exhausted all the time.

   _____

 4 **WRITE.** With a partner, make up a story about the next few years of Antonio's life. Use the past tense and *before, after, as soon as,* and *when.*

Example: *After they had their first baby, Antonio and his wife...*

 5 **WHAT ABOUT YOU?** Talk with a partner. Describe an important milestone in your life. What was your life like before the event? How did your life change after the event? Ask and answer questions about your life milestones.

 6 **WRITE** five sentences about your milestone from Activity 5. Use time clauses.

Example: *After finishing computer training, I got promoted.*

LESSON 3: Listening and Conversation

1 **TALK.** Look at the pictures. Why do you think the people are happy?

1 Luis

2 Emilia

3 Huong

4 Ben

TCD4, 32–35

2 **LISTEN** to the question. Then listen to the interviews of the people above. Then listen to the question again. Fill in the circle for the correct answer. Repeat each item if necessary.

1. (A) (B) (C)   3. (A) (B) (C)

2. (A) (B) (C)   4. (A) (B) (C)

TCD4, 36

3 **LISTEN** to Serena talking about how she became a nurse. Then number the events in the correct order.

_____ Got a scholarship	_____ Worked as a health aide
_____ Got a job in a hospital	_____ Took the RN (Registered Nurse) exam
_____ Attended community college	_____ Took the LPN (Licensed Practical Nurse) exam
_____ Got a high school diploma	

4 **LISTEN** again and take notes about Serena's career. Then ask and answer the questions about Serena with a partner.

What did Serena do…

…when she finished high school? _____

…before she decided to study nursing? _____

…after she got her LPN exam? _____

…after she started work in a hospital? _____

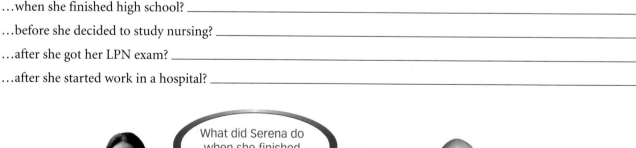

What did Serena do when she finished high school?

She worked as a health aide in a nursing home.

TCD4, 37
SCD47

5 **LISTEN** and read.

> *A:* Hi Petra! Did you hear about Alicia?
>
> *B:* No, what happened?
>
> *A:* She passed her driving test!
>
> *B:* That's wonderful!
>
> *A:* Yeah. And after she got her license, she took out a loan and bought a new car!
>
> *B:* Wow! That's great.

6 **PRACTICE** the conversation in Activity 5 with a partner. Use the information in the chart.

Person / First event (success)	Ways to respond to news of success	Second event
1. Brian / graduated from business school	That's great!	after he got his degree, he started his own business
2. Tino and Jim / traveled around the U.S. by bicycle	That's amazing!	after they got home they wrote a book about their trip
3. Anna / won the lottery	Good for her!	when she got the money, she quit her job

TCD4, 38 **Pronunciation:** Checking meaning

When you do not hear or understand a question, or when you need time to think about your answer, you can repeat the time clause at the end of the question to check that you understand. Look at the examples. Listen and repeat. Notice the difference in your voice.

Example: *A:* What did you do <u>when you finished school</u>? *B:* When I finished school?

TCD4, 39
SCD48 **A** **LISTEN.** <u>Underline</u> the time clause in each sentence below. Write it. Then draw arrows above each to indicate the voice. Listen and check.

1. *A:* Where did you live when you were a child? *B:* _____

2. *A:* Where did she study before she joined this class? *B:* _____

3. *A:* What did they do after they went home yesterday? *B:* _____

TCD4, 40 **B** **LISTEN** again and repeat. Then practice with a partner.

7 **WHAT ABOUT YOU?** List five events from your life. Do not list them in the correct time order. Then work with a partner. Ask *Did…?* questions to find out the correct order of items on your lists.

Example: *A:* Did you buy your car *before* you got your first job?

B: No, I bought it *after* I got my first job.

LESSON 4: Grammar and Vocabulary

1 GRAMMAR PICTURE DICTIONARY. What are the future plans of the people below? Listen and read.

1
As soon as we sell our home, we're going to **pay off** our **mortgage** and **relocate** to California.

2
You can borrow up to $5,000 for your **tuition.** You won't have to **repay** it until you finish school.

3
When I save enough money, I'll **make a down payment** on a home.

4
After I **get my GED,** I'm going to attend classes at a community college.

5
I'll **go back to work** when my kids grow up.

6
I'm going to **consult** with a career advisor before I register for classes.

2 TALK. Read the sentences in Activity 1 with a partner.

3 NOTICE THE GRAMMAR.

A. UNDERLINE the future forms *will* and *be going to* in the sentences in Activity 1. Then circle the main verbs in each clause.

B. READ the sentences again. Which event happens first and which happens second in each sentence?

Future Time Clauses with *after, when, as soon as, before,* and *not...until*

You can use *after, when, as soon as,* and *before* in time clauses to talk about the future. The time clause has a future meaning, but the verb is in the simple present form.

Main clause	Time clause
We're going to relocate	*as soon as* we sell our home.
I'll make a down payment on a home	*after* I save enough money.
She's going to consult an advisor	*before* she registers for class.

Don't forget to use a comma if the time clause comes first.

Time clause	Main clause
As soon as I save enough money,	I'll make a down payment.

Question forms

Will she go back to work	*when* her kids grow up?
Will she consult a career advisor	*before* she registers for class?

Not...until tells what you will do after, when, or as soon as something else happens, but <u>not</u> before. *Not* is used in the main clause and *until* begins the time clause.

We're **not** going to relocate to California **until** we retire.
(We're going to relocate to California *after* we retire.)

I **will not** make a down payment **until** I save enough money.
(I'll make a down payment *as soon as* I save enough money.)

Be Careful!
Do not use the future form of verbs in time clauses.

Incorrect ✗:
When I ~~will~~ get my diploma, I'll get a raise.

Correct ✔:
When I get my diploma, I'll get a raise.

---

4 **WRITE.** Combine the sentences using time clauses. Use the words in parentheses.

1. First, he will pass his driving test. Then he will buy a car. (after)

   After he passes his driving test, he'll buy a car.

2. First, they are going to save some money. Then they will repay their loans. (after)

   _____

3. First, Tom will get a full-time job. Then he will make a down payment on a house. (before)

   _____

4. First, Elena will get her GED. Then she is going to go back to school. (as soon as)

   _____

5. First, Ling will sell his house. Then he will pay off his mortgage. (not...until)

   _____

5 **TALK** with a partner. Ask and answer questions about the people in Activity 1. Use sentences with future time clauses.

Example: *A:* What will she do when her kids grow up?
   B: She'll go back to work.

LESSON 5: Grammar Practice Plus

1 **LISTEN** to Simon's career plan. Then tell a partner Simon's plan.

Simon's Career Plan

1   Simon's goal is to become a website designer. After consulting his career counselor, Simon made a plan to prepare for a career in web design. First, he's going to get his GED. Then he's going to apply to a community college to study web design. Before he applies, he's going to research several colleges

5   and compare them. He might try to speak with some students at the colleges or look at the college websites to get more information. He'll also compare the cost of tuition, the entry requirements¹, and opportunities for financial aid². Then he'll choose the best college for him, and he'll apply. While he's studying, he may get a part-time job. He could try to get an internship³ at

10   a web design company or an Internet advertising company, or he might get a work-study job at the college library. He won't apply for a full-time job until he graduates.

¹*entry requirements* = exams or grades you need to enter the college or school
²*financial aid* = 1. grants or scholarships (you don't have to repay these) 2. loans (you have to repay these after you stop going to school) or
   3. work-study programs (you work at the school while you study and the school pays some or all of the tuition)
³*internship* = a job as an assistant that prepares you for a position at a company

---

2 **READ** the paragraph.
Which plans are certain?
Which ones are possible?
Discuss in a group.

> We use the modals of possibility *may, might,* and *could* with time clauses to talk about possible (but not certain) future events.
> When I finish college, I **might** take some time off.
> I **may** look for another job after I get my GED.
> Before he gets a job, he **could** decide to take a trip.

3 **READ** the paragraph again. Check ☑ *True* or *False*.

	True	False
1. Simon made a career plan before he applied to college.	☐	☐
2. Simon isn't going to apply to a college until he gets his GED.	☐	☐
3. Before he applies to college, he'll research several colleges.	☐	☐
4. After choosing the best college, he'll find out about entry requirements.	☐	☐
5. He won't get a part-time job until he finishes college.	☐	☐
6. He'll apply for a full-time job after he graduates.	☐	☐

4 **WHAT ABOUT YOU?** Think about your goals. Write one in the space below. Use the chart to list three steps to reach your goal.

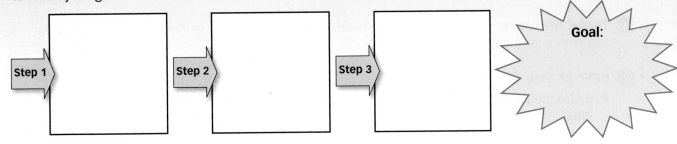

5 **TALK.** Tell your partner about the steps to reach your goal. Ask and answer questions. Use *after, when, as soon as, before,* or *not . . . until* and modals of possibility.

6 **TALK.** Walk around the class and ask your classmates about their future plans. Add *after, before, when,* or *as soon as* to each question. Complete the chart.

What are you going to do...	Answer	Classmate's Name
1. (when) you get out of class today?	study in the library	Eva
2. (...) you get home tonight?		
3. (...) you come to class tomorrow?		
4. (...) you have enough money?		
5. (...) you have some free time?		
6. (...) _____		

 7 **WRITE** six sentences about your classmates. Use information from the chart in Activity 6.

Example: *Eva is going to study in the library when she gets out of class today.*

Math: Compare tuition fees to determine unit cost

A **READ** the problem.

Simon compared the cost of two similar courses. One was at Cranfield Community College and cost $640 for 8 weeks, four hours a week. The other course was at Southfield Community College and cost $600 for 12 weeks, two hours a week.

B **CALCULATE** the cost per hour for each course.

Which course costs less per hour? _____

LESSON 6: Reading

1 **THINK ABOUT IT.** In a group, make a list of different ways you can get information about taking classes at a community college.

2 **BEFORE YOU READ.**

A. SKIM the text and course schedule on the next page. What information does the text give? What information does the schedule give? What abbreviations are there?

B. TALK. What abbreviations are there?

C. SCAN. Read the questions below. Then scan the text on the next page. Check ☑ the questions that are answered in the text.

- ☐ Do I have to take a test?
- ☐ How much is the tuition?
- ☐ What level of English do I need?
- ☐ Can I transfer credits?
- ☐ What do I need for registration?
- ☐ When can I meet an advisor?

3 **READ.**

A. READ the text on the next page. Then answer the checked questions in Activity 2B with a partner.

> **READING FOCUS: Understand and use information in a schedule**
>
> You can skim and scan a schedule to find the information you need quickly and easily. Read the column heads and learn the abbreviations. Then scan to find specific course information.

Reading Strategy Summary
Use prior knowledge.
Skim for the main ideas.
Scan for specific information.
Understand and use information in a schedule.

B. SCAN the schedule. What class is each student planning to take? Write the section number and class title.

1. Tran will take a class in the afternoon after 1 P.M. twice a week. _____

2. Elsa will take a class once a week in the afternoon. _____

3. Marta will take a class three times a week at night. _____

4. Carlos will take two classes. He needs 6 credits and will go to classes in the afternoon. _____, _____.

5. Luis needs 3 credits and will go to class Tuesday and Thursday mornings. _____

4 **AFTER YOU READ.** (Circle) the words in a–e in the reading. Match each word with the words in *italics* with a similar meaning.

1. _____ You must *hand in* your form.
2. _____ You must *fill out* a form.
3. _____ The computer will *print out* your scores.
4. _____ You must *make* an appointment.
5. _____ You can *enroll in* a course.

- a. schedule
- b. generate
- c. register for
- d. submit
- e. complete

http://www.scc.edu/enrollmentinfo

About Us	Admissions	Student Services	Course Schedule	More Information

Southfield Community College:
Four easy steps to enroll

1 **1) Complete the application form**

All students must first complete an application form and submit the form, along with a $30 application fee, to: Southfield Community College Enrollment Services, Main Hall, 4013 College Avenue, Spring View, MA 01108.

5 **2) Take the placement test[1]**

After your completed application form is received, you will be sent an acceptance letter. To schedule a time for the placement test, please call 843-555-1710. You will take the test on campus[2] in the computer lab. The computer will generate your test score[3] and will send you the titles of appropriate courses. The next step is to take your printed test score to an academic advisor.

10 **3) Meet with an academic advisor**

Before you can register for courses, you must meet with an academic advisor to discuss your score. After discussing your schedule and advising you on the appropriate courses, the advisor will give you a registration form. The advisor must sign the form. Advisors are available Monday through Friday from 8 A.M.–5 P.M.

4) Register for courses

15 After meeting with an academic advisor, you can register for courses. Complete the registration form, including the section numbers, class titles, and meeting times. Submit your registration form in person or by mail to Enrollment Services with full payment by check or credit card. If you have any questions, please call Enrollment Services at 843-555-1710.

Section	Class Title	Day	Time	Credits	Start	End
ESL 103-1	Beginning ESL	MWF	10 A.M.–11:50 A.M.	6	9/5	12/14
ESL 104-1	Intermediate ESL	MWF	6 P.M.–8:50 P.M.	6	9/5	12/14
ESL 105-1	Advanced ESL	MW	6 P.M.–9:15 P.M.	3	9/5	12/14
ESL 106-1	Oral Communication ESL	TTh	12 P.M.–1:20 P.M.	3	9/6	12/15
ACL 150-1	Academic Reading	MW	1:30 P.M.–2:50 P.M.	3	9/5	12/14
ACL 151-1	Study Skills	TTh	10:30 A.M.–11:20 A.M.	3	9/6	12/15
ACL 152-1	College Success	T	1:30 P.M.–3:20 P.M.	1	9/6	11/7
ACL 153-1	Critical Thinking	MW	11 A.M.–12:50 P.M.	3	9/5	12/14
VCL 190-1	Career Planning	S	9 A.M.–10:50 A.M.	1	9/10	11/10

[1]*campus*: area around college buildings   [1]*placement test*: test to find your skill level   [3]*test score*: test result; grade

---

DISCUSSION

1. How much does it cost to apply? Why?

2. What do you need to bring to the academic advisor? Why?

3. What documents do you need when you enroll? Where do you get them?

LESSON 7: Writing

1 **THINK ABOUT IT.** Read about these people's goals. What steps do you think they need to take to reach their goals?

> I want to buy my own home.

Meilin

> I want to be a chef in a big hotel.

Paola

> I want to set up my own business.

Ivan

> I want to be on TV.

Angelo

2 **BEFORE YOU WRITE.**

A. READ what Paola wrote about herself.

> Cooking is my hobby, and it is also my career. <u>I graduated from high school five years ago. Then I worked in a hotel for two months.</u> I loved to watch the chefs in the kitchen. <u>Summer ended and I got a job in an Italian restaurant in my hometown right away.</u> Now I often cook for my friends and my family. Last year, I prepared a meal for thirty people for my brother's wedding party. My goal is to get a job as a chef in a big hotel.
>
> There are several steps to reach my goal. <u>First, I need to improve my English. Then I'll try to get a job in a restaurant and save money.</u> Then I'll go to college and take classes in food and nutrition. <u>I'll get a diploma in culinary arts. With my diploma, I'll be able to apply for a job as a chef in a hotel.</u>

> **WRITING FOCUS: Use time clauses to sequence your writing**
>
> You can use both sequence words (*then, next, first,...*) and time words (*before, after, when,...*) to sequence ideas when you write. When you use sequence words, use a period between the clauses. When you use a time clause first, use a comma. When you use a time clause second, you don't need a comma.
>
> I finished high school. **Then** I worked in a hotel for two weeks.
>
> **After** I finished high school, I worked in a hotel for two weeks.

B. WRITE four sentences about Paola. Combine the underlined sentences or clauses in Activity 2A with time clauses. Use *after, when, as soon as, before,* and *not...until.*

After Paola graduated from high school five years ago, she worked in a hotel for two months.

C. DISCUSS these questions with a partner.

1. What kinds of skills and experience does Paola have?

2. What is her goal?

3. How many steps are in her plan? What are they?

3 WRITE.

A. ORGANIZE your writing. Follow these steps.

1. Talk in a group about your goals. Make a list of goals for the people in your group.

2. Write your own information in complete sentences below. Then read your sentences aloud to your group.

Paragraph 1

Your goal: _____

Why you chose this goal:

Reasons: _____

_____

_____

Your skills and experience: _____

_____

_____

Paragraph 2

Steps you need to take to reach this goal:

1. _____

2. _____

3. _____

B. WRITE two paragraphs about your goal in your notebook. Follow the example of Paola's paragraphs in Activity 2A. Write about your goal, your reasons for choosing that goal, and your skills and experience in the first paragraph. Write about the steps you need to take to reach your goal in the second paragraph.

4 AFTER YOU WRITE.

A. EDIT your work.

1. Was the meaning clear?

2. Did you present several steps in your plan?

3. Did you use time clauses?

B. READ a partner's paragraphs. Then ask and answer questions about your goals.

C. REWRITE your paragraphs with corrections.

1 **LISTEN** to the conversation. Then practice with a partner.

TCD4, 43

Augustine:	Where are you going?
Pierre:	I'm going to my computer science class.
Augustine:	Oh, I didn't know you were studying. What are you going to do after you graduate?
Pierre:	When I get my degree, I'm going to apply for a job… as a computer programmer.
Augustine:	That's great! So, are your classes difficult?
Pierre:	They're a lot of work. But I think it'll pay off. I love working with computers.
Augustine:	And you'll definitely get a better salary after you get your degree. Good luck!

2 **TALK** with a partner. Answer the questions about the conversation.

1. Where is Pierre going?
2. What does Pierre plan to do after he finishes studying?
3. How does Pierre feel about his classes?
4. What do you think a computer programmer does? What other types of computer jobs do you know about?

3 **DISCUSS** in a group. Look at the chart. Then discuss the questions.

1. According to the chart, how does a person's level of education affect his or her salary?
2. According to the chart, how does level of education affect unemployment rates?
3. What are some other things that can help someone get a higher salary?
4. What are some other reasons to get a higher level of education?

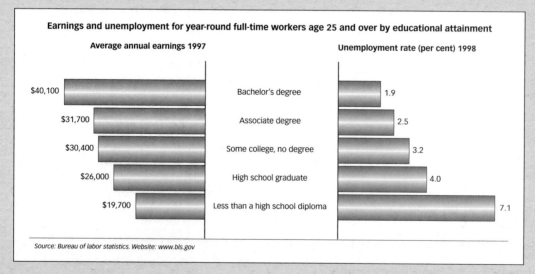

Earnings and unemployment for year-round full-time workers age 25 and over by educational attainment

Average annual earnings 1997		Unemployment rate (per cent) 1998
$40,100	Bachelor's degree	1.9
$31,700	Associate degree	2.5
$30,400	Some college, no degree	3.2
$26,000	High school graduate	4.0
$19,700	Less than a high school diploma	7.1

Source: Bureau of labor statistics. Website: www.bls.gov

4 **WHAT ABOUT YOU?** Tell your group about a job that you would like to have in the future. What qualifications or experience do you need for this job? How will the job improve your life? Have your group ask you questions.

Check Your Progress!

Skill	Circle the answers	Is it correct?
A. Use past time clauses.	1. We lived in an apartment before we **bought** / **buy** / **buys** a house. 2. **Before** / **As soon as** / **After** I got a job, I never worked. 3. When I got a car, I **stop** / **stopped** / **stops** riding the bus. 4. **Before** / **After** / **As soon as** I broke my ankle, I ran every day.	☐ ☐ ☐ ☐
	Number Correct	0 1 2 3 4
B. Use future time clauses.	5. He's going to buy a car **before** / **after** / **until** he saves some money. 6. I won't apply for college until I **graduate** / **graduates** / **graduating**. 7. **Before** / **After** / **When** she retires, she'll work very hard at her job. 8. Sue will cook better **before** / **after** / **until** she takes a cooking class.	☐ ☐ ☐ ☐
	Number Correct	0 1 2 3 4
C. Talk about milestones.	9. Before I **got promoted** / **took out a loan** I shared a workspace. 10. Jack is **exhausted** / **in a bad mood**. He got fired today. 11. I **eat out** / **socialize** a lot because I don't like to cook. 12. You shouldn't **consult** / **socialize** too much at work. Your boss won't like it.	☐ ☐ ☐ ☐
	Number Correct	0 1 2 3 4
D. Discuss plans for the future.	13. I don't have to **repay** / **relocate** my loan until I get a job. 14. We will **pay off our mortgage** / **make a down payment** so we can move after retirement. 15. When you buy a house, you have to **get your GED** / **make a down payment**. 16. My **tuition** / **mortgage** for school is $3,000.	☐ ☐ ☐ ☐
	Number Correct	0 1 2 3 4

COUNT the number of correct answers above. Fill in the bubbles.

Chart Your Success					
Skill	Need Practice	Okay	Good	Very Good	Excellent!
A. Use past time clauses.	⓪	①	②	③	④
B. Use future time clauses.	⓪	①	②	③	④
C. Talk about milestones.	⓪	①	②	③	④
D. Discuss plans for the future.	⓪	①	②	③	④

Grammar Reference Guide

Simple Present and Present Continuous Review

- Use the simple present to talk about facts or repeated actions.
- Use the present continuous to talk about actions that are happening right now.

Simple Present

We often use the simple present with the adverbs *always, usually, sometimes, never,* and *every day / week / month / year.*

Affirmative Statements

Subject	*be*	
I	am	
You	are	a student.
He / She	is	
We / You / They	are	students.

Negative Statements

Subject	*be + not*	
I	am not	
You	are not	a student.
He / She	is not	
We / You / They	are not	students.

Subject	Verb	
I / You	study	
He / She	studies	every day.
We / You / They	study	

Subject	*do + not* + Verb	
I / You	don't study	
He / She	doesn't study	every day.
We / You / They	don't study	

Present Continuous

We often use the present continuous with *now* or *right now.*

Affirmative and Negative Statements

Subject	*be* + (*not*) + verb*ing*	
I	am (not) using	
You	are (not) using	a computer.
He / She	is (not) using	
We / You / They	are (not) using	

Contractions with *be*

Affirmative	Negative
I'm	I'm not
You're	You're not / You aren't
They're	They're not / They aren't
He's	He's not / He isn't
She's	She's not / She isn't
We're	We're not / We aren't

Spelling rules for simple present:

1. Add *-s* to the base form of a verb (for *He, She, It*): start → start**s**, walk → walk**s**
2. For verbs ending in consonant + *-y*, change *-y* to *-i* and add *-es*: study → stud**ies**, carry → carr**ies**
3. For verbs ending in vowel + *-y*, add *-s*: buy → buy**s**, pay → pay**s**
4. For verbs ending in *-s*, *-z*, *-ch*, *-sh*, and *-x*, add *-es*: relax → relax**es**, watch → watch**es**

Spelling rules for present continuous:

1. Add *-ing* to most verbs: study → studying, mail → mailing, play → playing
2. Words with *consonant + -e*, drop *-e* and add *-ing*: take → taking, use → using
3. Words with *vowel + one consonant*, double the consonant and add *–ing*: run → running, stop → stopping

Simple Past Review

Remember to use the simple past to talk about actions in the past.

Affirmative Statements

Subject	Verb	
I / You / He / She	attended	class.
We / You / They		

Negative Statements

Subject	Verb	
I / You / He / She	didn't attend	class.
We / You / They		

Questions

	Subject	Verb	
Did	I / you / he / she	attend	class?
	we / you / they		

Short Answers

	Subject	Verb
Yes,	I / you / he / she	did.
No,	we / you / they	didn't.

Future with *be going to*

Use *be going to* + verb for future planned actions.

Affirmative Statements

Subject	*be*	*going to* + Verb
I	am	going to study.
You	are	
He / She	is	
We / You / They	are	

Negative Statements

Subject	*be*	*going to* + Verb
I	am not	going to study.
You	aren't	
He / She	isn't	
We / You / They	aren't	

Questions

be	Subject	*going to* + Verb
Are	you	going to study?
Is	he / she	

Short Answers

	Subject	Verb
Yes,	I	am.
No,	he / she	isn't.

Spelling Rules for adding *ing*

Rules	Examples
Verbs Ending in Silent -e If the verb ends in a silent -e, drop the final -e and add -ing.	shake → shaking
One-Syllable Verbs Ending in *C-V-C* In one-syllable verbs that end in a consonant-vowel-consonant pattern, double the final consonant and add -ing. Don't double the consonants -w, -x, or -y.	stop stopping fix → fixing
Two- or More-Syllable Adjectives For two- or more-syllable adjectives that end in C-V-C, double the final consonant only if the last syllable is stressed.	permit → permitting
Verbs Ending in -ie For verbs ending in -ie, change the -ie to y and add -ing	die → dying

Comparisons with Adjectives

> Two-syllable adjectives that end in –y follow the rules for short adjectives.
> heavy → heavier

Use comparative adjectives to compare two things. Short adjectives have just one syllable (*large, small*). Long adjectives have two or more syllables (*re-li-a-ble*).

Subject + *be*	Comparative (Short Adjectives)	
The Buzz mixer is	cheaper than	the Wizz food mixer.
cheap → cheaper, heavy → heavier, big → bigger		

Subject + *be*	Comparative (Long Adjectives)	
The Espressomix coffeemaker is	more complicated than	the Quick Cup coffeemaker.
The Quick Cup coffeemaker is	less complicated than	the Espressomix coffeemaker.
complicated → more complicated / less complicated (*less* is the opposite of *more*)		

Use *as…as* to say things are the same or equal.
The Espressomix coffee is *as good as* the Quick Cup coffee. (Both items are equal, or the same.)

Use *not as…as* to say things are not the same or equal.
The Colby microwave *isn't as powerful as* the Deluxe microwave. (The first item is less powerful than the second.)

Rules	Examples
1. Add *-er* or *-r* to most **one-syllable adjectives**.	old**er** large**r**
2. For most **one-syllable adjectives ending in consonant + vowel + consonant**, double the consonant and add *-er*. Do not double *w*.	big**ger** new**er**
3. For **two-syllable adjectives ending in *y***, change the *y* to *i* and add *-er*.	sunn**y** → sunn**ier** nois**y** → nois**ier**
4. For **adjectives with two or more syllables that do *not* end in *y***, use the word *more*.	**more** relaxed **more** stressful
5. Some comparative adjectives are **irregular**. See page xx for a list of irregular adjectives.	good → **better** bad → **worse**

Questions with Comparatives

Question	1st Choice	2nd Choice
Which are better,	regular toothbrushes	or electric toothbrushes?
Which is more expensive,	a CD player	or an MP3 player?

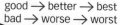

Remember:
Some adjectives are irregular in the comparative and superlative.
good → better → best
bad → worse → worst

Superlative Adjectives

Use superlative adjectives to compare one thing to two or more things in the same set or group.

Subject + *be*	Superlative with Short Adjectives (Use *the* + adjective+*est*)
The white sweatshirt is	the cheapest.

large → largest, heavy → heaviest, big → biggest

Subject + *be*	Superlative with Long Adjectives (Use *the* + *most / least* + adjective)
The black boots are	the most / least practical.

least expensive = cheapest (*least* is the opposite of *most*)

Questions and Answers

Often you can use *one* or *ones* instead of the noun in the answer. *One* or *ones* points to the noun in the question. This is more natural in conversation than repeating the noun.

Which **sweatshirt** is the cheapest? ↑ The white **one**.	Which **boots** are the most practical? ↑ The black **ones**.

Rules	Examples
Add *-est* or *-st* to most **one-syllable adjectives**.	the old**est** the safe**st**
For **one-syllable adjectives ending in consonant + vowel + consonant**, double the consonant and add *-est*.	the big**gest** the thin**nest**
For **two-syllable adjectives ending in -y**, change the *-y* to *i* and add *-est*.	busy → bus**iest** noisy → nois**iest**
For adjectives with **two or more syllables that do *not* end in -y**, use the words *the most*.	**the most** expensive **the most** dangerous
Some adjectives have **irregular** superlative forms.	good → **the best** bad → **the worst**

> We don't usually use some verbs, such as *be* and *have*, in the past continuous.

Past Continuous

The past continuous describes an ongoing action during a period of time in the **past**.

Affirmative and Negative Statements

Subject	Past of *be* + (*not*)	Verb +*ing*
I / He / She	was / wasn't	speeding.
We / You / They	were / weren't	speeding.

Affirmative and Negative Statements with *when* Clause

When introduces a second action. The second action interrupted the ongoing action. Use the simple past with the *when* clause. Use the past continuous for the ongoing action.

Past Continuous Clause			Simple Past Clause with *when*
Subject	Past of *be* + (*not*)	Verb +*ing*	*when* + Subject + Simple Past
I / He / She	was / wasn't	speeding	*when* the police officer *stopped* me / him / her.
We / You / They	were / weren't		*when* the police officer *stopped* us / you / them.

Use a comma after the clause beginning with *when* if it comes at the beginning of the sentence.

Simple Past Clause with *when*	Past Continuous Clause
When the police officer *stopped* me,	I was speeding.

Wh- Questions with Past Continuous

Use the past continuous to ask and tell about ongoing actions in progress at a specific time in the past.

Question

Wh- word	Past of *be*	Subject	Verb +*ing*	Time Phrase
What	was	he	doing	at 9:00 last night?

Answer

Subject	Past Continuous
He	was studying.

Past Continuous with *while* Clause

While means "during the time." *While* introduces the continuous action. Use the past continuous after *while*.

Simple Past Clause		Past Continuous Clause with *while*		
Subject	Simple past	*while*	Subject	Past continuous
She	cut her hand	*while*	she	was unpacking boxes.
He	burned his arm	*while*	he	was cooking dinner.

Use a comma after the clause beginning with *while* if it comes at the beginning of the sentence.

Past Continuous clause with *while*			Simple Past Clause	
While	Subject	Past Continuous	Subject	Simple Past
While	she	was unpacking boxes,	she	cut her hand.
While	he	was cooking dinner,	he	burned his arm.

May and *Can* for What is Allowed

Use *may* to say an action is okay or allowed. Use *may not* to say that an action is not allowed. It is common to use *may* and *may not* in formal writing or in listing rules. *May* and *may not* are less common in informal conversation. Use the base form of the verb after *may* and *can*.

Subject	*may (not)*	Base Verb
Employees / You / They	may may not	exchange shifts.

Use *can* to say that an action is allowed. Use *cannot* to say that an action is not allowed. *Can* is more common in informal conversation than in formal writing or listing rules.

Subject	*can (not)*	Base Verb
I / You / He / She	can can't	exchange shifts.
We / You / They		

Must and *Have to* for Requirements

Must and *have to* are similar. *Must* is stronger, and is more common in writing than in conversation.

Subject	*must / have to*	Base Verb
Residents	must / have to	park in assigned spaces.
Employees		wear safety glasses.

Must not and *May not* for Prohibition

Must not means that a person is prohibited from doing something. It is stronger than *can't* and *may not*.

Subject	*must not / may not*	Base Verb
Residents		run in the hallways.
Employees	must not / may not	use company cars on weekends.
Students		talk during the test.

Don't have to for Requirements

Don't have to means *don't need to*.

Subject	*don't / doesn't*	*have to*	Base Verb
I / You / We / They	don't	have to	wear a suit to work.
He / She	doesn't		

Modals of Possibility and Certainty

Use *must* to show that something is almost certain. Use *may, might,* and *could* to show that something is possible. The base form of a verb follows a modal.

Subject	Modal		Base Verb + Noun or Adjective
I / You / He / She We / You / They	must	certain	have pink eye. feel itchy.
	may could/might	↓ less certain	have bronchitis. need antibiotics. be infected.

Used to for Past Habits or Situations

Use *used to* to talk about past habits or situations that were different in the past than they are now.

Subject	*used to*	Base Verb		Subject	*did not + use to*	Base Verb
I / You / He / She	used to	take the elevator.		I / You / He / She	didn't use to	take the stairs.
We / You / They		buy frozen dinners.		We / You / They		buy fresh food.

Infinitives

An infinitive is *to* + the base form of the verb.

Subject	Verb	Infinitive
I / You	need / don't need	
He / She	intends / doesn't intend	to exercise.
We / You / They	want / don't want	

Infinitives often follow these verbs.

intend	plan
like	want
need	would like

Infinitives of purpose give a reason why.

Action	Infinitive of Purpose	
I'm going to the library	to return	some books.

Some verbs that are often followed by an infinitive (*to* + base form of verb)

afford	can't stand*	hate*	need	promise	stop*
agree	choose	learn	offer	refuse	suggest*
arrange	continue*	like*	pay	remember*	want
ask	decide	love*	prefer*	request	would like
begin*	expect				

These verbs can also be followed by gerunds.

Gerunds as Objects

A gerund is a noun. A gerund looks like the *-ing* form of a verb, but it takes the place of a noun in a sentence. Gerunds are always singular.

Affirmative

Subject	Verb	Gerund
I / You	like	hiking.
He / She	hates	

Negative

Subject	Verb	Gerund
I / You	don't like	hiking.
He / She	doesn't hate	

Questions

Do	Subject	Verb	Gerund
Do	you	enjoy	hiking?
Does	he / she		

Answers

Affirmative	Negative
Yes, I do.	No, I don't.
Yes, he / she does.	No, he / she doesn't.

A gerund often follows these verbs: *dislike, enjoy,* and *finish.*

An infinitive *or* a gerund can follow these verbs: *like, can't stand, love, hate,* and *prefer.*

Remember:
Count nouns have plurals.
3 cat**s**, 4 **people**
Non-count nouns don't have plurals.
pollution, housing

Count and Non-count Nouns with *too many, too much,* and *(not) enough*

Use *too* to say there is more than a good or normal amount. Use *enough* to say you have as much as you need, and *not enough* to say you don't have as much as you need.

Statements with *too many* and *too much*

Use *too many* before a count noun and *too much* before a non-count noun.

	Quantifier	Count Noun
There are	too many	old cars.
		people.

	Quantifier	Non-count Noun
There is	too much	crime.
		pollution.

Statements with *(not) enough*

Use *enough* or *not enough* before both count and non-count nouns.

	Quantifier	Count Noun
There are (not)	enough	trees.
		sidewalks.

	Quantifier	Non-count Noun
There is (not)	enough	housing.
		space.

Questions with Count Nouns

	Quantifier	Count Noun
Are there	too many	cars?
	enough	trees?

Questions with Non-count Nouns

	Quantifier	Non-count Noun
Is there	too much	pollution?
	enough	housing?

Too and (not) enough with Adjectives

Too comes <u>before</u> an adjective: *too* + adjective. *Enough* comes <u>after</u> an adjective: (*not*) + adjective + *enough*.

Statements with *too*

Subject	*be*	*too* + Adjective
The neighborhood	is (not)	too crowded.
The roads	are (not)	too busy.

Statements with (*not*) enough

Subject	*be*	Adjective + *enough*
The river	is (not)	clean enough.
The sidewalks	are (not)	wide enough.

Gerunds as Subjects

A gerund can be the object or the subject of a verb. When the gerund is the subject, always use the third person singular form of the verb.

Gerund as Subject

Subject	Verb	Adjective
Recycling	is	good.
Exercising		healthy.

Gerund as Object

Subject	Verb	Object
I	like	recycling.
We		exercising.

A gerund can also have its own object.

Subject		
Gerund	Object of Gerund	Verb + Object
Recycling	plastic	reduces trash.

Some verbs that are often followed by a gerund (base form of verb + *ing*)

admit	consider	explain	love*	practice	regret
appreciate	continue*	finish	mind	prefer*	remember*
avoid	delay	hate*	miss	prevent	report
begin*	dislike	keep	permit	prohibit	stop*
can't stand*	enjoy	like*	postpone	quit	suggest*

*These verbs can also be followed by infinitives.

Negative Gerunds

To form the negative of a gerund, add *not* before the gerund.

Negative Gerund	Object of the Gerund	Verb + Object
Not using	your dishwasher every day	saves energy.

Many verbs are irregular. You'll learn some irregular past participles in Lesson 2.

Present Perfect with *yet* and *already*

Use the present perfect to talk about completed past actions when the exact time of the action is either not important or not known.

Statements with *already*

Use the present perfect with *already* to talk about actions that have happened before now.

Subject	*have*	*already*	Past Participle	
I / You	have			
He / She	has	already	registered	for the class.
We / You / They	have			

Contractions

I have = I've
You have = You've
He has = He's
She has = She's
We have = We've
They have = They've

Statements with *yet*

Use the present perfect with *yet* in negative statements to say that something is still expected to happen.

Subject	*have + not*	Past Participle		*yet*
I / You	haven't			
He / She	hasn't	registered	for the class	yet.
We / You / They	haven't			

Questions and Answers

Use *yet* in questions. We don't usually use *already* in questions.

Have	Subject	Past Participle	*yet*
Have	you		
Has	he / she	registered	yet?

Yes / No	Subject	*have (not)*
Yes,	I	have.
No,	he / she	hasn't.

Present Perfect: *Have you ever...?*

We use *ever* with the present perfect to ask whether someone experienced something at any point up to the present time.

Have	Subject	*ever*	Past Participle	
Have	you			
Has	he/she	ever	taken	the bus?

Affirmative	Negative
Yes, I have.	No, I haven't.
Yes, he/she has.	No, he/she hasn't.

Present Perfect with *for* or *since*

Use the present perfect with *for* or *since* to describe situations or states that started in the past and continue to the present (and may continue into the future).

- Use *for* with a length of time (*one month, three hours, a long time, two weeks*).
- Use *since* with a specific past time (*yesterday, last week, 2:30, my birthday*).

Statements

Subject	*have*	Past Participle		*for/since* + time
I / You	have		retired	*for* six months.
He / She	has	been		
We / You / They	have		out of work	*since* last year.

Questions with *How long...?*

Use *How long* and the present perfect to ask about the length of time.

How long	*have*	Subject	Past Participle		Short Answers
	have	I / you		retired?	*For* six months.
How long	has	he / she	been		
	have	we / you / they		out of work?	*Since* last year.

How long... Questions with the Present Perfect

Present Perfect with *be* + Noun

How long	*have*	Subject	*be*	Noun	Short Answer
How long	have	you	been	a volunteer?	For five years.
	has	he		a diabetic?	

Present Perfect with Verbs other than *be*

How long	*have*	Subject	Past Participle		Short Answer
How long	have	you	lived	in Miami?	Since last year.
	has	she	had	diabetes?	

Present Perfect Continuous

Use the present perfect continuous to talk about actions or states that started in the past, continue into the present, and may continue in the future.

Affirmative and Negative Statements

Subject	have (not)	been	Verb + ing
I / You / We / They	have (not)	been	weeding.
He / She	has (not)		

You can use contractions with *have* and *has*.

She has been weeding. → She's been weeding.

They have been weeding. → They've been weeding.

Yes/No Questions

Have	Subject	been	Verb + ing
Have	I / you / we / they		
Has	he / she	been	weeding?
Have	we / you / they		

Short Answers

Affirmative	Negative
Yes, I / you have.	No, I / you haven't.
Yes, he / she has.	No, he / she hasn't.
Yes, we / you / they have.	No, we / you / they haven't.

Wh- Questions

Wh- Question Word	have	Subject	been	Verb + ing
What	have	I / you / we / they	been	doing?
Where	has	he / she		working?

Present Perfect Continuous for Repeated Actions in the Recent Past

Use the present perfect continuous to tell about actions repeated over a period of time up to the present. We often use an adverb, such as *recently* or *lately*, to tell what we've been doing in the recent past.

Subject	Present Perfect Continuous	Object	Adverb
I / You	have been playing	soccer	recently.
He / She	hasn't been baking	cakes	lately.
We / You / They	have been taking	a cooking class	recently.

Present Perfect Continuous with *How long...*, *for*, and *since*

Use the present perfect continuous with *for* or *since* to talk about how long something has been happening. Use it to focus on the *ongoing* situation.

Questions with *How long...*

How long	*have*	Subject	*been*	Verb+*ing*	Object
How long	have	I / you	been	designing	homes?
	has	he / she			
	have	we / you / they			

Answers and Statements with *for* and *since*

Subject	*have*	*been*	Verb+*ing*	Object	*for... / since...*
I / You	have	been	designing	homes	for ten years. / since 1998.
He / She	has				
We / You / They	have				

Present Perfect or Present Perfect Continuous?

We often use the **present perfect** to talk about quantity, or the number of times an action has happened. (She **has written** three books. I **have sent** five e-mails today.)

We use the **present continuous** to talk about continuing actions. We don't use it to talk about quantity or number of times an action has happened.

Present Real Conditional

Sentences with *if* have two clauses. The *if* clause gives a possible situation or condition. Use the simple present. The main clause can tell you what usually happens or what you should usually do in this situation.

Statements

If Clause		Main Clause	
If + Subject	Verb +	Subject	Verb Phrase
If the paper	gets stuck,	—	turn off the power. (imperative)
		you	turn off the power. (simple present)
		you	should turn off the power. (modal)

The *if*-clause can also be the last clause of the sentence. Do not use a comma in this case.

Main clause	*if* Clause
Turn off the power	if the paper gets stuck.

Wh- Questions

Wh- question word	Auxiliary	Subject	Verb	*if* + Simple Present
What	do	I	do	if the paper gets stuck?

Future Real Conditional

Use *if* + simple present and a main clause with *will* to talk about things that are probable in the future under a certain condition.

Statements

If Clause	Main Clause
If + Subject + Simple Present	Subject + Future
If I don't keep fit,	I will gain weight.

We can also put the *if* clause in the second part of the sentence. There is no comma when the *if* clause comes second.

Main Clause	*if* Clause
I won't gain weight	if I keep fit.

Wh- Questions

If Clause	*wh-* Question
If you lose your job,	what will you do?

Wh- Question	*if* Clause
What will you do	if you lose your job?

Separable Phrasal Verbs

Phrasal verbs are two-word verbs. They have a verb and a particle (a small word such as *on, in, off, out, over, out, into*). A particle changes the meaning of a verb.

Common Phrasal Verbs

drop off	figure out	pick out	put on	turn in	turn on
fill out	look over	pick up	take off	turn off	wake up

Some phrasal verbs are separable. This means an object can come after the phrasal verb or between the verb and the particle.

Subject	Phrasal Verb (Verb + Particle)	Object
He	filled out	the form.

Subject	Verb	Object	Particle
He	filled	the form / it	out.

When the object is a pronoun, it *must* go *between* the verb and particle.

I dropped off **the security deposit.**

Incorrect ✗:
I dropped off **it** this morning.
Correct ✓:
I dropped **it** off this morning.

Inseparable Phrasal Verbs

Some phrasal verbs are *inseparable*. This means the object always comes after the particle. It never comes between the verb and the particle.

Common Inseparable Phrasal Verbs

come over	get on	run into
get off	get up	grow up

Subject	Phrasal Verb	Object
I	ran into	my old teacher.
He	got off	the bus.

Reported speech: *asked... to... /told... to...*

Use reported speech to tell what someone asked or told another person to do. Asking someone to do something is more polite than telling. *Asking* is a request. *Telling* someone to do something is a command.

Statements

Subject	Simple Past Verb	Object	Reported Information
She	asked	you / him / her	(not) to remove a light fixture.
I	told	him	(not) to replace the showerhead.

Who questions

Who	Simple Past Verb	Object	Reported Information
Who	asked	them	(not) to remove the light fixture?
	told	you	(not) to replace the showerhead?

Past Time Clauses with *after, when, as soon as,* and *before*

Use *after, when, as soon as,* or *before* to tell when something happened in relation to something else. These words can connect two clauses and make a sentence.

After, when, and *as soon as* introduce an event that happened before another event. When you use *as soon as* or *when*, the second event is often very soon after the first event.

Time Clause (1st event)	Main Clause (2nd event)
After they had a baby,	they didn't go out anymore.
When I got a promotion,	I got my own office.
As soon as she got her license,	she bought a car.

Use *before* to introduce an event that happened <u>after</u> another event.

Time Clause (2nd event)	Main Clause (1st event)
Before I got my driver's license,	I went to work by bus.

It is also possible to put the main clause first.

Main Clause	Time Clause
They didn't go out anymore	*after* they had a baby.

We use the words *just* and *right* with *before* and *after* to mean that two events happen at almost the same time.

I got a job right after I graduated. (I didn't have to wait a long time.)

Just before I got home, Bob called. (I missed his call. I came home a short time later.)

Wh- Questions

What did she do	*before* she got the job?
How did you feel	*when* you got promoted?

Future Time Clauses with *after, when, as soon as, before,* and *not...until*

You can use *after, when, as soon as,* and *before* in time clauses to talk about the future. The time clause has a future meaning, but the verb is in the simple present form.

Main clause	Time clause
We're going to relocate	*as soon as* we sell our home.
I'll make a down payment on a home	*after* I save enough money.
She's going to consult an advisor	*before* she registers for class.

Don't forget to use a comma if the time clause comes first.

Time clause	Main clause
As soon as I save enough money,	I'll make a down payment.

Question forms

Will she go back to work	*when* her kids grow up?
Will she consult a career advisor	*before* she registers for class?

Not...until tells what you will do after, when, or as soon as something else happens, but <u>not</u> before. *Not* is used in the main clause and *until* begins the time clause.

We're **not** going to relocate to California **until** we retire.
(We're going to relocate to California *after* we retire.)

I **will not** make a down payment **until** I save enough money.
(I'll make a down payment *as soon as* I save enough money.)

Be Careful!
Do not use the future form of verbs in time clauses.

Incorrect ✗:
When I ~~will~~ get my diploma, I'll get a raise.

Correct ✔:
When I get my diploma, I'll get a raise.

Gerunds with *before* and *after*

A gerund can follow *before* or *after* if the subject of the main clause and the time clause are the same.

In these examples, *he* is the subject of both the main clause and the time clause. When this is the case, the subject (*he*) + verb (*moved*) can become a gerund (*moving*).

Main Clause	Time Clause
He lived in a small town	before **moving** to the city. (before *he* **moved** to the city.)

Wh- Question	Time Clause
What did *he* do	after **getting** engaged?) (after *he* **got** engaged?)

Irregular Verbs

Base Form	Simple Past	Past Participle	Base Form	Simple Past	Past Participle
be	was/were	been	keep	kept	kept
become	became	become	know	knew	known
begin	began	begun	leave	left	left
bleed	bled	bled	lend	lent	lent
break	broke	broken	lose	lost	lost
bring	brought	brought	make	made	made
buy	bought	bought	meet	met	met
choose	chose	chosen	pay	paid	paid
come	came	come	put	put	put
cost	cost	cost	read	read	read
cut	cut	cut	ring	rang	rung
do	did	done	run	ran	run
drink	drank	drunk	see	saw	seen
drive	drove	driven	sell	sold	sold
eat	ate	eaten	send	sent	sent
fall	fell	fallen	set	set	set
feel	felt	felt	shake	shook	shaken
fight	fought	fought	shut	shut	shut
find	found	found	sleep	slept	slept
forget	forgot	forgotten	speak	spoke	spoken
fry	fried	fried	speed	sped	sped
get	got	gotten	spend	spent	spent
give	gave	given	take	took	taken
go	went	gone	teach	taught	taught
grow	grew	grown	tell	told	told
have/has	had	had	think	thought	thought
hear	heard	heard	wear	wore	worn
hold	held	held	write	wrote	written
hurt	hurt	hurt			

Audio Script

Unit 1

LESSON 2 Grammar Practice Plus Activity 1 (Page 8)

A. Nancy is talking about an assignment with a tutor.
B. Ben is meeting with his study group. They are studying for a test next week.
C. Pam is listening to a CD. She's sitting in a chair near the magazines.
D. Denise is studying the information in her textbook. She's highlighting important information with a yellow highlighter.
E. Andy is writing notes on index cards. He uses the cards to study.
F. Nick is drawing illustrations of new words. The pictures help him remember the words.
G. Kevin is sitting working on his computer. He is typing his notes.
H. Kate is using a computer. She's using a CD-ROM to practice grammar.

LESSON 3 Listening and Conversation Activity 1 (Page 10)

1. What is the teacher going to talk about?
   A: Welcome to Intermediate ESL. My name's Mr. Smith, and I'm your instructor. I'd like to give you some advice that will help you succeed in this course.

   What is the teacher going to talk about?
   A. He's going to talk about his name.
   B. He's going to talk about being an instructor.
   C. He's going to talk about how students can succeed.

2. What should you do if you are absent?
   A: First, try to come to every class and participate. Of course, you might have to miss a class sometime. If you do, please call the school to say you will be absent.

   What should you do if you are absent?
   A. Participate in class.
   B. Call the instructor.
   C. Call the school.

3. Who can the students call about homework?
   A: Second, it's important that you do all your class and homework assignments. Third, get to know your classmates. Call them about the homework if you miss a class. Meet with them to study for tests.

   Who can the students call about homework?
   A. the teacher
   B. their classmates
   C. study for tests

4. When will students tour the computer lab?
   A: Another suggestion is that you use the computer lab. We will take a tour of the lab next week. The librarians can help you with resources. Finally, develop good study skills. Schedule time to study every day.

   When will students tour the computer lab?
   A. at the library
   B. to develop study skills
   C. next week

Activity 2 (Page 10)

Welcome to Intermediate ESL. My name's Mr. Smith, and I'm your instructor. I'd like to give you some advice that will help you succeed in this course. First, try come to every class and participate. Of course, you might have to miss a class sometime. If you do, please call the school to say you will be absent. Second, it's important that you do all your class and homework assignments. Third, get to know your classmates. Call them about the homework if you miss a class. Meet with them to study for tests. Another suggestion is that you use the computer lab. We will take a tour of the lab next week. The librarians can help you with resources. Finally, develop good study skills. Schedule time to study every day.

Activity 4 & 5 (Page 15)

A: Hi, Jim. Have a seat.
B: Thank you.
A: You passed your class last term, but you didn't do very well. You were absent a lot, and you didn't complete all of your assignments. Did you have to miss class because of work?
B: No . . . I didn't always understand, so I couldn't do some assignments. That was my biggest problem.
A: Well, that's a *really* big problem. Did you get any kind of help or support?
B: No.
A: Well, that's why you had problems.
B: Because I didn't get support?
A: Yes. You're smart. I know you have the ability to do better. You just need to ask for help from the people who can help you! To start, you can ask your instructors for help. You can always make appointments during their office hours. And there are lab assistants in the computer lab to help. Also, writing tutors work in the writing lab.
B: I didn't know that. Or maybe I forgot.
A: What about your classmates? Or your family? Can they help you?
B: Maybe.
A: Well, *ask* them, okay?
B: Okay.
A: Okay. So tell me what you plan to do.
B: Well, I'm going to ask my instructor for help when I need it.
A: That's a good start. What else?
B: I'm going to study in the computer lab and maybe get a tutor. But first, I'm going to ask my wife for help. And I'm going to complete all my assignments.
A: That sounds great. It's important to complete your assignments and to make studying a priority. And I hope you're not going to miss class.
B: No, I'm going to attend every class, and I'm not going to forget my homework.
A: And what about *in* class? I heard you had some problems working with other students.
B: I know. That's true. But this term I'm going to be friendlier.
A: Great! A good attitude can go a long way!

Unit 2

LESSON 2 Grammar Practice Plus Activity 1 (Page 24)

a. This yellow sofa looks comfortable, but it isn't as comfortable as the white one.
b. Hmm . . . this black hairdryer is smaller and lighter. It's very easy to carry. It's more convenient than the red one because it's so easy to carry. I can take it anywhere.
c. A: This brown vacuum cleaner isn't as heavy as the red one.
   B: Yes, but I think it's also less powerful.
d. Look at this flat-screen TV. This silver color is more modern and it has a better picture. But is it as reliable as a smaller TV set?

LESSON 3 Listening and Conversation Activity 1 (Page 26)

1. Which word describes the furniture store?
   A: Is your sofa looking tired and old? Time to buy something more comfortable? Come visit us at Friendly Furniture showrooms—we're friendlier than other furniture stores.

   Which word describes the furniture store?
   A. friendlier
   B. tired
   C. old

2. Which word describes the burgers?
   A: Come to Alfredo's Burger Bar for the best hamburgers in town. We aren't as famous as some other hamburger restaurants, but we're just as good. In fact, people say that our burgers are tastier than any other burgers in town. Try one of our burgers, and you'll come back for more!

   Which word describes the burgers?
   A. more disappointed
   B. more famous
   C. tastier

3. Which word describes the windows?
   A: Save time and money with Window Lite, our new window installation service. Save money on your fuel bills. Window Lite windows are just as safe as regular windows, but they're easier to install, and they're less expensive. Satisfaction guaranteed or your money back.

   Which word describes the windows?
   A. more expensive
   B. less expensive
   C. safer

Activity 2 (Page 26)

1. What does the man want to buy?
   A: Excuse me. How much are these vacuum cleaners?
   B: The Dustfree vacuum cleaner is $39.50, and the Kleanvac is $49.99.

   What does the man want to buy?
   A. a microwave
   B. a computer
   C. a vacuum cleaner

2. Which vacuum cleaner is more powerful?
   A: Which one is better?
   B: They're both good. The Dustfree isn't as heavy as the Kleanvac and it's less expensive, but it's also less powerful.
   A: What about the Kleanvac?
   B: It's more powerful, but it's also more expensive.

   Which vacuum cleaner is more powerful?
   A. the Kleanvac
   B. the Dustfree
   C. They're both powerful.

3. Which vacuum cleaner does the man buy?
   A: Does the warranty cover parts and labor?
   B: The Dustfree warranty covers parts only. The Kleanvac warranty covers parts and labor but only for one year.
   A: I think I'll get the Dustfree.

   Which vacuum cleaner does the man buy?
   A. the Kleanvac
   B. the Dustfree
   C. the warranty

Activity 3 (Page 26)

A: Excuse me. How much are these vacuum cleaners?
B: The Dustfree vacuum cleaner is $39.50, and the Kleanvac is $49.99.
A: I see. Which one is better?
B: They're both good. The Dustfree isn't as heavy as the Kleanvac and it's less expensive, but it's also less powerful.
A: What about the Kleanvac?
B: It's more powerful, but it's also more expensive.
A: Does the Dustfree have a warranty?
B: Yes, they both have a warranty included in the price.
A: Does the warranty cover parts and labor?
B: The Dustfree warranty covers parts only. The Kleanvac warranty covers parts and labor but only for one year.
A: I think I'll get the Dustfree.

LESSON 5 Grammar Practice Plus Activity 2 (Page 30)

A: I always use Everclean laundry detergent. It's not the cheapest, but I think it has the nicest smell. My laundry comes out clean, but the most important thing is that it smells great.
B: I usually buy what's on sale. . . . I just buy the least expensive one like Brite Lite. But I hate cleaning windows!
C: I love tomato sauce and it always gets on my clothes. I buy Stainaway because it cleans even the toughest stains. It's the best one for tomato stains anyway.
D: I love Spa Bath Oil because it has the most colorful bottle. Purple and pink are my favorite colors! And it matches my bathroom.

LESSON 7 Writing Activity 2 (Page 34)

A: Keepcool Air Conditioner Company. Can I help you?
B: Yes, I have a complaint about my air conditioner. I only bought it three weeks ago. It's smaller and quieter than my old air conditioner, but now there's a problem. It just isn't working.
A: Do you have a warranty?
B: Yes, I do.
A: Okay, we'll send out a repair person to take a look at it, but first you need to send us a copy of your receipt and a copy of the warranty information.
B: Okay.
A: Good. Now what is your name and address?
B: My name is Rachel Gomez.

Unit 3

LESSON 3 Listening and Conversation Activity 1
(Page 42)

1. What does the officer ask to see?
   A: Hello. Are you hurt? Do you need to go to the hospital?
   B: Thank you, officer. I'm not hurt.
   A: May I please see your license?
   B: Of course. Here you are.

   What does the officer ask to see?
   A. the man's car
   B. the man's license
   C. two different I.D. cards

2. What did the man hit?
   A: Please tell me what happened.
   B: Well, a cat ran in front of the car, and I tried not to hit it. I hit this tree.
   A: How fast were you driving?

   What did the man hit?
   A. a cat
   B. the front of a car
   C. a tree

3. How fast was the man driving?
   B: I was driving about 35 miles per hour.
   A: The speed limit here is 25 miles per hour. It's a school zone.
   B: I didn't know that. I'm sorry.

   How fast was the man driving?
   A. 25 miles per hour
   B. 35 miles per hour
   C. slowly

4. What does the officer tell the man to do?
   A: It's important not to go over the speed limit in a school zone. There are many children who have to cross the street or get on and off of school buses.
   B: I'll be more careful in the future.
   A: All right. I'm not going to give you a ticket. I didn't really see you while you were speeding. But please drive safely.
   B: Yes, officer. Thank you.

What does the officer tell the man to do?
A. take the bus to work
B. buy a ticket
C. drive safely

Activity 2 (Page 42)
A: Hello. Are you hurt? Do you need to go to the hospital?
B: Thank you, officer. I'm not hurt.
A: May I please see your license?
B: Of course. Here you are.
A: Please tell me what happened.
B: Well, a cat ran in front of the car, and I tried not to hit it. I hit this tree.
A: How fast were you driving?
B: I was driving about 35 miles per hour.
A: The speed limit here is 25 miles per hour. It's a school zone.
B: I didn't know that. I'm sorry.
A: It's important not to go over the speed limit in a school zone. There are many children who have to cross the street or get on and off of school buses.
B: I'll be more careful in the future.
A: All right. I'm not going to give you a ticket. I didn't really see you while you were speeding. But please drive safely.
B: Yes, officer. Thank you.

LESSON 7 Writing Activity 2A (Page 50)
A: Cindy, I'm writing my accident report summary, and I'd like to ask you some questions about Jim's accident.
B: Sure, Mr. Miller.
A: You were with Jim, right? What happened? I understand that he broke his leg.
B: That's right. His left leg.
A: And where did the accident happen?
B: It happened outside, on the steps in front of the building.
A: How did it happen? Did you actually see the accident?
B: Yes. I was talking to him when he fell. There was snow and ice on the steps, and he slipped on the ice while he was climbing them.
A: I see. And when did this happen?
B: It happened on Wednesday afternoon.
A: Wednesday, January 18th. . .
B: Yes. . .
A: About what time?
B: Around 1:30. While we were coming back from lunch.
A: Thank you, Cindy. And I'll be sure to have snow and ice removed in the future, but be careful on those steps!

Unit 4

LESSON 3 Listening and Conversation Activity 1 (Page 58)
1. A: Hey, Julia. Did you read about the summer dress code?
   B: Huh? You mean the dress code changes in the summer?
   A:
   A. No, I didn't mean it.
   B. Yes, it changes for June, July, and August.
   C. I like summer dresses.
2. B: Can we wear open-toe shoes?
   A: Yes. Women can wear open-toe shoes and sandals. But we can't wear flip-flops.
   B:
   A. What about sneakers? Can we wear them?
   B. I will wear my flip-flops tomorrow.
   C. But my flip-flops are old.
3. B: Where can I get information about the summer dress code?
   A: It's in the employee handbook. It's also on the bulletin board in the kitchen.
   B:
   A. I want a new dress.
   B. I need to get a handbook. I don't have one.
   C. It's too cold in summer.

4. A: But some new rules aren't in the handbook.
   B: Like what?
   A:
   A. The rules are in the handbook.
   B. For example, I go swimming in summer.
   C. For example, employees can't smoke in front of the building.

Activity 2 (Page 58)
A: Hey, Julia. Did you read about the summer dress code?
B: Huh? You mean the dress code changes in the summer?
A: Yes, it changes for June, July, and August.
B: Can we wear open-toe shoes?
A: Yes. Women can wear open-toe shoes and sandals. But we can't wear flip-flops.
B: What about sneakers? Can we wear them?
A: I don't remember.
B: Where can I get information about the summer dress code?
A: It's in the employee handbook. It's also on the bulletin board in the kitchen.
B: I need to get a handbook. I don't have one.
A: Yeah. That's a good idea. But some new rules aren't in the handbook.
B: Like what?
A: For example, employees can't smoke in front of the building. We can only smoke in the smoking area.
B: That's OK. I don't smoke.
A: Oh, and now employees can't exchange shifts.
B: Not ever?
A: We can only exchange shifts in emergencies or for doctors' appointments.
B: I didn't know that.
A: Well, the new rules are on the bulletin board. I saw them there for the first time last week.

Pronunciation Activity A & B (Page 58)
1. We can make personal calls.
2. We can't send personal e-mails during break.
3. Can't they wear jeans to work?
4. They can wear flip-flops to work.
5. Can employees wear headphones at work?
6. We can't make personal phone calls at work.

Unit 5

LESSON 2 Grammar Practice Plus Activity 2 (Page 72)
1. A: I feel so tired every day.
   B: I see. You might need more iron in your diet. We sometimes advise pregnant women to take an extra vitamin: an iron supplement. But let's get you a blood test to make sure.
   A: Thank you.
2. A: His throat really hurts. It may be infected.
   B: Does he have a fever?
   A: No, not really.
   B: Okay, let's take a look. Open your mouth wide and say ah!
   C: Ah!
   B: Well, it definitely looks sore.
   A: Is it serious?
3. A: The x-ray shows your rib is not broken.
   B: But why does my chest hurt?
   A: I'm not sure. We will have to do more tests.
4. A: Stretch your leg all the way out. And step up . . . and slowly down. . .
   B: Is this right?
   A: Yes, but keep your other leg straight.
   B: Ow, that hurts.
   A: It might hurt a bit at first, but you'll need to do twenty of those on each leg.
   B: Twenty?

5. A: Do you think I might have a heart problem?
   B: We're going to do a test now. Don't move.
   A: Okay.
   B: Now just hold still. Don't move while I set this up for you.
6. A: That rash looks painful. Is it?
   B: Yes, it's very itchy, too.
   A: It may be some sort of allergy.
   B: It just started yesterday morning.

LESSON 3 Listening and Conversation Activity 1 (Page 74)
1. Why is the woman calling?
   A: Good morning. General Hospital Radiology.
   B: Hello. I have an appointment for April 24, but I need to reschedule.
   A: What's your name please?
   B: Erin Matthews, m-a-t-t-h-e-w-s.
   A: Oh yes, 4:00 P.M. The appointment is for your wrist x-ray.
   B: Yes, that's right.
   A: The first available appointment is 10:00 A.M. on May 2. Can you come in on that day?

   Why is the woman calling?
   A. She wants to make a new appointment.
   B. She wants to cancel an appointment.
   C. She wants to change an appointment.
2. Why is the woman calling?
   A: Good morning. Dr. Smith's office.
   B: Hello. I need to make an appointment right away. I have a bad rash on my face. I think I might be allergic to something.
   A: Could you come in tomorrow at 8:30 A.M.?
   B: Yes, that's great. My name is Benson, b-e-n-s-o-n. My first name is Elaine.
   A: All right we'll see you tomorrow at 8:30.
   B: Thanks very much. Good-bye.

   Why is the woman calling?
   A. She wants to make a new appointment.
   B. She needs to cancel an appointment.
   C. She wants to change an appointment.
3. Why is the man calling?
   A: Dr. Petersen's office.
   B: Hello, my daughter has an appointment for next week, but I want to cancel it.
   A: Would you like to reschedule?
   B: No, that's Okay. My daughter had a sore throat so I made an appointment, but she's feeling better now. I don't think she needs to see the doctor.
   A: I see. What's your daughter's name please?
   B: Sarah Cadina, c-a-d-i-n-a.
   A: Okay. I cancelled the appointment. Thanks for calling.

   Why is the man calling?
   A. He needs to make a new appointment
   B. He wants to cancel an appointment
   C. He needs to change an appointment

Activity 2 (Page 74)
1. What type of health care provider is the woman calling
   A: Good morning. General Hospital Radiology.
   B: Hello. I have an appointment for April 24, but I need to reschedule.
   A: What's your name please?
   B: Erin Matthews, m-a-t-t-h-e-w-s.
   A: Oh yes, 4:00 P.M. The appointment is for your wrist x-ray.
   B: Yes, that's right.
   A: The first available appointment is 10:00 A.M. on May 2. Can you come in on that day?

   What type of health care provider is the woman calling?
   A. a dermatologist
   B. a radiologist
   C. a pediatrician

2. What type of health care provider is the woman calling?
   A: Good morning. Dr. Smith's office.
   B: Hello. I need to make an appointment right away. I have a bad rash on my face. I think I might be allergic to something.
   A: Could you come in tomorrow at 8:30 A.M.?
   B: Yes, that's great. My name is Benson, b-e-n-s-o-n. My first name is Elaine.
   A: All right we'll see you tomorrow at 8:30.
   B: Thanks very much. Good-bye.

   What type of health care provider is the woman calling?
   A. a dermatologist
   B. a radiologist
   C. a pediatrician
3. What type of health care provider is the man calling?
   A: Dr. Petersen's office.
   B: Hello, my daughter has an appointment for next week, but I want to cancel it.
   A: Would you like to reschedule?
   B: No, that's Okay. My daughter had a sore throat so I made an appointment, but she's feeling better now. I don't think she needs to see the doctor.
   A: I see. What's your daughter's name please?
   B: Sarah Cadina, c-a-d-i-n-a.
   A: Okay. I cancelled the appointment. Thanks for calling.

   What type of health care provider is the man calling?
   A. a dermatologist
   B. a radiologist
   C. a pediatrician

Activity 3 (page 74)
   A: Hello, Dr. Jackson.
   B: Good morning, Mr. Freeman. How are you feeling today?
   A: Terrible. I have a fever and a bad cough. My whole body hurts. I can't go to work.
   B: It could be the flu, or you might have bronchitis.
   A: I feel really sick.
   B: Let's just take your temperature . . . Okay, I'm going to prescribe an antibiotic.
   A: How often do I take it?
   B: Twice a day, morning and evening, for two weeks. You must finish all the tablets. You mustn't drink any alcohol. Then make a follow-up appointment to see me again in two weeks.
   A: Okay! Thank you very much, doctor.

Unit 6
LESSON 2 Grammar Practice Plus Activity 1 (Page 88)
1. A: Hi, Sharon.
   B: Oh, hi, Tim!
   A: Where are you going?
   B: To the clinic. I want to donate blood.
   A: That's a really good thing to do.
2. A: Hey, where are you going, Carlos?
   B: I'm going to the fire station.
   A: Why?
   B: I want to join the volunteer fire department. There's a volunteer registration at the station today.
3. A: Nadia, hi!
   B: Oh, hi, Bob. How are you?
   A: I'm great. I'm on my way to the youth center. I volunteer there on Saturdays.
   B: Really? You like to work with teenagers?
   A: Yeah. I love it.
4. A: Hi.
   B: Hi, Pam. How are you?
   A: I'm great. How are you?
   B: Fine. How is everything at work?

A: It's Okay. I'd love to talk longer, but I need to go to the animal shelter. I volunteer there. I walk dogs.

B: That's great. Have fun.

A: Thanks. Bye. . .

5. *A:* Stephen?

B: Hey, Howard. What are you doing in this neighborhood?

A: I'm going to the senior center.

B: Why?

A: To help out the elderly. I'm a volunteer.

6. *A:* Marci! Hi!

B: Claudia! Good to see you!

A: You, too! Are you walking my way? I'm going to the farmer's market.

B: Actually, I'm going there, too. I went to the supermarket this morning, but I like to go to the farmer's market to buy fresh vegetables.

7. *A:* Hi, Zach. Are you going to the park?

B: Yeah. I'm going to meet some friends there to play basketball. Do you want to play?

A: Oh, thanks, but not today.

8. *A:* Hey, Richard, are you going to the library?

B: Yes. I want to check out some books. I plan to start a restaurant, and I want to read about starting a small business.

9. *A:* Hi, Elizabeth. Where are you going?

B: To the gym. I want to get in shape.

10. *A:* Where are you going, Bianca?

B: To the community center. I want to sign up for art classes.

11. *A:* Hi, Kathy.

B: Hi, Kevin. How are you?

A: Good. How about you?

B: I'm fine. I'm going to the nature center to meet a tour group. I volunteer to guide people on the trail.

12. *A:* Hi, Rebecca. Where are you going?

B: To the homeless shelter.

A: What are you going to do there?

B: I hope to volunteer. I want to cook meals for homeless people.

LESSON 3 Listening and Conversation Activity 2 (Page 90)

1. What is the holiday?

A: Oh, hi, Barbara. I'm surprised to see you shopping so late!

B: Hi, Paula. I usually try to shop earlier, but I wanted to shop when the store was not so busy. There's always a big Fourth of July sale here. Are you going to go to the neighborhood picnic tomorrow?

A: We sure are. I just need to buy a few things. Then I plan to go home and make potato salad.

What is the holiday?

A. The Fourth of July

B. Memorial Day

C. Labor Day

2. What is not true about Barbara's husband?

B: You're going to be up all night.

A: Oh, not really. Tom can help. You know, Barbara, when I married him, I didn't intend to do all the shopping and cooking and cleaning alone!

B: Well, Dave doesn't like to shop or clean. But he *does* like to barbecue. He plans to barbecue tomorrow, so I have to buy some chicken.

What is not true about Barbara's husband?

A. His name is Dave.

B. He doesn't like to shop.

C. He doesn't like to barbecue.

3. What does Paula need to do?

A: Bye. I'll see you tomorrow. I need to go home and make the potato salad for the picnic.

B: I can't wait, Paula. You make the best food in town!

What does Paula need to do?

A. clean her home

B. make a salad

C. buy food

Activity 3 (Page 90)

A: Oh, hi, Barbara. I'm surprised to see you shopping so late!

B: Hi, Paula. I usually try to shop earlier, but I wanted to shop when the store was not so busy. There's always a big Fourth of July sale here. Are you going to go to the neighborhood picnic tomorrow?

A: We sure are. I just need to buy a few things. Then I plan to go home and make potato salad.

B: You're going to be up all night.

A: Oh, not really. Tom can help. You know, Barbara, when I married him, I didn't intend to do all the shopping and cooking and cleaning alone!

B: Well, Dave doesn't like to shop or clean. But he *does* like to barbecue. He plans to barbecue chicken tomorrow, so I have to buy some.

A: Bye. I'll see you tomorrow. I need to go home and make the potato salad for the picnic.

B: I can't wait, Paula. You make the best food in town!

LESSON 5 Grammar Practice Plus Activity 3 (Page 95)

A: What do you usually do in your free time, Antonio?

B: I don't have free time. I have two children! They enjoy playing at the park, so we go there a lot. How about you? Do you have family here?

A: No. I usually just hang out with my friends. But I'd like to meet some new people, so I want to volunteer somewhere.

B: Are you interested in working with young people?

A: Actually, I prefer working with old people.

B: Maybe you should think about helping out at the senior center.

Unit 7

LESSON 3 Listening and Conversation Activity 1
(Page 106)

1. What is the customer calling about?

A: Home Energy Services. This is Rita. How can I help you?

B: I have a question about my gas bill.

What is the customer calling about?

A. The customer is calling about his electric bill.

B. The customer is calling about his phone bill.

C. The customer is calling about his gas bill.

2. What is the customer's problem?

A: Could you tell me your name and account number, please?

B: My name is Park. Jim Park. My account number is 6745980.

A: How can we help you today?

B: I think there's a mistake on my bill. It's too expensive. Could you check it for me?

What is the customer's problem?

A. His bill has the wrong name.

B. His bill has the wrong account number.

C. His bill is too expensive.

3. Why is the customer's bill high?

A: Okay, let me check that . . . Yes, your gas usage went up from 16 units to 25 units. Did you use a lot of heating this month?

B: No . . . but maybe I used too much hot water for my washing machine and dishwasher.

A: I'm sure that's the reason.

B: Okay, thanks a lot. Goodbye.

Why is the customer's bill high?

A. The customer used more hot water this month.

B. The customer used more heating this month.

C. The company is going to send him a new bill.

Activity 2 (Page 106)
1. What is the problem with Danny's bill?
   A: Maria, did you get your electric bill this month? Why is my electric bill so high? I don't understand. There's a big difference from last month.
   B: Yeah, Danny, my electric bill was high this month, too. Did you check your bill carefully?

   What is the problem with Danny's bill?
   A. It's too high.
   B. It's for the wrong customer.
   C. It has a mistake.
2. What is the reason for Danny's problem?
   A: I don't know. Let's look at the usage . . . Yes, it looks like I used more kilowatts this month.

   What is the reason for Danny's problem?
   A. He used more electricity last month.
   B. He used more electricity this month.
   C. The company billed him for the wrong number of kilowatts.
3. Why does Danny use so much electricity?
   B: Maybe you are using too many appliances.
   A: Well, we have two air conditioners. Maybe that's why.
   A: Yeah, I'm trying to use less air conditioning. It uses too much electricity.

   Why does Danny use so much electricity?
   A. He has two appliances.
   B. He has two air conditioners.
   C. He uses less air conditioning.

LESSON 5 Grammar Practice Plus **Activity 2** (Page 110)
Good morning and welcome to our new radio show about energy-saving tips for your home.

First, make sure your home is well-insulated. Reducing air leaks around windows, doors, and fireplaces will lower your heating bills. Insulating your roof can also cut down your bills by up to 25 percent.

Another place to save energy is in the bathroom. Taking short showers instead of baths really cuts down on water consumption. An average bath uses 15–25 gallons of hot water, while a five-minute shower uses less than 10 gallons. Leaky faucets can also waste a huge amount of water. Fixing just one leaky faucet can save 250 gallons of water a month, or 3,000 gallons per year. And don't forget the hot water tank. Wrapping insulation around your hot water tank reduces heat loss and saves on your heating bills, too.

In the kitchen, leaving the refrigerator door open makes the refrigerator warmer, and wastes energy. Closing the door saves energy! Your dishwasher uses a lot of energy and water, too. Only run your dishwasher when it is full. The same thing goes for your washing machine. Only use it when it is full. Using cold water in your washing machine also helps to reduce energy costs.

Finally, get into good energy-saving habits. Leaving the lights on when you go out wastes electricity. Turning off the lights when you leave the room or go out saves energy. Saving energy makes sense because it saves money, too!

Unit 8

LESSON 2 Grammar Practice Plus **Activity 1** (Page 120)
1. Mrs. Johnson is going to the Community Center. She loves taking fitness classes and working out there.
2. Mr. Johnson is staying home tonight. He has spent hours doing his taxes, but completing the forms is very difficult for him. He is thinking about getting help with tax preparation at the library this evening.

3. Max and Lily went to the library earlier today. They joined the summer reading program a few weeks ago. They're reading in the living room now.
4. Their new dog, Bingo, is in the kitchen. He has new license tags on his collar, and he wants to play.
5. Evan has been very happy with his new computer. He talks to friends online almost every night and he visits a lot of chat rooms.

LESSON 3 Listening and Conversation **Activity 1**
(Page 122)
1. What type of agency is Sam calling?
   A: Hello. Midtown Health Clinic.
   B: Hello. I'd like to make an appointment to see a doctor.
   A: Have you been to our clinic before?
   B: No, I haven't.
   A: All right. Do you have medical insurance?
   B: No, and I don't have a lot of money. How much will it cost to see a doctor.

   What type of agency is Sam calling?
   A. Community center
   B. Clinic
   C. Health insurance office
2. What is Sam's yearly income?
   A: We use a sliding scale here. Do you know what that is?
   B: No, not really.
   A: It means we ask you to tell us your income — how much money you make every year.
   A: What's your income?
   B: About $14,000.

   What is Sam's yearly income?
   A. $44,000
   B. $40,000
   C. $14,000
3. What percentage of the cost will Sam have to pay?
   A: Are you married?
   B: No, I'm single.
   A: Okay, then. A single person making $14,000 a year has to pay 50 percent of the cost. The cost of the visit is $75.00. So you would pay half of that.
   B: I see.

   What percentage of the cost will Sam have to pay?
   A. 0 percent
   B. 50 percent
   C. 100 percent

Activity A (Page 122)
1. Joe makes $13,400 a year, and his medical bill is $150.00.
2. Maria makes $36,000 a year, and her medical bill is $268.00.
3. Raul makes $16,100 a year, and his medical bill is $98.00.
4. Gina makes $22,400 a year, and her medical bill is $212.00.

LESSON 5 Pronunciation **Activity A** (Page 126)
1. They've bought tickets
2. He read the book.
3. Jan's received the letter.
4. Li and Su enrolled in the class.

Activity 1 & 2 (Page 128)
1. *A:* I've lived in this country for almost a year, and I like my life here. I go to school and I work part-time, so I don't have much free time. I was really happy for the first six months, but lately, I've been bored and lonely on the weekends. I'd like to meet some new people.
   B: Have you thought about volunteering? A lot of places need volunteers.
   A: That's a great idea. Where could I get information about that?
   B: Well, I think the library might have information. You should contact the reference librarian.
   A: Thanks. I'll do that.

2. A: I don't know what's wrong with my son. He's had a rash and a fever since yesterday. I want to take him to the doctor. But no one in my family has gone to a doctor in this town yet. How can I find one?
   B: I think you can look in the phone book. Look under "clinics." You can call them and ask if they are taking new patients. Or, I think you can call the hospital and ask how a new person in town can find a doctor.
   A: I think I'll try that first.
3. A: I like my job, but I've already had it for two years, and I haven't had a promotion yet. I talked to my boss, but he said there won't be any promotions for two years. Maybe I should start looking for another job. I think I'll go to some companies and ask for applications.
   B: Well, you could do that. But it might be better to go to the employment agency first.
   A: The employment agency?
   B: Yes. There are counselors there who can help you find a job that's a good match for you. I think the agency also offers some training programs and help writing resumes.
   A: Sounds great! I'll call tomorrow!
4. A: I don't have enough money to send my daughter to preschool, but I know she'd love it. She's been able to read simple picture books since last summer.
   B: Have you heard of Head Start programs? They're programs that help young children get ready to start school. They're free or very inexpensive.
   A: Should I call a school to get information?
   B: No, actually, you should call the Board of Education. Just ask them to send you information about Head Start. You could also check out their website online.

Unit 9

LESSON 3 Listening and Conversation. Activity 2 & 3
(Page 138)
1. What is the manager doing?
   A: Look at this mess!
   B: Yes, I really have to clear this up today.
   A: I guess you haven't been filing documents lately?
   B: I've been attending training sessions and I got behind with the filing. . .
   A: Okay, well you may have to stay late.
   B: Yes, of course, ma'am.

   What is the manager doing?
   A. complaining about the assistant's work
   B. giving the assistant advice
   C. asking the assistant for help
2. What is the teacher doing?
   A: Why haven't you been doing your homework this semester?
   B: Don't know, sir.
   A: You don't know! And what about you?
   C: I've been training for the soccer team every day.
   A: That's no excuse. You still have to do your homework if you want to get a good grade.

   What is the teacher doing?
   A. asking students about soccer
   B. asking students about their grades
   C. asking students for an explanation
3. What is the boss doing?
   A: Perry, which tools have you been using to dig the flowerbeds?
   B: This small shovel, ma'am.
   A: Well that's not the best way. You'll go faster if you use the pitchfork and the large shovel, okay?
   B: Yes, ma'am. Thanks!

What is the boss doing?
A. giving advice
B. complaining about work
C. asking for help
4. What is the supervisor doing?
   A: Stan, why haven't you been wearing your safety helmet?
   B: It's just too hot to wear it in this weather, sir.
   A: I'm sorry, but you have to wear it. It's an important safety rule.
   B: You're right. I'll put it on now.
   A: I'll try to find better helmets for next week, okay?
   B: Thanks a lot, sir.

   What is the supervisor doing?
   A. asking about the weather
   B. asking about safety rules
   C. expressing concern

Pronunciation Activity B (Page 138)
1. Where's she been eating?
2. What's he been baking?
3. What's she been weeding?
4. Where's he been studying?

LESSON 5 Grammar Practice Plus Activity 5 (Page 143)
Good afternoon and welcome. Today I'd like to introduce Elsa Martinez. Elsa started a small business twenty years ago. She started with just one small store, but now owns twenty-three stores all over the state and employs 141 people. She's won the Best Businesswoman award three times and she created a successful company that is still going strong today! She retired three years ago, but she hasn't been sitting at home watching TV! For the past two years, she's been traveling around the state, giving motivational talks to help other people start small businesses. She believes that anyone can do what she's done if they have the right advice and the right motivation. So she's been sharing the wealth of her experience with small business owners like us all. Whether you own a pet store or a hair salon, I'm sure her advice today will help all of you get ahead.

For the last year she's also been working for the organization Parents Against Drugs. She's been raising money to create educational programs to stop young people from using drugs. This year she's raised over $50,000 for drug education programs in high schools. She has so much energy and is a truly inspirational person for us all. Today she's going to tell us about her experience as a business owner and about her fundraising work. She has also written a book about her experience. Signed copies of her book will be available at the end of her talk. So. . .I'd like to welcome. . .Elsa Martinez!

Unit 10

LESSON 2 Grammar Practice Plus 2 Activity 4 (Page 153)
Okay everyone. Can I have your attention, please? I'm going to tell you about the first aid kit in the break room. Of course I hope you won't need to use it, but just in case there is an emergency, you should know what's in the kit.

First we have bandages and antibiotic cream. This is in case you get a small cut on your hand or arm. If you burn yourself, you should use the burn cream. The aspirin is in case you have a fever or a headache, or for small aches and pains. The cold pack will help to reduce the swelling if you sprain your ankle or wrist, for example.

In addition to these basic medical supplies, we also have a flashlight. If the electricity doesn't work and it's dark, it's useful to have one here. There is also a first aid guide. Please look at it if you aren't sure what to do. Of course, if there is a serious medical emergency, you must call 911 right away. Okay?

LESSON 3 Listening and Conversation Activity 1
(Page 154)

1. If you want to hear the message again later, you have to save it.
2. If you call someone who isn't there, you can leave a message.
3. Do you want to erase the massage, or do you want to hear it again?
4. At the end of a message, you sometimes have to press the pound sign.
5. If you don't know someone's phone number, you can often find it in a directory.

ACTIVITY 2 (Page 154)

1. How do you save a message?
   - A: You have 1 new message and 2 saved messages. To listen to new messages, press 1. To listen to saved messages, press 2. New message received Thursday May 27 8:10 P.M.
   - B: Hi Miki. It's Bob. Call me back.
   - A: To hear this message again, press 1. To save this message, press 2. To erase this message, press 3. Your message will be saved for 19 days.

   Which is correct?
   - A. Press *2*.
   - B. Press *1*.
   - C. Call back.

2. Where is the person calling?
   - A: Thank you for calling Citysaver Bank. For account information, press 1. To transfer funds, press 2. For checking accounts, press 1. For savings accounts, press 2. To hear this menu again, press 9. Please enter your account number followed by the pound key.

   Where is the person calling from?
   - A. The person is calling a bank.
   - B. The person is calling a school.
   - C. The person is calling a library.

3. What does the caller want to do?
   - A: Thank you for calling the Weston Library. For library hours press 1. For directions, press 2. You have pressed 2. For directions from Weston town center, press 1. From Weston town center, follow Route 138 past Weston City Mall and up the hill to Spring Street. Take a left at the traffic light, onto Main Street, then your third right onto Mill Avenue. The library is in Weston Central Park to your right. To return to the main menu, press 2.

   What does the caller want to do?
   - A. The caller wants to find out the library's hours.
   - B. The caller wants to get directions to the library.
   - C. The caller wants to leave a message.

4. What does the caller want to do?
   - A: This is Bellman and Williams. Our office hours are 8 A.M. to 6 P.M. Monday through Friday. If you know your party's extension, please dial it now. Press 1 for a directory by name. Dial the first three letters of the name followed by the pound key.
   - B: Pia Larson. Hello?
   - C: Hi, Pia. This is Don. Do you have time to meet for lunch today?

   Which is correct?
   - A. The caller wants to know the office hours.
   - B. The caller wants to talk to an employee of the company.
   - C. The caller wants to leave a message.

Pronunciation Activity A & B (Page 154)

1. If I want start the computer, do I press this button?
2. If I need to change the number, which button do I press?
3. If the machine breaks down, what should I do?
4. If I make a mistake, do I press *Cancel*?

LESSON 5 Grammar Practice Plus Activity 4 (Page 159)

I have lots of plans to improve my life. First, I'm going to take math classes at night. If I improve my math skills, I'll get a better job. If I don't study math, I'll never get promoted. Second, I'm going to cut down on snack foods. I eat too many snacks, especially potato chips. If I eat fewer snacks, I'm sure I'll lose weight. If I don't, I'll gain weight and have health problems. Third, I'm going to stop using all my credit cards. If I stop using them, I'll save money. If I keep using them, I won't be able to pay my bills.

Unit 11

LESSON 2 Grammar Practice Plus Activity 4 (Page 169)

- A: Hi. How are you doing?
- B: Not great. I bought a new bookshelf, and I can't put it together. I've been trying to do it all day
- A: Were there any instructions?
- B: Yes, but I can't figure them out. Hey can you come over and help me tonight? I'll order pizza.
- A: Sorry. I'm busy this evening. And after work I have to take my friend Jack to the airport.
- B: What about after you drop him off? Would that be too late?
- A: No. I could stop by on my way home.
- B: Great!
- A: Oh! I need to go.
- B: Okay. See you later.

LESSON 3 Listening and Conversation Activity 2
(Page 170).

1. What does Jill say about the utilities?
   - A: Oh, here's an ad for an apartment that sounds good. It's in a great neighborhood. The deposit is two months' rent, but the rent is cheap and utilities are included in the rent.
   - B: Well, you should call and make an appointment before you stop by. Do you want me to go with you?
   - A: No, that's Okay. My friend Keith will go with me.

   What does Jill say about the utilities?
   - A. They're cheap.
   - B. They require a deposit.
   - C. They are included in the rent.

2. What does Jill's father tell her to do?
   - A: Dad, if I like the apartment, should I sign the lease right away?
   - B: No, don't sign it right away. Tell the landlord you're interested in the apartment. Ask to take the lease and look it over at home.

   What does Jill's father tell her to do?
   - A. sign the lease right away
   - B. ask to take the lease home and look it over
   - C. write a check

3. When might you not get your security deposit back?
   - B: Here's some more advice, Jill. It's usual for a landlord to ask for a security deposit. But if you break or damage something, you will not get your full security deposit back when you move out. You need to be a careful tenant.
   - A: Thanks for your advice, Dad.

   When might you not get your security deposit back?
   - A. if you stay too long
   - B. if you break something
   - C. if your stove needs repairs

4. What advice does Jill's father give her?
   - B: Also, find out which utilities are included in the rent.
   - A: It's usually heat and water and gas, right?
   - B: Well, sometimes gas and electricity aren't included in the rent for apartments.

A: Well, the ad says all utilities are included.

B: Yes, but it's important to be sure.

A: You're a great dad. I appreciate all your advice!

What advice does Jill's father give her?

A. Find out which utilities are included in the rent.

B. Ask if the apartment has heat and water.

C. Electricity is expensive.

Activity 3 & 4 (Page 170)

A: Oh, here's an ad for an apartment that sounds good. It's in a great neighborhood. The deposit is two months' rent, but the rent is cheap and utilities are included in the rent.

B: Well, you should call and make an appointment before you stop by. Do you want me to go with you?

A: No, that's Okay. My friend Keith will go with me. Dad, if I like the apartment, should I sign the lease right away?

B: No, don't sign it right away. Tell the landlord you're interested in the apartment. Ask to take the lease and look it over at home. Here's some more advice, Jill. It's usual for a landlord to ask for a security deposit. But if you break or damage something, you will not get your full security deposit back when you move out. You need to be a careful tenant.

A: Thanks for your advice, Dad.

B: Also, find out which utilities are included in the rent.

A: It's usually heat and water and gas, right?

B: Well, sometimes gas and electricity aren't included in the rent for apartments.

A: Well, the ad says all utilities are included.

B: Yes, but it's important to be sure.

A: You're a great dad. I appreciate all your advice!

LESSON 5 Grammar Practice Plus Activity 1 (Page 174)

A: Hello, You have reached the landlord, Tom Compton, at 555-9908. I can't come to the phone right now. Please leave your name, your phone number, and a short message. Thank you.

B: First message. Call received at 9:20 A.M.

C: This is Eli Blake in apartment 2B. I'm calling again to ask you to paint the bathroom. The old paint is coming off the wall, and it looks very bad. I asked you to paint the bathroom several months ago. I hope you can do it soon. Please call me. My number is 555–4689. Thank you.

B: Second message. Call received at 10:45 A.M.

C: Hello . . . This is Regina in apartment 4E. I have a problem with my toilet. Can you please come over and fix it as soon as possible? My number is 555–2475. Thank you.

B: Third message. Call received at 1:36 P.M.

C: Hello. This is Susan Shelby in Apartment 4G. I have two requests. Could you help me install a ceiling fan? That's the first request. The second is more important. Could you please replace the locks on my door? I'm having a problem with my boyfriend, and I don't want him to come in while I'm not home. My number is 555–0018. Thank you very much.

B: Fourth message. Call received at 4:12 P.M.

C: This is Mark Raynor in Apartment 6B. My number is 555–3359. I need you to inspect my fire extinguisher. I asked you to do this last week, but I am still waiting. Please call me. Again, my number is 555–3359.

Unit 12

LESSON 2 Grammar Practice Plus Activity 1 (Page 184)

I was born in August 1982. I grew up in a small town. My family knew everyone in the town and I had a lot of friends. We lived in a big house with a yard. But I thought the town was boring. I left home as soon as I graduated from high school. That was in July 2000. After I left home, I moved to the city. I didn't know anyone there, and it was difficult to make friends. In August 2001, I got a scholarship to business school and I got a job. I went to school at night and worked in a computer software company during the day. That's where I met Amy. She was working there as a website designer. That was in April 2003. As soon as I saw her, I knew she was the one for me. We got engaged in January 2004. Right after I graduated from college in June 2006, we got married. About a year after we got married, we moved out of the city—to the suburbs. Amy worked from home and I kept my job in the city, but it was very difficult. There was so much traffic; the commute was sometimes over two hours! I was exhausted when I got home. So in September 2008 I quit my job, took out a small business loan, and started my own company. Now I work from home and go to the city once or twice a month. We're very happy in our new neighborhood. It's safe and friendly. We know all the neighbors. Now we've decided to start a family. Our first child is due in five months. I'm so excited about becoming a dad and watching my kids grow up!

LESSON 3 Listening and Conversation Activity 2 (Page 186)

1. How did Luis's life change after getting a scholarship?

   A: What's been the most important event of your life so far?

   B: I don't know about the most important, but definitely one of the key events in my life was when I got a scholarship to drama school.

   A: Why was that so important?

   B: Well, before I went to drama school, I had no idea what I wanted to do with my life. Then I applied for the scholarship and was totally amazed when I got it! It paid for all my tuition for three years. And while I was there, I realized that I loved acting. I found out I wanted to be an actor and nothing else.

   A: So it helped you to choose your career?

   B: That's right. Before I got the scholarship, I was thinking of becoming a doctor.

   How did Luis's life change after getting a scholarship?

   A. He didn't know what to do.

   B. He had a lot of money.

   C. He decided to become an actor.

2. How did Emilia's life change after she quit smoking?

   A: Emilia, what's been your biggest achievement so far?

   B: My biggest achievement was to quit smoking.

   A: Really? How did it change your life?

   B: Well, before I quit, I was always in a bad mood and I coughed all the time. I felt very unhealthy.

   A: And how do you feel now?

   B: As soon as I stopped, I started to feel better. Now I have more energy and I'm in a better mood. I save a lot of money, too!

   How did Emilia's life change after she quit smoking?

   A. She has more energy.

   B. It was difficult.

   C. She is in a bad mood.

3. Why was it difficult for Huong to get her bachelor's degree?

   A: Huong, was it difficult to get your bachelor's degree?

   B: Yes, it was. It took me six years, and there were many times when I thought I just wouldn't make it.

   A: Was that because you were you working full-time?

   B: Yes, that's right. I went to class every day after I finished work. I was always exhausted. And then there were assignments and exams. . .

   A: And how do you feel now? Was it worth it?

   B: Definitely! I feel I really achieved something. Graduation day was the happiest day of my life.

   Why was getting her bachelor's degree difficult for Huong?

   A. It took six years.

   B. She was working full-time.

   C. She wanted to give up.

4. How does Ben feel after getting promoted?

A: How did your life change after you got promoted, Ben?

B: Well, obviously I'm earning more money now. And that's very good. As an associate manager, I have to attend more meetings, and I have to wear a suit, and . . .I have to stay late if there's a problem. . .

A: So do you feel that your work life has improved?

B: Well, it was less stressful before, that's for sure. But now I feel I'm learning more. I'm climbing the job ladder and that's a good feeling.

A: So you're looking forward to your next promotion?

B: Absolutely.

How does Ben feel after getting promoted?

A. His work is less stressful.

B. He has too many problems.

C. His work is more interesting.

Activity 3 & 4 (Page 186)

A: Serena, thanks for letting me interview you today.

B: You're welcome. No problem.

A: Can you tell me how you became a nurse?

B: Sure. Let's see. I started working as a health aide after I finished high school. I had my high school diploma, but I didn't have any nursing qualifications. It was mostly on-the-job training. I worked in a home for senior citizens. I was mainly cooking and cleaning to begin with, but later I started taking care of the residents, helping them eat and walk, that kind of thing. I really enjoyed the work, so I decided to attend classes at a community college to study nursing.

A: What kind of classes did you take?

B: I studied to be an LPN—a Licensed Practical Nurse. It took a year. I had to take out a student loan to pay the tuition. When I finished the course, I took the LPN nursing exam.

A: What did you do after you completed your LPN exam?

B: When I became an LPN, I got a job in a hospital. After I started working in the hospital, I applied for and got a hospital scholarship. It paid for my tuition.

A: You mean the hospital paid for your training?

B: Yes, that's right. So I studied for another year to become an RN; that is a Registered Nurse, and when I finished that, I took the RN exam.

A: You make it sound easy, but it was a lot of work, wasn't it?

B: Yes! I had to study every night and go to class after I finished work. I didn't have time to socialize—I had no free time at all!

A: Do you like your work now?

B: Yes, definitely. I get paid more and the work is more interesting. It's more challenging and I have more responsibility, too. Sometimes I have to solve difficult problems and make some difficult decisions, but I'm happy to be helping people.

Pronunciation Activity A & B (Page 187)

1. *A:* Where did you live when you were a child?

   B: When I was a child?

2. *A:* Where did she study before she joined this class?

   B: Before she joined this class?

3. *A:* What did they do after they went home yesterday?

   B: After they went home yesterday?

Vocabulary

Numbers in parentheses indicate unit numbers.

academic counselor (1, 6)
accidentally (10, 161)
advice (1, 6)
affordable housing (7, 102)
after (12, 183)
air conditioner (11, 172)
air pollution (7, 102)
allergy (5, 70)
antibiotic (5, 70)
area (3, 48)
as soon as (12, 183)
assigned space (4, 60)
assignment (1,6)
assistant (1, 6)
associate manager (12, 182)
asthma (5, 70)
attended every class (1, 12)
auditory learner (1, 17)
award (9, 140)
bake (9, 134)
bath oil (2, 30)
before (12, 183)
best value (2, 28)
beverage (7, 112)
blood sugar (5, 76)
boots (2, 28)
bridge (7, 104)
brochure (8, 120)
bronchitis (5, 70)
build a fire (4, 62)
bump (3, 46)
buy fresh vegetables (6, 88)
cafeteria (1, 6)
call in sick (10, 158)
camp (4, 62)
car seat (3, 38)
cardiologist (5, 72)
career advancement (8, 118)
CD-ROM (1, 6)
championship (9, 140)
change-of-address
     form (11, 166)
changing lanes (3, 38)
chat with each other (4, 54)
check out (8, 118)
check out books (6, 88)
chest pain (5, 70)
childhood obesity (5, 80)
choose (11, 174)
click (10, 150)
coaching (9, 140)
coffeemaker (2, 22)
colored (1, 16)
colorful (2, 28)
common area (4, 60)
commute (10, 156)
complete (1, 14)
complicated (2, 22)
confused (10, 161)
conjunctivitis (5, 70)
consult (12, 188)
contact (8, 118)

cook meals for homeless
     people (6, 88)
cooperate (1, 14)
copier (4, 56)
cough (5, 70)
counselor (1, 9)
courteous (1, 14)
create (9, 140)
crime (7, 102)
crosswalk (7, 104)
curbside (7, 112)
curtains (11, 166)
cuts down on (7, 108)
dermatologist (5, 72)
design (9, 140)
dessert (5, 76)
diabetes (5, 78)
diabetic (8, 124)
dial (10, 150)
difficult (12, 182)
dining area (4, 54)
direct movies (9, 140)
discrimination (11, 177)
dislocate (3, 44)
disturb (2, 32)
donate blood (6, 86)
(be) down (8, 124)
down the hall (3, 44)
driving alone in a carpool
     lane (3, 38)
driving with a child (3, 38)
drop off (11, 166)
dumpster (4, 60)
durable (2, 28)
earbuds (4, 56)
eat out (12, 182)
eczema (5, 70)
elevator (5, 76)
emergency exit (10, 152)
energy efficient (2, 22)
enroll (8, 118)
entry (11, 177)
eviction (11, 177)
exceeding (7, 112)
exhausted (12, 182)
express (2, 32)
extermination chemicals
     (11, 172)
factory (7, 104)
faucet (7, 110)
fax machine (10, 150)
figure out (11, 166)
fill out (11, 166)
fire alarm (10, 152)
fire extinguisher (11, 172)
fireplace (7, 110)
first aid kit (10, 152)
fitness class (8, 118)
flashlight (10, 152)
flip-flops (4, 54)
food label (5, 76)
free meal (4, 54)

frozen dinner (5, 76)
gain weight (10, 156)
garbage (4, 60)
garbage can (7, 102)
generate (12, 192)
get a scholarship (12, 184)
get engaged (12, 184)
get fired (10, 158)
get in shape (6, 86)
get my GED (12, 188)
gets stuck (10, 150)
glass cleaner (2, 30)
go back to work (12, 188)
government (4, 64)
grill (3, 46)
grow up in (12, 184)
gym (5, 76)
gynecologist (5, 72)
had support (1, 12)
hair dryer (2, 24)
hammer (9, 136)
hand out flyers (9, 134)
hang up (10, 161)
hanging out (6, 92)
hard time (8,128)
hazardous (7, 112)
headset (3, 38)
help out at (6, 86)
high blood pressure (5, 78)
high-calorie soft drink (5, 76)
hiking (6, 92)
history (4, 64)
hitchhiking (3, 40)
homeless shelter (6, 86)
hook up (11, 168)
hot water tank (7, 110)
hunt (4, 62)
hurt (3, 44)
illegal (4, 64)
immediately (10, 161)
improve (10, 156)
in a bad mood (12, 182)
indoors (4, 60)
informed (3, 48)
inspect (11, 172)
install (11, 172)
instructor (1, 6)
insulating (7, 110)
Internet service (8, 120)
invest (10, 156)
itchy (5, 70)
jams (10, 150)
join the PTA (6, 86)
join the volunteer fire
     department (6, 88)
junk food (5, 80)
keep a record (9, 144)
keep fit (10, 156)
keep your job (9, 144)
keep up to date (9, 144)
keep someone busy (9, 144)
keeps (7, 108)

key (1, 16)
kinesthetic learner (1, 17)
lab assistant (1, 9)
ladder (9, 136)
laptop (10, 150)
laundry detergent (2, 30)
lease (11, 166)
leisure activity (8, 128)
librarian (1, 9)
license (8, 120)
lift (3, 44)
light fixture (11, 172)
local event (8, 118)
location (10, 161)
look over (11, 166)
lowers (7, 108)
made learning a priority
     (1, 12)
make a down payment
     (12, 188)
make an outside call (10, 150)
make sure (10, 150)
make up (1, 16)
making small talk (6, 92)
microwave (2, 22)
mixed feelings (5, 80)
mixer (2, 22)
motivated (1, 14)
moving (11, 177)
music festival (6, 92)
neighborhood watch
     group (8, 120)
obscene (4, 56)
office hours (1, 6)
on hold (8, 124)
on leashes (4, 60)
on strike (8, 124)
organize (9, 134)
out of an elevator (3, 44)
out of breath (5, 70)
out of work (8, 124)
pace (1, 16)
paintbrush (9, 136)
parking garage (7, 104)
parking in a handicapped
     parking space (3, 38)
passing in a no passing
     zone (3, 40)
pay attention (to) (1, 14)
pay off our mortgage (12, 188)
pediatrician (5, 72)
personal belonging (4, 60)
personal call (4, 54)
personally (3, 48)
photocopier runs out of
     (10, 150)
physical therapist (5, 72)
pick (9, 134)
pick out (11, 166)
pick the flowers (4, 62)
pink eye (5, 70)
play basketball (6, 88)

playground (7, 104)
powerful (2, 22)
practical (2, 28)
pretty (2, 28)
printer (10, 150)
priority (1, 14)
program (8, 118)
proud of (8, 128)
public transportation
    (7, 102)
put away (11, 168)
put in (11, 168)
put together (11, 168)
put up (11, 168)
quit (12, 184)
radiologist (5, 72)
railing (11, 172)
raising (money) (9, 140)
rash (5, 70)
reading program (8, 120)
receive (8, 118)
record (1, 16)
recycling (7, 108)
reduces (7, 108)
refuse (7, 112)
register (8, 118)
reliable (2, 22)
relocate (12, 188)
remove (11, 172)
repair (11, 172)
repay (12, 188)
replace (11, 172)
requirement (4, 64)
resident (4, 60)
resource (1, 6)

retire (10, 156)
retired (8, 124)
reusing (7, 108)
risky (2, 32)
roof (7, 110)
runny nose (5, 70)
save (10, 150)
scanner (10, 150)
schedule (12, 192)
school income (5, 80)
security deposit (11, 166)
senior shuttle (8, 124)
set goals (1, 12)
set up (11, 168)
shift (4, 54)
shovel (9, 136)
showerhead (11, 172)
sidewalk (7, 102)
sign (9, 140)
sign up for (6, 86)
sleeping at the wheel (3, 40)
slip (3, 44)
small talk (2, 32)
smoke (7, 104)
smoke detector (10, 152)
socialize (12, 182)
socks (2, 28)
sofa (2, 24)
speeding (3, 38)
sprain (3, 46)
spray (11, 172)
stain remover (2, 30)
stairwell (4, 60)
start a business (12, 184)
stranger (6, 92)

stuck to a schedule (1, 12)
study group (1, 6)
stylish (2, 28)
submit (12, 192)
subscribe (8, 118)
subscription (8, 118)
suitcase (2, 28)
support (1, 14)
surf the Internet (4, 56)
swollen (5, 70)
take a day off (10, 158)
take a walk on a trail (6, 88)
take down (11, 168)
take out (11, 168)
talking on his cell phone
    (3, 38)
tax preparation (8, 118)
tear (3, 48)
tenant responsibilities
    (11, 177)
thermostat (7, 108)
took out a loan (12, 182)
took responsibility (1, 12)
tour (1, 6)
traffic (7, 102)
translate documents (9, 134)
trash collection service
    (7, 102)
tray (3, 48
trip (3, 44)
trouble (10, 161)
tuition (12, 188)
turn in (11, 166)
turn signal (3, 38)
turning down (7, 108)

tutor (1, 6)
tutor teenagers (6, 86)
TV (2, 24)
underline (1, 16)
unlimited (2, 32)
unload (3, 44)
unpack (3, 46)
unplugging (7, 108)
vacuum cleaner (2, 24)
vegetarian (5, 78)
visual learner (1, 17)
walk dogs (6, 88)
warning sign (10, 152)
was motivated (1, 12)
washing machine (7, 110)
wasting money (6, 92)
water pipe (7, 108)
wearing a helmet (3, 40)
wearing a seatbelt (3, 40)
weatherproofing (7, 108)
website (9, 140)
weed (9, 134)
wheelbarrow (9, 136)
when (12, 183)
win (9, 140)
window shopping (6, 92)
without electricity (8, 124)
work out (5, 76)
work overtime (10, 158)
work tool (9, 134)
work with teenagers (6, 88)
wrap (7, 110)
wrench (9, 136)

Index

Career Skills

Credits

Illustrators: Ian Baker, Richard Beacham, Steve Bjorkman, David Cole, Janise Gates, Jerry Gonzalez, Jim Haynes, Mike Hortens, Kevin Kobasic, Karen Lee, Tania Lee, Eric Olson, Shelton Leong, Pat Lewis, Scott McBee, Chris Murphy, Rich Powell, Bot Roda, Jon Rogers, Phil Schever, Theresa Seelye, Pete Smith, Jem Sullivan, Steve Sweny, Ron Zalme, Jerry Zimmerman.

Photo credits:

3 Dave & Les Jacobs / Getty Images; **10** Dynamic Graphics / Jupiter Images, McGraw; **11** Mark Pierce, Alamy; **11** (bottom left) [**23, 40** (bottom left), **55** (bottom left), **68** (bottom right), **71** (bottom left), **77** (bottom left), **121** (bottom left), **141** (bottom left), **171** (bottom right)]: AAGAMIA / Getty Images; **11** (bottom right) [**30, 40** (bottom right), **63** (top left), **73** (bottom right), **87** (bottom right), **107** (bottom right), **111** (middle right), **119** (bottom right), **135** (bottom left), **148** (bottom right), **157** (bottom right)]: Jose Luis Pelaez Inc/Blend Images/Corbis **14** (lower left): Andersen Ross, Digital Vision, Getty; **14** (upper right): Jessica Miller, Taxi, Getty; **15** (bottom left), **29, 47** (bottom left), **63** (top right), **77** (bottom right), **89** (bottom right), **93** (bottom right), **121** (bottom middle right), **139** (bottom left), **148** (bottom left), **157** (bottom left), **186** (bottom left)] Jose Luis Pelaez Inc/Blend Images / Corbis; **15** (bottom right), [**40** (top), **46** (bottom right), **55** (bottom right), **71** (bottom right), **73** (bottom left), **89** (bottom left), **104, 111** (middle left), **119** (bottom left), **137, 142** (top left), **152, 173** (bottom left), **179** (bottom right)]: Jose Luis Pelaez Inc / Blend Images / Corbis; **17** (top): Jon Feingersh, Photography, Inc., Blend Images, Alamy; **17** (middle): Jacky Chapman, Janine Wiedel Photolibrary, Alamy; **17** (bottom): Manchan, Digital Vision, Alamy; **18** Marty Heitner / The Image Works; **20** Jack Hollingworth, Photodisc, Getty; **25** (far left): Ingram Publishing / Alamy, McGraw; **25** (far middle left): StockByte / PunchStock, McGraw; **25** (middle left): Corbis; **25** (middle): Corbis; **25** (middle right): Ryan McVay / Getty Images, McGraw; **25** (far right): NiKreationS / Alamy, McGraw; **26** (top): Jean Maurice, Red Cover, Getty; **26** (bottom): Ingram Publishing / Fotosearch, McGraw; **27** (top): Tobi Zausner; **27** (bottom): Tobi Zausner; **31** (left): Tony Cordoza, Almy; **31** (middle): D. Hurst, Alamy; **31** (right): Cre8tive Studios, Almy; **31** (bottom): Tobi Zausner; **33** Peter Griffin, Alamy; **36** Sigrid Olsson, PhotoAlto, Alamy; **41** (top): Corbis, McGraw; **41** (left): Dynamic Graphics, Jupiterimages / Creatas, Alamy; **41** (middle left): Andersen Ross, Digital Vision, Getty; **41** (middle right): Jon Feingersh, Blend Images, Getty; **41** (right): moodboard, Corbis; **43** Christa Knijff, Alamy; **46** (bottom left), [**59, 75, 79** (bottom right), **87** (bottom left), **107** (bottom left), **121** (bottom middle right), **135** (bottom right), **142** (top right), **164** (bottom), **173** (bottom right), **179** (bottom left), Anderson Ross / Blend Images/Corbis; **47** (bottom right), **68** (bottom left), **79** (bottom left), **93** (bottom left), **109, 121** (bottom right), **141** (bottom right), **151, 171** (bottom left), **186** (bottom right): John Lund/Tiffany Schoepp/Blend Images/Corbis; **50** Christa Knijff / Alamy; **52** BananaStock, Jupiterimages / BananaStock, Alamy; **62** Carolyn Woodham / Getty Images; **63** (left): Comstock / Superstock; **63** (middle left): Image Source Black / Getty Images; **63** (middle right): Comstock / Superstock; **63** (right): Jeff Greenberg / The Image Works; **65** (top): JMarvin E. Newman / Getty Images; **65** (top middle): Brooklyn Museum / Corbis; **65** (bottom middle): Joseph Sohm / Visions of America / Corbis; **65** (bottom): Seth Wenig/ Reuters / Corbis; **66** BananaStock / PictureQuest; **68** Brand X Pictures / PunchStock; **73** (left): SSPL / The Image Works; **73** (middle left): age fotostock / SuperStock; **73** (middle): Bob Daemmrich/ The Image Works; **73** (middle right): Michel Gaillard / REA / Redux; **73** (right): Donn Thompson / Getty Images; **81** Justin Sullivan / Getty Images; **82** (left): age fotostock / SuperStock; **82** (middle left): Popperfoto / Alamy; **82** (middle right): Roy Ooms / Mastefile; **82** (right): Minnesota Historical Society / Corbis; **82** Thinkstock / Corbis; **90** (left): John E. Kelly / FoodPix; **90** (middle left): Tobi Zausner; **90** (middle right): Photodisc / SuperStock; **90** (right): David R. Frazier / The Image Works; **90** (bottom): Roy Morsch / Corbis; **91** (left): Sean Just¬ice / Corbis; **91** (right): Picturenet / Getty Images; **94** Robin Lynne Gibson / Getty Images; **95** Rubberball / Getty Images; **96** Mitch Wojnarowicz / Amsterdam Recorder / The Image Works; **97** (top): Skjold Photographs / The Image Works; **97** (bottom): Syracuse Newspapers / The Image Works; **98** Daniel Dempster Photography / Alamy; **100** Corbis Premium RF / Alamy; **107** Helene Rogers / Alamy; **111** Edward Pond / Masterfile; **114** (top left) Image Source Pink / Superstock; **114** (top middle) David Hoffman Photo Library / Alamy; **114** (top right) Medioimages/Photodisc/Getty Images; **116** Comstock Select/Corbis; **121** Chris Carroll / Corbis; **123** Blend Images / SuperStock; **129** Carlos Goldin / Corbis; **130** Itani / Alamy; **132** moodboard / SuperStock; **138** (left to right) David Woolley/ Getty Images; M. Thomsen / zefa / Corbis; Mark Hall / Getty Images; GoodShoot / SuperStock; **139** Creatas / SuperStock; **143** Cultura Limited / SuperStock; **148** ColorBlind Images / Getty Images; **159** BananaStock / SuperStock; **155** (left) Stockbyte / Alamy; **155** (right) age fotostock / Superstock; **158** (left to right) MM Productions / Corbis; Michael Prince / Corbis; Michael Prince / Corbis; Redlink Production / Corbis; **160** (left) age fotostock / SuperStock; **160** (middle) Willie Hill Jr./ The Image Works; (right) Gregor Schlaeger/ VISUM/The Image Works; **164** WoodyStock / Alamy; **171** GOGO images / SuperStock; **174** (left) Amy Eckert / Getty Images; **174** (top middle) D. Hurst / Alamy; **174** (bottom, left middle) T. Ozonas / Masterfile; **174** (bottom middle right) Photodisc / SuperStock; **174** (right) Datacraft / Getty Images; **175** Blend Images / SuperStock; **177** Marc Romanelli / Getty Images; **178** Blend Images / Alamy; **186** (left to right) Comstock / SuperStock; AFP Getty Images; Photographers Choice RF / SuperStock; Formcourt (Formcourt Advertising) / Alamy; **187** Creatas / SuperStock; **190** Redchopsticks.com/SuperStock; **194** (left to right) Glow Images / Alamy; Photodisc / SuperStock; David Frazier / The Image Works; Stockbyte / SuperStock; **196** Blend Images / SuperStock

Cover photo:
Hand: Corbis
Picture in hand: (MMH provided)
Female Pharmacist: Jupiter images
Mother and daughter at graduation: Corbis
Businessman reading book: Corbis
Grandma, Mother, Granddaughter: Corbis